ADVAN ...
THE WA...........WOMB

"Each essay is a lens through which we are invited to view in Joycean detail the author's deeply personal present, yet at the same time to ponder and to rethink larger worlds of history and cultures. It's a collection that often is wry but never cynical, acutely learned and always alert to humor and wonder."—David Toomey, author of *Weird Life: The Search for Life That Is Very, Very Different from Our Own*

ADVANCE PRAISE FOR THE WANDERING WOMB

The Wandering Womb

THE

WANDERING

WOMB

ESSAYS
IN SEARCH
OF HOME

S.L. WISENBERG

UNIVERSITY OF MASSACHUSETTS PRESS

Amherst and Boston

ISBN 978-1-62534-735-0 (paper)

Designed by Deste Roosa
Set in Athelas and Trade Gothic Next LT
Printed by Books International, Inc.

Cover design by adam b. bohannon
Cover art by Roseanne Kenny, *Brown Body Abstract,* courtesy of the artist.
RoaseanneKenny@_rosiekenny.

Library of Congress Cataloging-in-Publication Data
Names: Wisenberg, S. L. (Sandi L.), author.
Title: The wandering womb : essays in search of home / S.L. Wisenberg.
Other titles: Essays in search of home
Description: Amherst : University of Massachusetts Press, [2023] | Series:
  Juniper Prize for creative nonfiction | Includes bibliographical
  references.
Identifiers: LCCN 2022044972 (print) | LCCN 2022044973 (ebook) | ISBN
  9781625347350 (paper) | ISBN 9781685750268 (ebook) | ISBN 9781685750275
  (epub)
Subjects: LCSH: Wisenberg, S. L. (Sandi L.) | Jewish
  women—Texas—Houston—Biography. | Jewish
  women—Illinois—Chicago—Biography. | Jews—Texas—Houston—Biography.
  | Jews—Illinois—Chicago—Biography. | Jews—Identity. |
  Jews—Psychology. | Houston (Tex.)—Biography. | Chicago
  (Ill.)—Biography.
Classification: LCC F394.H89 J519 2023 (print) | LCC F394.H89 (ebook) |
  DDC 305.892/40773311092 [B]—dc23/eng/20220920
LC record available at https://lccn.loc.gov/2022044972
LC ebook record available at https://lccn.loc.gov/2022044973

British Library Cataloguing-in-Publication Data
A catalog record for this book is available from the British Library.

What I am trying to strike at Sandi, is the manner in which you deal with you[r] feelings. You seem to let them overwhelm you. Why? How important are they really? What do they mean to your day to day existence or your more purposeful role in life? Surely feelings are important but only in so much as they relate to our workings in a broader world. . . . In the world I say, not inside yourself. Perhaps in the end you will know more about your feelings than anyone else knows about theirs. What will you have gained? What will your life have meant to you? See you soon. Love, Paula

—typed letter, December 7, 1976

CONTENTS

*Author's note: These essays are not presented
chronologically. In most pieces I've tried to locate
the reader in time by noting my age when events
took place or by giving the year as a reference point.*

The Wandering Womb

FEMALE PROTECTION

Istanbul

We were strangers and our eyes met as we both left the tourism office. He smiled and I smiled and it was very early in the morning and I'd just arrived and didn't have plans. He was Austrian, spoke English, was tall with acne still on his baby face. I was in my early thirties. His name was Stephen. He asked if the American dollar was strong—physically—if it would hold up to washings if he sewed it into his clothing. We walked through bazaars and tea gardens and ate in cheap restaurants I couldn't find again after he left. We talked about the Big Things you talk about with strangers because you don't have enough intimacy to talk about the petty stuff. The morality of violence, World War II, the Baader-Meinhof Gang. I was his first Jew in the flesh. He'd seen a rabbi once—on TV, part of a series. He left a day before I did and after that I realized he had been my protection. Because I wasn't wearing a headscarf and skirt the men knew I was western and therefore hounded me

Vienna

Five years later: I stayed with Stephen and his sister. He took me to the Naschmarkt for sheep-cheese sandwiches; to his medical school, a building that smelled of formaldehyde and had worn stone steps. He wanted to show me daily things and tourist things and I wanted to Do Research. Jewish Research. But to come to Vienna and not want to see Saint Stephen's Cathedral or view the Klimts and Persian miniatures in the Belvedere Palace—instead, to concentrate on tribal history—that seemed narrow, parochial, stuck in the past.

I had my period. I didn't know where to throw my tampons and pads. There was no trashcan in the bathroom. I was afraid the tampons would plug up the toilet. I was too embarrassed to ask Stephen what to do with them. His sister wasn't around. I stuffed my used feminine hygiene products into the bottom of the kitchen trash. I put some in my knapsack and tossed them into garbage bins on the street. That whole week I felt very bloody, very Jewish. Once we passed by the Jewish Welcome Service on Stephansplatz and I wanted to stop in but not while he was with me. My Jewish Shame seemed the same as my menstrual shame, the clot that I scrubbed from the floor of the square bathtub. What to do with the unmentionables? Why bring up the Jews, those unmentionables? There was an outdoor exhibit downtown on the reconstruction of the city after the War. There were giant panels of blown-up black-and-white photos of rubble and after. Stephen told me he was tired of the War being thrown into his face. In school he'd always had to write essays about it. The past was past. And here I was, come from the New World, wallowing in it. He didn't say that. I thought that.

It had been interesting to talk about Jews when we first met, in Istanbul, I imagined him thinking. But once was enough. On to the next topic.

(I didn't leap then from the personal to the body politic. Unlike Germany, the defeated power, Austria, as an "occupied" country, has not had to examine its anti-Semitism and eager participation in the Final Solution. After all, it was an occupied country. Not their responsibility, no need to mea-culp like Germany. And even German historians had started: *Enough is enough, how long must we be guilty?*)

It still felt like the Cold War, back when Vienna was supposedly full of spies. The heart of Europe. I was a spy in old empire, a Jew masquerading as an innocent American tourist, pretending concern for Sachertortes and baroque palaces and Their history, visiting, say, the resistance museum and looking impassively at the artifacts: chess sets molded from bread, pretending a lack of scorn for the veneration of Communists and Catholics to the exclusion of the Jews. Nothing. *Judenrein.*

I went by myself to Freud's apartment. The good doctor had taken most everything with him when he and his family left, after much difficulty, for London in 1938. Now, instead of Freud's furniture and statues, there were black-and-white photographs of his furniture and antiquities all along the walls, roughly where the real objects had once been. A binder with multilingual pages gave the history of the absent artifacts.

I needed to use the restroom. I went to Freud's. It was large, like in an American house, clean white tiles. With a perfect metal trash basket for my American/Jewish/female unmentionables.

What does a woman want? Freud asked.

See above: a clean bathroom, a lined trash basket.

THE WANDERING WOMB

Hysterikos

If women are troubled in mind or body, the Kahun Gynaecological Papyrus (circa 1820 BCE) advises its readers to look to the wandering womb. In the fourth century BCE, Hippocratic physicians wrote that women who were ill might be plagued by a wanderlustful womb, which had loosened itself from its mysterious moorings to cause trouble in the parts of the body where it had set up shop. If the womb strayed into the head, it would cause headaches; if it sat in a woman's chest, it could cause near-suffocation. A misplaced womb could steal breath. Bind up a throat. Make everything difficult. *Give it a child and it will be happy.* Sometimes treatment was performed via the orifices. Affected women would be given something foul-smelling to breathe, so that the womb would be repulsed, would high-tail it back down to where it belonged. Another treatment was to expose the vulva to something pleasant-smelling, to lure the womb down to its rightful place, the way a woman incites a lover with sweet perfumes. Intercourse was proposed as a cure. After all, the womb longed to be of use. It wanted to be a nest. In the age before dissection, men could not divide its mysteries.

The womb, said Plato, is a wild animal. The womb, according to physician Aretaeus the Cappadocian four centuries later, is "like some animal inside an animal."

> *Hustera, hystera* (Greek) = uterus, womb
> *Hysterikos* = hysteric = coming from the womb, suffering caused by the womb
> Muff. Beaver. Pussy.

Bowl

I cannot imagine how surgeons remove the uterus. Because it is an embedded bowl. Or pear, as it is referred to in much of the literature about hysterectomies.

The womb as animal—as marten, say, weasel, ferret. It pokes its nose into corners and burrows, looking for a child to carry. It holds an empty bowl, or it is transformed from animal to bowl, looking like the fur-lined teacup created by a surrealist.

The womb as empty bowl, like a beggar's bowl. The beggar's bowl is mostly a man's bowl, a monk's bowl, or tool, equivalent to a shovel, perhaps, because it is with the bowl that he earns his daily bread. The beggar's bowl is a symbolic and a real bowl. It is philosophical so it deserves mention; it deserves not to be put out into the street.

A beggar's bowl is what the monk or nun takes out, empty each morning. They start anew. With hope and prayers. The bowl reminds the monk that all must be asked for, all must be given. The monk (or nun) asks for sustenance. They ask for enough. The person who gives enough, or part of enough, is blessed. The Torah tells Jews to leave the corners of their fields unharvested so that the poor could gather wheat for themselves. Are we blessed on the nights that we leave our bags of restaurant leftovers on the top of the dumpster so that they're easier for the homeless people to reach?

Each morning the begging bowl shines with waiting. If you are a monk you are confident. The universe will provide. In a film on the largest prison in India, I saw inmates learning Vipassana meditation, en masse; they emerged from their ten-day silence cleansed, quiet, humble, willing finally to admit that they had harmed society. That it had not done them wrong. In this prison, population 10,000, in suburban New Delhi, a pickpocket can wait six years for his case to come to trial, knowing that the sentence for his crime is only one year. Ten percent of the inmates are convicts; the others are awaiting trial. The film's narrator makes a statement about the slow wheels of justice in India. As if the slowness were just. The prisoners tell the camera: *This was meant to be. With Vipassana I no longer have revenge in my heart. This is what I was looking for. I was put here for a reason.*

The teacup, *Lunch in Fur,* was made by Méret Oppenheim in 1936 and titled by André Breton. Oppenheim used the pelt of a Chinese gazelle to cover a dime-store cup, saucer, and spoon. It brought her fame. Many years later, she hosted a small dinner party/performance during which guests ate a meal from the body of a nude woman lying on a table; thus the body was a table on a table, but unlike a table, the woman was able to partake of the meal along with the guests.

We all feast on the female body, at least once. The gazelle eats only grasses; it tries to outrun hunters. It is known for its gracefulness and for being endangered.

Perspective

It must be added that Plato also considered the penis to be a separate living thing. (Who wouldn't?) For Aristotle, the heart was like an animal. Medical historian Helen King charges that too much has been made by us moderns of the notion of the animal nature and the wandering womb among the ancients, blaming faulty scholarship and "our fascination with womb movement." She reminds us that intercourse and childbirth were prescribed as antidotes for almost all that ailed the female.

"The language may shift—the womb travels, vapors rise, sympathy transmits symptoms through the body—," King writes, "but the message remains the same: women are sick, and men write their bodies." Nineteenth-century hysteria was "a parasite in search of a history"—not evolving directly from earlier beliefs, but dipping into them, at will.

Global Wombing

Throughout the world, myths and legends persist, telling of vaginal teeth or fangs devouring the penis. Freud believed that the stories represented a universal fear.

In Vietnam, a rumor ran among GIs that prostitutes lined their vaginas with razors. In Japan, female ninjas were said to stuff theirs with sharp wire. Or somehow to insert daggers, pointing outward. *Women pretending to love the enemy. Women pretending not to be the devious creatures they were known to be.*

The Music Next Door

She began coughing for the first time when once, as she was sitting at her father's bedside, she heard the sound of dance music coming from a neighboring house, felt a sudden wish to be there, and was overcome with self-reproaches.

—Josef Breuer, "The Case of Anna O.," in Joseph Breuer and Sigmund Freud, *Studies in Hysteria*

There is always music next door.

That is the condition of humankind.

Anna O. is sitting next to her father, who is suffering from TB. It is possible that his weakened condition is caused by syphilis. Both ailments are known variously as the Viennese disease and the Jewish disease. Mr. O.'s Viennese-Jewish body has become home to rod-like tuberculosis bacilli, maybe to snake-like spirochetes, invisible bacteria both. This is still the age of enlightenment; the physicians know that sickness comes not from humors—too much blood, yellow or black bile, phlegm—or from the gods, but grows from invisible filaments, thriving as the body diminishes, from the inside out. Father and daughter are in his bedroom in a four-story chalet in Bad Ischl. *Bad* means "bath," and Ischl is a resort town where the kaiser vacations. When he's not in residence, you can visit his summer villa and see the desk where he declared war on Serbia. But not yet. It is only 1880. The war that split his hyphenated empire is more than a generation away, the 1.2 million sons of the empire who die in battle are not yet born. Ischl is a little boomlet hamlet, put on the map after a

local doctor sent word to the capital that the mineral salts would
be good for what ailed royalty. And it seemed so: the archduke's
wife bathed in the springs and became pregnant. Now the elite
come here, artistes, theatrical people, musical luminaries such
as Brahms. Ischl is the alpine resort of the genteel gentile high
bourgeoisie as well as the Jewish. Mahler, who is both, it seems
(born Jewish, converted, afraid that he still gestures like a Jew)
will summer here. But back in 1880, he is not yet composing here.
Anna's father is spending the summer decomposing. This night
in July no one in the family is awake except for the night nurse,
Anna, who is the only surviving daughter (two sisters died in
childhood), is twenty-one years old, generally bored with her life,
and this night she is sitting, waiting for a surgeon to arrive from
Vienna to drain her father's lung. She is nodding off, her arm
hanging on the back of her chair. Perhaps she's been knitting, or
sewing, is contemplating the shade of blue she will choose for
her father's dressing gown. Her contemporary Freud pronounced
rather nastily that women who did needlework idled their time
away with fantasy. He also said that women began to weave in
the first place because they were ashamed that they didn't have
penises. In their embarrassment, they wove their pubic hair.
They were ashamed that they had been castrated—what else
could have happened to their phalluses?

(Or perhaps those dangling parts had been eaten by the
vagina dentata. No wonder the womb wandered so—it was afraid
of all those teeth.)

So Anna, during this alpine summer, has been symbolically tatting her pubic hair. Maybe she's been embroidering an
edelweiss, a nice big one, the famous alpine daisy, surrounded by
a border. It is also the badge of the Austrian army and mountain
troops. About eighty years hence, in America, girls (including my
sister and me) will weave potholders on blue metal looms that
come with printed directions. Over under, over under; make a
little loop to hang it on and it will protect our mother's Jewish
fingers from kitchen burns. Anna O. will complain later she
did not learn any useful household arts, she learned how to
embroider, not how to mend; the laws of keeping kosher, but not
how to cook. Girls in Austria could attend school only through

age sixteen. Anna went to a Catholic school, the only second-
ary education available to females, where girls were polished,
made ready for society or prepared for jobs as governesses: they
learned French, Italian, music appreciation. It was assumed they
were schooled at home in the more subtle arts—prinking and
preening and lowering their lids when approaching boldness.

One thing Anna has learned to do is wait. To wait up. To
sleep by day if she is watching over. She has also learned to dance.
Did she learn, too, how to sit still while next door she can hear,
wafting, the sound of music?

Not the movie, though this is near Salzburg, the town
where the movie will be filmed. This is the real sound of music,
night music, wafting, waltzes, maybe mazurkas, even, when the
band feels adventurous. Young people Anna's age are dancing,
changing partners. Are laughing, are eating sweet cakes, perhaps
babas au rhum, tortes heaped with cream, mille-feuilles, napo-
leons from the famed Zauner pastry shop in town, perhaps sug-
ared violets, are drinking punch with lemon slices floating in the
silver bowl, a dash of red wine. Sashes, lace, swooshing taffetas
over whalebone that shapes the women into young hourglasses;
they have plenty of time. Hands, fingers, waists, shoulders. Does
Anna drop a stitch? She is not Madame Defarge working in a
code, or maybe she is but who can decipher it? Dr. Breuer hasn't
arrived yet in her life to untangle her secret messages. Her skirt
is still, her feet in place, her arm falls asleep, her eyes droop.
Then she's suddenly attentive to the sounds, as if they're smells
that wend their way to her room, her father's room. He is asleep,
practicing for his future role, of dead man; she practices being
an old woman while friends her age (she loves to dance, too, and
ride horses, hike in the meadows and mountains, play piano,
though not well) float through the evening. She is partnered
with her father.

He is feverish, has an abscess in his lungs, they are awaiting the arrival of the train carrying the doctor from the city. A
surgeon from Vienna. The train whistle awakens her, and she
begins to cough.

Tussis nervosa. Tussis hysterica. That's how it developed.
That night. The music. Why, she can't go dancing tonight, she

must stay inside where she belongs. With that cough. What can she be thinking of, going out with that cough? Instead of staying home to nurse it—and her father.

She awakens with a start, tries to check the time, but her eyes are filled with tears that distort the numbers under the crystal of her watch; they are blurry, unreadable. Across the room she seems to see a black snake about to attack her father. She looks at her fingers, they have turned into death's heads and squirming little snakes, she is coughing, she brushes off the hallucinations; but the next day, outside, playing a ring-toss game, she finds that sticks turn into snakes, snakes and death are everywhere, and soon she takes to her bed. She loses her language, develops a squint, paralysis; she becomes a hysteric. Which means, in the late nineteenth century, that her psychological state has created physical symptoms.

But maybe her womb, metaphorically or not, wandered next door while she was asleep; maybe it dressed up and went to the ball, this Cinderella-animal of Bad Ischl. Furry, weasel-like, it slips in between the dancing feet. Sniffs at them, slides in and out, careful to avoid being stepped on. Her escaped womb is licking up the crumbs fallen from all those tortes. It does not want to return to the deathlike bedroom, close with the faint iron-like smell of coughed-up blood. The womb loves being out, it is petted and cooed over, but watch for its tiny sharp teeth. Oooh! A girl flings it down, crying prettily to her dance partner. Awful. Wild animal. *Vilde khaya.* Her own womb is, thank you very much, snugly and smugly tucked in below her abdomen.

The Wombs of Bad Ischl

Bad Ischl houses secrets. During the Second World War the nearby Lauffen salt mine held art treasures that were looted from Jewish households; the plan was that after Hitler's victory such objects would be displayed in the Führermuseum in Linz. After the collapse of the Reich, Jewish survivors of the death and concentration camps were installed by the U.S. Army in the sumptuous villas of Bad Ischl that had been inhabited by Nazis. The furniture remained, as well as the gardeners. But the Jews had to leave—bad for tourism, said the Bad Ischlites. When a

U.S. Army chaplain addressed the European Jews, he referred to the locals as "Goddamned Austrians" and "khayas"—animals. He knew his audience. He knew the Austrians, too. In the late 1940s, when the residents of the nearest city, Salzburg, were polled, two-fifths reported that Jews were "profiteers." Half agreed that the Nazis had gone too far, but still "something had to be done to place limits" on Jews. Angry Bad Ischlites converged at a Jewish hostel and at city hall, the latter as a reaction to an unfounded rumor that the natives would have to make do with powder while the Jews would continue to receive whole milk.

Two decades after the War, before he became a notorious right-wing politician, Jörg Haider attended a private high school in Bad Ischl. There he joined a nationalistic fraternity that practiced fencing moves on a straw dummy, which was labeled "Simon Wiesenthal"—the renowned Nazi hunter

The Vanishing Womb

The wandering bowl, the animal that is a bowl, that escaped the bowl, that escaped being the bowl

    The wandering pear, a pear when it is ripe, ready

    There are animals—the common wolf, the fossa from Madagascar—that have been slandered and libeled through time; they were said to sneak into houses and steal human babies. Cats have been said to slink up to a cradle and steal the breath of infants. You can still buy amulets to ward off Lilith, the she-devil, who steals babies, kills babies, eats them.

    Méret Oppenheim declared at eighteen that she did not want to have children, and she never did. Women suffer, she said in her sixties, partly because men have not accepted their own feminine side. Her father once sent her to see Jung, who concluded that nothing was wrong with her, she was just an artistic type. Breton, the father of surrealism, celebrated hysteria as the "supreme vehicle of expression." Psychotic speech, he wrote in 1930, might "replace the ballad, the sonnet, the epic."

Anna O., aka Bertha Pappenheim, opened a school for wayward girls in Germany. She had them learn useful trades so that they could break from their fates. Sometimes it worked. She joined with other early twentieth-century feminists to stop the "white slave trade"—sexual trafficking of young women. In 1911 and 1912 Pappenheim visited Jewish prostitutes around Europe and Asia and the Middle East and reported on conditions to the Jewish feminist group that she founded. (Freud made fun of her crusade in a letter to a friend. He wrote that she'd never married, and now look what she's doing—trying to stop prostitution! A classic case of sublimation.) In one of her missives to her organization, Bertha tells of meeting Jolanthe, one of the most beautiful Jewish girls she had ever seen, at a brothel in Salonika. The girl was illiterate; she could not read or write her way out of her life, she could not keep men from paying to annihilate her soul. How can this person, Bertha asked, who is only twenty years old, offer her body, which is her most beautiful and precious possession, for sale?

Jolanthe is a princess in a fairy tale, imprisoned. By the world. But there is no one to save her, and each day, each night, there will be a bit less of her to save. Until she will disappear. Bertha tried once to save another young prostitute named Manya. Pappenheim brought her to her school, treated her as a daughter, but Manya went back to the streets, ended up in an institution.

Princess Jolanthe is dirt-ignorant, does not know her letters, any letters, in any language. She waits for men to choose her, for her seductive clothing, her smile, her dimples; she is a prisoner in an ancient land. Does she even think to pray to God for deliverance? Unlike Bertha, she does not write to Martin Buber to discuss theology, does not translate the ultimate feminist manifesto, *A Vindication of the Rights of Woman,* by Mary Wollstonecraft. Jolanthe in white, dark-eyed, dark-haired. A child. Bertha, white- haired, blue-eyed, descended from the famed poet Heinrich Heine, correspondent of Martin Buber, lover of music and opera, who is imperious in her dark Victorian skirts, who lives among carved antique furniture but is not afraid to travel half the world in dogcarts through muddy barely-roads. After she meets Jolanthe, Bertha dreams of her. In darkness, their lives join.

Promised Land

I am spending another summer in Elmwood in Berkeley, renting a large studio behind a house. It is so easy to live here, in summer, renting. I am envious of a Chicago acquaintance who spends summers in San Francisco. But my husband and I are rooted in Chicago, and deep into middle age.

Outside the little gourmet grocery store, the one where Michael Chabon and Ayelet Waldman's children run a tab, a man named Josh is sitting on a bench. He has three dogs with him. Two are furry shepherdy animals with pointy faces that are black on one side, white on the other. They are mirror images. They are both from a shelter, he says he waited a year for the second black-and-white dog. He put in his request to the online list for a border collie with a split black-white face and got it. When the supply is abundant you can afford to be picky. The third is a little brownish mop-haired dog hiding under the bench who didn't match up with anyone. He is a temporary foster dog.

Later I buy a silver gelatin print of Frida Kahlo processed by the man, Joshua Partridge, who prints pictures taken by his grandmother, Imogen Cunningham, decades before. Frida's photo was from 1931, when she was twenty-three or twenty-four, had already damaged her spine and pelvis in a bus accident, had started painting as she recuperated, and had already lived more than half her life; more or less the same as age as Méret Oppenheim when she lined the dime-store teacup. When does an artist grow into herself, and can we only discern this stage in retrospect?

China is starting to notice the absence of girls, many of whom were abandoned and taken West. It is predicted that in two decades some 30 million unmarried and unmarriageable men—uneducated, unemployed *guang guan* or "bare branches"—will form a tide of unrest, crime, violence. Unanchored, unmoored, these migrants will gather in cities, will not be lured back home with vials of sweet smells.

Song of Solomon

What was inside Bertha's dream of Jolanthe? Did she dream of her smooth twenty-year-old skin, her flashing black eyes, her wavy black hair, her exoticness? The girl must not have been so exotic to her customers; Sephardic Jews like Jolanthe made up more than half the population of Salonika then. The men who paid for her must have been drawn by her beauty, which they knew was fleeting. How do you separate the desire for her from the desire to join with such beauty, to own it, even for a few minutes—the clock ticking, the bare mattress stained and a little damp, the customer's sperm unthinkingly swimming toward the womb, as if the survival of the very species depended on it?

GRANDMOTHER RUSSIA/SELMA

I

It is 2020 and we are in the midst of Covid—reading about it, fearing it, masking against it, suffering from it, grieving from it, arguing about it, hiding from it, and hoping for a vaccine.

And I have been thinking about Russia. Or more precisely— I've been imagining Russia, its vastness, its grayness, its feature- lessness.

I know I have been imagining it inaccurately and as viewed from a large distance, bird's eye. I see it as if on a faraway map, without my glasses. I'm extremely nearsighted; if the best I could see *with* glasses were the way I see without them—I would be legally blind.

In their naturalization (as if they were unnatural before- hand) papers, my grandparents (and great-grandparents, depend- ing on which side of the family) had to renounce their loyalty to the czar of all the Russias. It was no great loss; the czar was no friend to the Jews.

Jews in Russian lands were relegated to living behind the pale, or fence, of settlement. It was a rare Jew who had permission to settle *beyond the pale.* My grandmother always said we were aristocracy; we were descended from the Vilna *Gaon,* the genius of Vilna, Lithuania. The gaon was a rabbi with a puckered-face personality, filled with so much learning that he condemned the happy dancing new sect called Hasidism. Its adherents believed that a yearning joyful soul would get you to God faster than learning what this rabbi and that rabbi had said about what the other rabbi had said about the Torah. In other words, the jumping Hasids were horning in on the territory of the genius.

And in the land of the Jews in the eighteenth century, there was little land, only people; thus territory meant followers. Lithuania was Russia. Poland was Russia. Romania was Russia, all depending on the time and portion of the smaller countries. Everything was Russia, even if it wasn't. Everything was empire, until it split, from rebellion or war.

I have read Tolstoy, Dostoevsky, Chekhov. I have tried to convince students that Chekhov was the father of the modern (western) short story. Freshman year (as we called it) in college, first quarter, I took a class on literature of the Soviet Union: Gorky, Sholokhov, Zoshchenko, Bulgakov, and yet I still see Russia as a vast plain. I see the characters animated by those stories as small dots amid the vastness. The mind's eye and heart have their own logic; they form the gulf between knowledge and imagination.

> *I do not know how I ever gained the impression that America was composed of a number of large and small islands, inhabited by a semi-barbaric people, free and brave but very much below the standard of the Europeans.*
>
> —Jewish-American Bernhard Goldgar on his circa 1878 voyage from Kodna, Russian Empire, to Macon, Georgia

We left the empire and didn't go back, didn't look back—because we were not Russian, we were Jews. They wouldn't let us be Russian. Russia did not care. Mother Russia was a large and blue-cold mother who had millions more at home she could treat indifferently, millions living and starving in the blue-cold folds of her shawls. Dying of cholera and overwork. Mother

Russia did not care for her Jews, any more than she cared for her unbelievers. Mother Russia could not be made to care. She went to sleep. She woke up and looked the other way. She looked up, sniffing for her next warm bite. We, on the other hand, were already on our way, with a few pieces of china and a pot or two and recipes in our heads, in the heads of our women.

I say that *we* left the Russian empire. It sounds like I was there, back in the dusty or muddy wooden shtetl with its chickens scratching, and potatoes and onions waiting in the cellar, then on the ship with its smells, ploughing through the Atlantic. But the Russian empire lived and died before I was born.

We—one—people—define ourselves by whom we are a part of. And that can change, and change, over time.

My grandparents and great-grandparents were tiny bits of the huddled masses who got into America before the gates were closed—to keep out the swarthy Mediterraneans, alien Asians (Jews were considered both), suspect Catholics and Eastern Orthodox, non-WASPS, though that term didn't exist yet. Unlike most of the masses, my grandparents and great-grandparents ended up in the southern United States. They arrived only thirty and forty years after the end of the Civil War. The Jews in the South, like the Jews in the North, often started out as peddlers, then became merchants. Jews in the South were few. In a Black-white society, they were deemed white. They wore their bestowed whiteness fearfully, then naturally. They adapted, hiring servants who were Black, who sometimes lived in shacks or small houses behind the white family home.

At the turn of the nineteenth-into-twentieth century, my great-great-uncles and great-grandfather traveled from Pashvitin near present-day Kaunus, Lithuania, to Selma, the bustling Queen City of the Black Belt. They had a relative who'd settled nearby. My great-grandfather Zelman/Sidney Mindel had been ordained as a rabbi but had heard that he wouldn't be able to find a pulpit with his limited English. In Selma he read a help-wanted ad in a Yiddish newspaper for a ritual slaughterer job in Louisiana, and traveled there. He didn't last a week. *The work was against his nature*, my grandmother said. He became a peddler. As he traveled from small town to town, he would introduce himself to Reform rabbis and coach them in Torah. My grandmother, his eldest daughter, lowered her voice on the cassette tape as she said this, as if there were something shameful about the situation, that Reform rabbis were so ignorant. After earning money peddling, my great-grandfather opened a grocery store on Water Avenue in Selma, near the Alabama River. I don't know if he made much of a living. His brother-in-law in Selma did not do well as the owner of another grocery store; he was apparently a head-in-the-sky intellectual. The brother-in-law died young of heart disease; then his widow died young when a car ran into her. She was taking her kids home from a movie matinee. She died in the hospital that is now the Vaughan-Smitherman Museum in Selma. In 2013 I stood in the museum for the first time, during Pilgrimage, the annual tour of historic homes and buildings. I realized: my great-great aunt Libby died here.

During the blockade, we couldn't get any decent thread, said the white woman. She was in period costume on another of my visits to Selma, this time for the Battle of Selma re-enactment, and she was one of the sutlers, or merchants, who set up shop next to the battlefield in a park. She was talking about the Civil War ship blockade that cut off the Confederacy from overseas trade with Europe. We? *We?* How could she identify so closely with many generations past, who, she didn't seem to acknowledge, were on the wrong side, the side of white people who believed in owning other, darker people, who believed it was right and good?

Sometime around 1916 in Selma my great-grandfather Sidney had the idea for a southern conference of Zionist Jews. He helped plan it, and he told his daughter Bessie to come with him to the meeting in Savannah, Georgia, so that she might meet a nice young man there. She did: my grandfather—Sol Wisenberg, who was living in Macon, Georgia, at the time.

I have seen the courthouse in Macon where my grandfather became a citizen. I have his official renunciation of loyalty to the czar in a frame on my wall. At the courthouse a generic Confederate soldier statue used to stand, facing South. It's since been moved elsewhere in town, *near an area where African-American human beings were bought and sold*, a local professor told a reporter. The erecting of the statue was part of a nationwide post-Reconstruction revanchism, the reassertion of white supremacy throughout the former Confederacy, reanointing their Civil War heroes who had become the embodiments of the Lost Cause. What did my grandfather think of the soldier standing there? Did he think: *American*? What did he think of the Confederate monument next to the courthouse in Laurel, Mississippi, the next place he lived? Laurel originated in 1882 as a timber town, with midwesterners fueling its growth. Its school superintendent was from the North. My aunt, born in 1918, remembered being taught in school in Laurel that the South was wrong during the war.

She also remembered going with her father to hear Governor Theodore Bilbo—Klan member, spewer of race-baiting bombast. My grandfather, she said, would predict what Bilbo would say, and he'd be right. *It was fascinating*, she said.

My family, the Wisenbergs, moved around the South, leaving a foreclosed house in Mississippi in 1932 to start over in Houston, Texas. That is where I was born, in a hospital downtown, at the end of 1955. I used to place my birth as ten years after the end of World War II. Several years ago I realized: it was also two weeks after Rosa Parks set off the Montgomery bus boycott.

On the bus that day Parks was tired, tired from tailoring in the basement of the Montgomery Fair department store but also soul-tired after working for the local NAACP for more than a decade, not believing that the timid Blacks of Montgomery, cradle of the Confederacy, would ever organize or "stand together." She'd been refreshed and strengthened, earlier that year, by her time at a summer workshop on school desegregation at the Highlander Folk School in Tennessee, where she ate, slept, and met with whites as equals.

After she came back home that summer, Emmett Till was kidnapped, tortured, and murdered in Money, Mississippi.

And three months later I was born. The hospital was segregated.

> *I am an American, Chicago born, and go at things as I have*
> *taught myself, free-style.*
>
> —Saul Bellow, *The Adventures of Augie March*

I did not teach myself much. I let myself be pushed along the waves of others' approval. That's what a girl-child does, a Jewish girl-child with asthma and shyness, who is tall for her age, gawky. Who loves to read and loves to catch grasshoppers and lizards, but dares not let the other kids find out. Because popular girls don't do such things. They spend most of their time giggling.

Oh my hair! It's so frizzy! That's what you were supposed to lament while standing in the bathroom mirror at school or synagogue. That was the chorus line you had to learn. The communal female Jewish wail about the humidity of Houston. This was an early-teen world of ID bracelets exchanged, phone calls waited for, notes passed, clothes and albums bought, boy-girl parties anticipated. These were the preoccupations of the young Jews, even those of us who were bar and bat mitzvahed. We paid passing attention to the words of the Torah, the conundrums in *Ethics of the Fathers*. Our religious inheritance was assigned to the margin. What was more important in Hebrew school was to make C feel self-conscious because D kept looking at her when she was whispering to E. That is a scheme I observed play out. The official lessons did not penetrate our self-absorption, our devotion to status building. Every so often an idea would float from the teacher's mouth into our brains, would lodge there: that we Jews don't refer to the Torah as the Old Testament because we don't accept the New Testament; that there are Jewish rules that govern life-and-death decisions: when two people are dying in the desert, the water should go to the person most likely to survive, no matter his (it was never her) status. That was interesting. We did not wonder why girls and women were not allowed to read from the Torah in public, why women could not be rabbis or cantors. We thought it was more interesting that our teacher, a short, thin, ill-at-ease British man who appears in my mind's eye in a tacky plaid suit, had been arrested for going through a stop sign on his bicycle, and ticketed. He was what was in front of us.

It is Jewish tradition that a person (a man) must wait until he is forty years old with a family to study the Kabbalah, the system of Jewish mysticism. He must be grounded, so that he doesn't float away. What if we had learned Kabbalah? Might that have kept our interest? We were surely tethered to the material world and our future in it.

Recently I found a Hebrew school quiz in my old papers. Now I would be able to match the men (women were not listed) on the list with the descriptions of their Jewish significance. Back then I missed almost half the matches. I have taught myself Jewish history, freestyle. I have visited many Jewish communities, but never gone back as far east as Kishinev, Slutsk, Pashvitin, Plungian—the places my family lived in the former empire. I would find what others have—overgrown cemeteries with faded or broken headstones, a young guide who might be Jewish or more likely not, maybe an active synagogue; I would wander in the former Jewish quarter wondering if my family might have lived here, or here, or where this parking lot sits.

My former synagogue is now the largest Conservative one in the country. There were so many thirteen-year-olds that two unrelated kids would be bar/bat mitzvahed together. My bat mitzvah partner, whom I'd met in the synagogue nursery school, who was born a month before me, had a Russian grandmother whom I don't remember meeting. At our *b'not mitzvah*, "double bat mitzvah," I must have seen her as just an old lady with a corsage. A few years ago I came across a transcript of an interview with her. She talked about having been a teenage socialist in Klimovichi, Belarus. She agitated against the czar. She helped organize a strike. She immigrated to Houston after the Bolshevik revolution, after World War I. In the 1976 interview she spoke of the people back in the USSR. She said, *I have there a left-behind family, I raised six children from my mother and father. In two years I lost three brothers and a sister so I was always in mourning. I keeped on sending money home all mine life. Mine sister died at sixty-five and three weeks ago, mine brother passed away in Russia. I'm the only.*

    I had no idea.

In seventh grade I had a friend named Jay who was best friends with our next-door neighbor. Jay's German-Jewish family were longtime Texans; an ancestor fought with Terry's Texas Rangers, a volunteer Confederate States Army cavalry regiment. I didn't know that then. I mention this just to show how close we were in Houston to the Confederacy.

    In Judaism we are taught to take our biblical ancestors' experience into our bodies. On Passover we read that you should feel that you were there in Egypt, that you were liberated and tentatively stepping your foot into the Red Sea, which had opened for the fleeing Jewish slaves. Our rabbi, a literal man, took up a staff and led synagogue members on a hike along Brays Bayou to reenact the Exodus. At the end of the march was the promised land of the Houston Jewish Community Center, and instead of manna, the weary Jews were proffered bagel and cream cheese provided by the Men's Club. This rabbi loved acronyms. There was a group called Put On Tefillin—Let's Start Davening (praying).

    Jay and his best friend had a bar mitzvah reenactment in 2019, fifty years after the event. The two of them gave relevant and thoughtful speeches; their children spoke.

Bar mitzvahs are wasted on the young.

Everyone else called it a second bar mitzvah. I called it a reenactment because I thought it was funny. But there is a hollowness at the center of reenacting. You are playing a role. This was a sincere reexperience, an excavation, dipping at the same well half a century later, for meaning.

My grandmother, the one from Pashvitin-Selma-Laurel, then Houston, was our tie to the Old Country, inaccessible behind the Iron Curtain as I was growing up. In the 1960s, in New York City for a family wedding, we saw *Fiddler on the Roof* on Broadway, and were sure she would feel warm about the depiction of her previous life. When the lights came on we saw: she was asleep.

When the movie version of *Fiddler* came to Houston, some friends went to see it with their grandmother Rose. She cried throughout. Her grandson Michael Newman said, *I remember her saying it was just like her life, except that they didn't sing and dance as much.* He was quoted in a local newsletter.

In my grandmother's time, in the time of *Fiddler on the Roof*, in the vast Russian empire, Cossacks and other locals ransacked the shtetls and raped Jewish women, laid waste to towns and houses and synagogues, slit necks and chests and genitals. Did not care. Did not see us—*us!*—as individuals. They sought to and succeeded in annihilating us. Some of us. They were so wild we could not reason with them, so wild they were savages. In Kishinev, Romania/Bessarabia, where the Wisenbergs (frequently known as Waysenbergs) came from, there was a violent pogrom in 1903 that shocked people around the world and spurred emigration. My grandfather told my aunt he remembered as a small boy pouring boiling oil on the marauders. A Houston friend told me that his grandfather said he remembered seeing rows of the dead outside the Jewish hospital in Kishinev. Another pogrom there in 1905 was met with Jewish resistance—which was quashed by police.

And obviously, the true murderers of Jews en masse, the crafters of full-fledged genocide, were the Germans decades later, aided by others. Jews from Kishinev and throughout the region were massacred; survivors were transported to ghettos and camps. The victims included the family my grandfather had left behind. In 1992 I met my third cousin in Israel, an emigree from Kishinev. She said her family didn't talk about the War; it was too sad and traumatic.

In Houston my grandmother wore dark short-sleeved dresses that were plain or had simple geometric patterns. This is what I remember, at least. She stuffed a Kleenex into a sleeve for access at all times. She also kept Kleenex in her pocketbook. She had large breasts that we became cognizant of only when we found her bra in a drawer when she was staying with us once when our parents were out of town. Size D, I think. She was not cuddly but she was friendly. She took us out for lunch and clothes shopping after Shabbat services on Saturday mornings. I remember eating at Hebert's Ritz "A-Bear" Cajun restaurant near downtown Houston. She probably ordered trout amandine and I, fried chicken. We didn't eat shellfish. After the meal I would carefully remove a square of sponge cake from the after-services reception. It would be wrapped in a paper napkin, and I would set it on my plate and eat it. The staff at Ritz "A-Bear" didn't object. Then we'd go shopping at one of the downtown stores—Neiman's, Battlestein's, Sakowitz, Foley's, Joske's—all founded or run by Jews. I remember once she bought me a blue dotted-swiss low-slung dress, size 6x, that I loved. It had a white sash around the hips I didn't have. The dress reminded me of the 1920s, whose fashions I knew from illustrations in *The World Book Encyclopedia*. Our grandmother lived in an apartment complex with a pool and I remember swimming with her there. She was fleshy, sturdy. Not exactly fat. We called her Grandma Baeky, though her peers called her Bessie. Sometimes she was Grandma Houston, to differentiate her from my mother's mother,

Grandma Dallas. She was at home in Houston. She traveled from grocery store to grocery store, buying bargains, mostly in fresh fruit, and delivering them to her daughter and daughters-in-law. She frequently baked a short, dense, lemon-glazed cake made with wine-soaked prunes and delivered it to her friends. She also sold the cakes to raise money for Hadassah. She made mandel bread, hamantaschen, gefilte fish, matzah ball soup, and various experimental dishes made from matzah meal on Passover, when you are not allowed to use leavening. My aunt remembered that her mother drove a car early on, in the 1920s, when the family was living in small-town Mississippi. When I knew her, she would pump on the gas pedal every few seconds, as if she believed that the proper way a car should move was bit by bit, that you had to be cautious to keep it from running away from itself. My aunt drove in the same way. My grandmother avoided freeways.

She spoke with a heavy accent. Most of the time it was a Deep South accent. When she spoke about Russia, it would get a slight Yiddish tinge. By the time I met her, she was a widow. I was named for her husband.

When I was first applying for jobs and the interviewers asked me to tell them about myself, I always wanted to say: *I was named after my grandfather Solomon Louis Wisenberg, who emigrated from Kishinev.* That was where I thought I'd started, with the grandfather I never knew, in a place I'd never been. My grandfather died a year and a half before I was born and, per Ashkenazi Jewish custom, a baby in the family was named for him. I have the same initials and same last name. My father idolized his father and I looked for ways to tie my life to this grandfather who was buried in the Beth Yeshurun cemetery. I remember once I had a brain freeze from eating ice cream and I asked my father if Grandpa Sol had had the same kind of headache. *Yes,* he said. Virginia Woolf be damned—she who said that *women think back through their mothers.*

I knew in job interviews that I wasn't supposed to start with my grandfather. I should say that I'd always wanted to write, I was curious about people, I wanted to cover housing or health for a newspaper, I wanted to be a great feature writer like _____ or a

columnist like _____ or I loved teaching writing because I loved
when the students _____. I was never good at job interviews.
        I can imagine this grandfather because I've heard about
him and seen pictures.

I can't imagine the entirety of Russia. Maybe I'm thoroughly
a child of the Cold War, can't shake the worldview that we
Americans (the shapeshifting *we*) are up against a large menacing nemesis. We Americans believed in democracy, rugged
individualism, each family settled in its own home with TV, on
which to watch *Father Knows Best*, and with a father who went
to work in a coat and tie and did know best. These families were
white, as American Jews became. The Soviets believed in mass
movements. Citizens were like ants on an anthill. If we were to go
there, to the USSR, and we wouldn't, we would be swallowed up.
        And thus, now, the heir to the Soviet Union is the undif-
ferentiated gray mass.

Sometimes my grandmother said we were from Europe, or would
say, *Back in Europe*. Recently I found to my surprise that she was
accurate: western Russia, the area where she was from, is considered to be Europe by geographers; calling it that always seemed
like a prettying up, an evasion. Russia as wannabe Europe. Peter
the Great was known for his westernization of the empire: from
fashion to the army to the alphabet. Members of the Russian
aristocracy were certain of their Europeanness, their superior-
ity to the peasants. At the beginning of *War and Peace*, they're
speaking French. Nabokov's parents spoke to their young child
in English. My ancestors spoke Yiddish and Russian.
        In *To the Finland Station*, Edmund Wilson writes about
Lenin's father, an education official: "he succeeded in getting the
better of the laziness and ignorance whose vacuity matched the
vast flat spaces of Russia."

He also writes, "As Germans, [Marx and Engels] had at the same time always cultivated a contempt for the Slavs."

As Hitler did.

Soviets sought to create the New Soviet Man, the man without history, no longer tied to the feudal, czarist system. However, the leaders were individuals. We certainly know their noms de guerre: Lenin, Trotsky, Stalin. There was opportunity, in waves, for the Jews to become Soviet Men, to join together, to shed what made them different.

Individuals mattered so little that 10 million of them could be murdered by the Georgian Ioseb Besarionis dze Jugashashvili, aka Stalin.

In the camps the Nazis infamously numbered everyone they could—Jews, Jehovah's Witnesses, gays, political dissidents, anyone who did not conform mentally or physically, who was not a member of the devoted Aryan tribe.

You were associated with a number, like an animal, because that's what Jews were.

In 1961 the non-Jewish Soviet poet Yevgeny Yevteshenko wrote about Babyn Yar or Babi Yar, the pit in Kiev where 33,000 Jews were thrown after they were murdered by the Nazis. He wrote, "I seem to be Anne Frank"—the modern German-Dutch girl who collected photos of western movie stars, whose name has become so emblematic that she is the star, the individual, in the poem about a mass execution and a mass grave. We want an individual to stand for the whole, the genius, the martyr. In the poem Yevteshenko also wrote that he seemed to be Dreyfus, another martyr, another Jew—eventually pardoned for a trumped-up crime. Yevteshenko was writing as witness to the past killing of Jews. The murdered adults and children pushed and kicked into Babi Yar were not merely Soviet citizens, as the government had said. They were Jews. No one knew their names, so he named two famous Jewish martyrs. The government was

trying to hide them, trying to dissolve their features, just like the
lime the Einsatzgruppen threw between the bodies to speed up
their disintegration. I first read the poem during the Cold War.
Back then both the poet and Kiev were considered Soviet. Later
I found that Yevteshenko was born in Siberia and came from a
multiethnic background. Now Kiev is the capital of Ukraine, a
country helmed by a Jewish former comic and actor.

The Red Army liberated Auschwitz, all wearing the Soviet
uniform.

I've seen names on local Civil War, World War I and II memorials, and they are the bedrock of contemporary memorials:
the Vietnam Veterans Memorial, the 9/11 Memorial, the AIDS
Quilt, the National Memorial for Peace and Justice (lynching
memorial), and so many Holocaust memorials.

The names of people who were enslaved, deracinated,
given new names—they were lost. By design.

On the website of Yad Vashem—the World Holocaust Remembrance Center—you can look up the European town your family
is from and you can look for people. You can look for people in
that town who have last names similar to those in your family,
and you can make a reasonable assumption. I looked at the list
of people from Slutsk (Russian empire, Soviet Union, Belarus)
where my Grandma Dallas was from. There was a girl born the
same year as my mother, with the family's name. I consider her
my mother's shadow twin, the one who didn't leave, who didn't
grow up in Dallas, who left the world instead, wrenched violently
from it, when she was fourteen.

Say their names, those who were killed by racist police, the system, by history, those who were both example and symbol of
what is wrong with society, during what we call peacetime.

During the pandemic we have been in quarantine, we have been restricting our movements, waiting in limbo, waiting for Godot to arrive and lift the lockdown. Time stretches on and on and maybe that is why I am imagining Russia as a large blank snowy land, its vastness equivalent to the sea of time where we are living now.

I know several Jewish women from the Soviet Union. One of them told me that she'd just observed the anniversary of her mother's death: *Yesterday I light twenty-four-hours candle*—the *yortzeit* memorial candle. She sounded a lot like the old ladies in synagogue when I was a child. She sounded like my bat mitzvah partner's grandmother. She sounded like I would, if our family had not emigrated earlier, and if we had survived the War. I would have her life. Or my cousin's.

My husband and I live a couple of blocks from Graceland Cemetery where Chicago city fathers and elites are buried. It has become a playground, full of masked, mostly white people jogging, biking, pushing strollers, walking fast and walking slowly, walking dogs. Singles, couples, families.

I lived in Houston through high school, have spent most of the rest of my life in Chicago. I belong to both cities, and neither. I don't have a plot in Chicago. I asked my mother if I had a plot in Houston. She said no, then the next day she offered to buy me one. I demurred. I am donating my organs. Or I might become the semester companion of a med student, who will (odds are) give my body a name. This naming is a way of coping with the fact of having an assigned dead body to slice and dice. Preparing the student to scalpel into real, living flesh, which has become half-dead through anesthesia.

Though I've never been there, I still want to say I'm from Russia. I need a place to be from. Not my birthplace but a deep, mysterious place, as mysterious as life and death. I need a place I don't know. I need a place in the past that goes back further than I can see. I need to be reassured that I am part of a what I see as a thick gray skein of family and pastness. I need to feel, to know, that I have a place in a river of family. Because I can't float. I can't live just being a person without a crowd of before and after. I need to be moored. Because otherwise—because otherwise when I die I leave no trace. I have no children.

This feeling accounts for the desire for connection to the past. Our horror is death. Our horror is that we will no longer exist, will no longer be named or remembered.

Death is the great shapeless mass, the nothingness.

II

There are others who identify closely with the past, feeling it in their bones. In the Vaughan-Smitherman Museum in Selma I went upstairs to the Confederate Room. *The slaves were not mistreated*, a man dressed as a Confederate told me. He was a history teacher. He was wearing a long-sleeved white shirt and a canteen attached to a bandolier that went across his chest, Sam Browne–style. He was a volunteer during the annual Pilgrimage weekend, when historic buildings are open to the public, and select local girls (white, one Black, according to a photo in the brochure) wear long, pastel, vaguely period antebellum dresses and supplement the guides.

When he was a young Baptist preacher, he visited old ladies, Blacks, who told him that the slaves were punished only if they deserved it. Your most valuable property—why would you ruin it, make it unfit for work? *Roosevelt sent people to interview former slaves*, he said, *and they are remarkably not bitter*. I have read many of these WPA interviews, and there is indeed some love expressed for the masters, but those instances are overwhelmed by descriptions of torture, savagery, inhumanity, cruelty, evil— fueled by slavery and white supremacy, during and after the Civil War. These interviews are compromised because most of them were conducted by whites, and it's hard to say how much the formerly enslaved elders felt free to express.

The man's great-great-grandfather had volunteered to fight in the Civil War, and after it, returned home to Georgia, finding that General Sherman had burned down the house and that one baby had starved to death. The man said he'd met a woman who had told him about her father's experiences at the Battle of Selma.

The trauma of the long-ago battle is felt by the man in front of me. It is perpetual, this trauma. The federal troops raided Selma. It was called Wilson's Raid; they burst in on a Sunday and kicked open the doors of churches and killed the men and boys. The ministers invited the troops in to pray, though at least one minster took off his pastor's robe to reveal the uniform beneath it and fought the enemy. The bodies piled up and the women and children were not allowed to bury their dead. After three days the bodies, hot and rank in the sun, attracted vermin, and then they were dumped into a communal grave in Live Oak Cemetery, where long beards of Spanish moss hang from the trees.

The feds also slaughtered horses, piling them in the very same streets. *And we couldn't bury them,* the man says.

I think of Antigone. I think how American Jews feel so personally about the Holocaust; I think about trauma traveling down the generations. I think of the way I say I'm from Russia, we're from Kishinev.

There is regular time that we splash our way through and there is deep time that connects this moment to the past, that collapses distance. There is homage to the past that is redemptive. Less than a mile from this museum is the Slavery and Civil War Museum. It has a slave ship room in which a reenactment of cap- ture and voyage takes place. The actor who created the original reenactment now does it on her own and in her own space. And down on Broad Street is a belly of the ship in a long tin shack that is Charlie Lucas's studio. He's an artist who's Black and is known as the Tin Man. There are no whips or chains; there's no rusty smell of blood. *It is beyond that, beyond the tragedy,* says the Tin Man. *There is the spirit that the slaves brought with them, their ancestors, their culture and traditions.* The room has wooden beams on the floor lengthwise and orange fabric that suggests sails, which reaches up alongside a few vertical pieces of wood and is tied loosely. The artist is still working on the captain's area—you can see the wheel. On the wall are paintings and paintings with assemblages, faces abstracted, mostly. They are not sad. They are red and black and green and yellow. They are beyond. What is beyond? What is beyond is soul. What is beyond is muse. It's hard for a semi-northerner to understand the origin of the name Tin Man. It has to do with having only $10 in his pocket at one point. Alabamans pronounce both words the same: *tin* and *ten.*

I think of the ten spot that I saw in the Selma museum, which a white volunteer guide said was the most reliable antebellum bill, issued by a bank in New Orleans. It said *D-i-x* on it, French for "ten," the *x* vocalized in the southern region where it was honored, as opposed to in France. It's one origin story for the word *Dixie.* In a bank down the street from the Tin Man's studio, next to the new Coffee Shoppe run by a Black woman and leased from a group of activist Catholic clergy, there are two pictures of fox hunters and a framed grouping of Confederate dollars.

In Selma, the Confederate says, the feds raped and pillaged; the war was fought over the wealth of the South, which the Northeast coveted, still covets, still tries to take from beneath the Mason-Dixon Line. *Look at the presidents, even Jimmy Carter was educated in the Northeast. And Obama, Harvard.* He says this to me and to a few other visitors to the Confederate Room. The year is 2013. Controversy has brewed in this town over Nathan Bedford Forrest, a hero of the Confederacy, wizard of the saddle, untaught master general. Forrest is considered to be the founder of the KKK, though that was when the organization was for the protection of citizens, and he dropped out later, when it got rough, the Confederate explains. Forrest was charged with massacring Black troops at Fort Pillow, Tennessee, though he was cleared by a congressional investigation. He has not been cleared by Black activists in Selma, who suggest that a bust of him was set on a column in an effort to see-you-one-and-raise-you-one in response to the bust of Martin Luther King, Jr., in front of the Brown Missionary Baptist Church. The bust and column were moved to Live Oak, and then the bust of Nathan Bedford Forrest was stolen, a $40,000 reward offered. He will be moved again, to a slab just behind the empty column, near the rebel flag, in the Confederate portion of the cemetery, if he is returned.

I have people there, in the cemetery—two Rosenbergs and two Rosenburgs. Selmians will tell you that there was no anti-Semitism, that the Jews were accepted and still are, though there are only a half-dozen left, no one under the age of sixty-two. The youngest member of the Jewish community is automatically the president of the temple. (In 2021, only four Jews in remain in Selma.)

What is me and what is not me. The Tin Man drew and painted and made toys out of wire and cans and sticks as he was growing up, worked odd jobs and worked maintenance at a hospital until he was laid off. Then he cut down and hauled logs and fell from the truck, breaking his back. He was paralyzed from the waist down, he prayed, he prayed to God that he could be reborn, that he could create, and he told his friends that his life was changing, he promised God he would give him credit, that he would teach others if he would be redeemed, and he was. Which takes us back to the $10 in his pocket. He could use his arms and hands and leaning over the side of the bed he made animals out of wire. He painted. He felt God moving within him. He felt the duty to feel joy, though he does not say it that way. He is walking now (he had back surgery), is thin and almost rangy, is always in pain, he says, but he has discipline, he listens to that voice within, allows God to work through him. Discipline is something like hewing to the path that your special gift is carving out for you. He works alone and he works with young students in school and at camp. They build funkified dinosaurs of yarn and wire and wooden leg joints. And metal. Like tin.

The connection from soul to soul is larger than voting rights is larger than politics, he says. He is not bitter, he does not hold anything against anyone.

The Confederate leaps through time, too, he feels con-
nections, he says that Black and whites should join together
stand against the Northeast, the Northeast again; it is the section of the country that is trying to destroy the culture of the
South, he says. The way the feds burned libraries, he says. He
asks, *Why would they burn libraries if not to tell the enemy that
they will be absolutely destroyed, the equivalent of being bombed
back to the Stone Age?*

The federal government is always wanting to tell the
South what to do, taxing it and deciding how to spend the taxes,
he says. When FEMA came to northern Alabama, he says, the
locals told the volunteers they weren't needed. The northerners
were shocked about how people in the South took care of one
another. They had that *bond of blood and fire*, he says.

Down the street is the studio of Afriye Wekandodis. It looks out
onto the Alabama River through glass doors. The walls inside
are mostly painted light blue, with some of the brickwork visible
in front, and painted blood red in the back. She's started hosting
concerts and talent shows there, in her By the River Center for
Humanity. There's a small stage with microphone and djembe.
What she uses in her work—in other words, where she guides
people in reenacting the dismal and torturing Middle Passage
ship journey from Africa to the New World—is the brown-
painted room, along a wall, that you reach via stairs. Once you're
there, you can pull open the trap door and walk down another
set of stairs. On the wall in front of the "ship" is a postcard that
is a photograph of a plaque of the Elmina slave castle in Ghana:
*In everlasting memory of the anguish of our ancestors. May those who
died rest in peace. May those who return, find their roots, may humans
never again perpetuate such injustice against humanity.*

Afriye grew up in Chicago. Racism is the same in her
native and adopted homes, she says. Her family was from
Selma, and after being gone for sixty-eight years, her mother
wanted to move back home. Afriye traveled with her mother

to Selma in June 2004, left and came back on a Greyhound, $20 in her pocket. She started volunteering at the National Voting Rights Museum and Institute and then she got a job at the Slavery and Civil War Museum. In June 2005 she felt God calling her to re-create the Middle Passage experience. She did that for the museum as an independent contractor. One day a downtown property owner stopped her on the street and told her she needed her own dedicated area for this work. He had just the place, along the river.

She starts outside. People usually come in groups with others they know. She tries to break down alliances. Then she brings everyone inside her studio, into the dark slave hold, on the ground level and upstairs. She repeated for me what she says there, a chant:

Can you imagine being taken away from your family, from your friends, never to see them again?

Can you imagine being on the Middle Passage in the bottom-most of the slave ship?

Can you imagine being chained to someone who has died or perhaps might be in the process of dying?

Can you imagine rats biting at you night after night, day after day? Can you imagine looking down and seeing maggots?

Can you imagine all of this—because of the color of your skin? And to justify their madness they said it was because you are godless people.

Can you imagine standing up and fighting for your right to be treated as a human being like so many enslaved Africans did but who did not make it into the history books? There are cases where they would not only kill you but they would chop your body up into pieces and force the others to eat you. If you decided to take your destiny into your own hands by starving yourself to death they had a way of fixing you by knocking your teeth out, putting hot coals down your throat.

Can you imagine all this because of the color of your skin? And to justify their madness they said you are godless people.

Can you imagine?

Can you imagine as a man hearing your womenfolk cry out for help and there's nothing you can do about it?

Can you imagine as a mother hearing innocent babies crying out?

Can you imagine all this because of the color of your skin? And to justify the madness they said it was because you are godless people. Yet in spite of the circumstances, in spite of the shackles and chains, the enslaved Africans never allowed their spirits to be broken, it was bent, it was crushed, but never never broken because they knew that someday God would answer their prayers, and even if they would never know the joy of physical freedom again they knew that someday, someday that their children's children's children's children would be free and that's why they were able to sing. But can you imagine—all because of the color of your skin?

Then she sings: *They stole my body, Lord, but I'm still here. They stole my body Lord, but I'm still here. They stole my body Lord, but they couldn't steal my soul. They stole my body Lord, but I'm still here.*

At that point she tells them they have arrived in North America. They are standing in the dark, and then Afriye becomes an old wraith mourning her children: *I will go through the dark and sob, "I want my babies." Or even I'll say, "Your mamma ain't never stop lookin' for you, she looked for you until the day she died, yes she did." And then they hear this young mother searching for her children.*

The she sings:
Sometimes I feel like a motherless child.
Sometimes I feel like a motherless child, such a
       long way from home.

Later she asks: *What shackles have you put on yourselves?*

She tells me, *They don't answer. That's just something you have to probably spend the rest of your life trying to answer. But then I turn on the lights and make eye contact with everyone because sometimes especially for African Americans they travel and for the first time in their lives they're really connecting with the history—even though they saw "Roots" and they saw all the other pictures and they read the books—but to go through this experience just for thirty to forty-five minutes made them realize how powerful we are as a people and that we have come a long way but we have a long way to go.*

I need at least twenty minutes but sometimes they go for an hour or more because we're not only talking about the enslavement of

*African Americans, we're talking about what's going on with people's
personal lives—that you're not embracing who you are.*

School groups are always touring Selma as part of civil rights history, and some of these groups sign up for Wekandodis's Middle
Passage experience. I talked to Marta Repoletto, who experienced
the journey twice. Repoletto teaches multicultural history at
Grant High School in Portland, Oregon, and was accompanied
by students and other teachers—most of them white. *It's the
best educational and emotional experience you can have in terms
of understanding what slavery was like,* she said. *I saw this as a
teacher, seeing how to teach it, how to empower kids of color so they
don't feel victimized. It's led by this powerful Black woman that takes
you through that journey.*

Wekandodis's studio is on the same street where my ancestors'
Red and Blue grocery stores sat. I imagine my grandmother as a
teenager—whose fellow students made fun of her in the Selma
High School yearbook, mocking her immigrant accent—walking
down Water Avenue, where thousands of pilgrims, including me,
have walked, on our way to reenact the historic bridge-crossing
of 1965. Maybe one day Grandma Baeky passed Afriye's grandmother there. It is the 1910s; the streets smell of horse dung,
resound with the thump and smack of hooves and footsteps, bits
of drawling conversation that overlap in this booming Queen
City of the Black Belt. The two young women in wide flat hats
are facing one another from a distance, one walking east, the
other west, blowing in from two different continents.

 The darker woman steps off the sidewalk, to allow the
so-called white woman to pass.

 That is the custom, the rule. If you live in the South you
know the expectations about back doors and front doors, about
eye contact, ways of addressing, gender and sexual protocols and
taboos; such written and unwritten mandates are bred into you.
If you are an immigrant you learned such things, as you learned
English and learned your place in the hierarchy of white supremacy, painfully or gently or unconsciously. All was decided for you.
If you are Black you learned the restrictions and requirements

of Jim Crow when you were a babe in arms; you learned the deadly consequences of breaching decorum. The rules, the way of life: immutable. Until you realized that customs and beliefs are created, and can be resisted, and fought, no matter the cost, even right here, in Selma.

Afternote: The whole meaning of Russia has changed since I wrote this. There is now too much to say about Russia, the bloody, aggressive Goliath led by a fascist twenty-first-century czar.

NOTES ON CAMP

For many years I didn't understand the appeal of summer camp. The rituals and traditions, which kept some children and later their children returning year after year, were alien, unfathomable. The vocabulary was strange. At camp they taught us how to make something called lanyards but never told us what they were or why our parents would want them as gifts.

I went because I was supposed to go. My sister had gone before me. Nevertheless, I was "exited" [sic], as I wrote in my diary the day before I left for Echo Hill Ranch in the Texas Hill Country. I was eight years old, tall for my age, bookish and shy. Echo Hill was a (Jewish) camp and was about three hours from our house in Houston. The parentheses mean that all of the campers seemed to be Jewish but the fact wasn't mentioned much, though we recognized the Sabbath by wearing white. The more Zionist and serious local kids (or those who had parents who were) went to Camp Young Judea. The more religious went out of state to Camp Ramah, which from secondhand descriptions sounded like living in an open-air synagogue.

The morning before I left for camp that first time, I looked in the mirror and noticed a small lump under my jaw. I thought maybe I had mumps, which had been going around. I doubted it, though, because I doubted myself most of the time, and I didn't mention my suspicion to my parents. I felt slightly guilty that I didn't. They drove me to a parking lot where I hesitantly boarded the bus for Echo Hill near Austin. After mechanical delays, we arrived, were assigned our cabins, and so on. Years later the owners' son Kinky Friedman—singer, author, and outrageous gubernatorial candidate—described Echo Hill as a camp for overprivileged kids. We were mostly middle-class kids (some upper-middle) who went to public school; most of our parents were the children of Eastern European immigrants. At camp we met kids whose parents our parents knew—through Jewish fraternities and sororities at the University of Texas, via other certain but mysterious ways that Jewish parents knew other Jewish parents in Texas.

My career as an asthmatic began when I was three days old. The affliction still comes upon me after a cold or when I'm exposed to dust, mold, or pollen. Because I was sick so often I missed one-third of my nursery-school classes; I have the mimeographed illustrated report card to prove it. I also get asthma upon exertion, especially running. I don't have asthma attacks. My asthma creeps, not leaps. I start wheezing; then my chest gets tight and congested. When I was young, my mother would give me a Tedral pill dissolved in a spoonful of Coke. That medicine was later taken off the market. If the Tedral didn't help enough, I'd take prednisone and maybe an antibiotic. I still take those two for bronchitis. Then, as now, the cough would break up and within a week or two or three I'd be back to normal, breathing clearly and being wary, and continuing to take preventive meds.

I started getting allergy shots when I was three years old. I stopped at thirteen after spending a night in the ICU on an oxygen tank, but that's another story. (There is something, too, about the number 3 going on here, but I'll ignore it.) The first night at Echo Hill I was wheezing and miserable. No one had considered that the Great Outdoors would be rife with mold and pollen, the cabin with dust and more mold. As I lay on my bunk bed, I silently repeated, to comfort myself, *Someday I'll be as famous as Louisa May Alcott*. As always I imagined there was a miniature German village in my chest. The wheezing reminded me of accordions. I felt a counselor slip a second pillow under mine, to elevate my chest.

The next day my glands were swollen. My self-diagnosis was confirmed and I packed up my shorts and tops with name tapes my mother had sewn on, and I moved into the infirmary. A friendly denatured skunk moseyed around, as domesticated as a cat. The place was air-conditioned, which helped filter out allergens. I lay in bed and read the books on hand. I read *Pollyanna*. Instead of "said with feeling," the author often used the term *ejaculated*. I was only a rising third grader, and a naïve one at that, but the verb seemed more than strange.

And the day after that, my parents picked me up.

The next year I went back for free. Echo Hill had a strong affection for the story of the *Titanic*, which I didn't question because I liked singing about the doomed ship, one of many versions of a folk song about the disaster:

It was sad. It was sad.
It was sad when the great ship went down
to the bottom of the sea.
Husbands and wives,
little children lost their lives.
It was sad when the great ship went down.

And there was Titanic Night, which was a themed talent show. For my performance I found a white rag and colored it with yellow crayon. I took to the stage and said I had been on the *Titanic* diapering my baby when the ship hit the iceberg, and my child went overboard. *And* (fake moaning) *all I had left was her dirty diaper*.

My performance was deemed the funniest and I was awarded a certificate, which found its way into my scrapbook.

I had asthma the entire two weeks of the session. Let me just say that having asthma at a place that's supposed to be fun, isn't. Suffering gives you a bad attitude and you question everything. As they say, nihilism means nothing to the dancing peasant, and I think that holds true for the average camper.

I don't think that the emphasis on the *Titanic* will hold up to much scrutiny, but I wonder if I registered, on some unconscious level, that we were celebrating a disaster that involved people dying after their lungs filled up with water and they could no longer breathe.

Around the same time in my life I read *Anne Frank: The Diary of a Young Girl*. My parents' friends, the Rosenbergs, brought the book to them one night. It was gray-black, hardcover, missing the paper cover. I confirmed its appearance the last time I was in Houston. Apparently my family never returned it. Let's say that possession for more than half a century is permanent. Or we can call it a gift.

I tried to model my life on Anne's. She had an older sister, and so did I. She wanted to be a writer (and was one) and so was I. The book ends before the group is betrayed, discovered, and most of the families murdered. But I knew what had happened to her, and that was both relevant and beside the point. I absorbed it thus: The Franks were afraid of the Nazis. They were Jewish, like us. There were parents and two sisters, like us. Therefore, we should be afraid of the Nazis.

That there were no obvious Nazis in Houston in the mid-1960s was irrelevant. (There may well have been American Nazis; Houston was home to Klan members and sympathizers. The city's racist police chief from 1964 to 1974 was a George Wallace supporter and alleged Klan member. He and his ilk spent their violence on African Americans, not Jews.) Nazis were alive in my imagination. They were the face of the bogeyman. My sister and I and our friends used to sit in our carpeted, walk-in closets and pretend we were hiding from the Nazis in the forest. That was during the day. At night I was afraid that they would take me away and I would die in a concentration camp without my medicine. Underneath that fear was the belief that I didn't deserve to live because I needed medicine to sustain me.

I remember one summer night when our air conditioning wasn't working and we opened the windows. I heard scratching against the screens all night, likely mosquitos, moths, and other night creatures, but I knew they were Nazis working their way inside my bedroom.

Several years after my fortnight at Echo Hill, a bunch of children and pre-teens in the neighborhood turned their attention to another (Jewish) camp, Wa-Kon-Dah, in Rocky Mount, Missouri. Kids came to the camp from the greater cities of the South (Houston, Dallas, Memphis, Atlanta, Chattanooga) and the lesser cities of the Midwest (St. Louis, Kansas City, downstate Illinois towns). Part of Camp Wah-Kon-Dah's appeal was that Missouri was allegedly cooler in the summer than Texas was, and there were more water sports there than at Echo Hill. I went for two years, and again I was confused. This "quietly Jewish" camp (a scholar's term) served bacon, which I knew I wasn't supposed to eat. Toward the end of the session, this same camp (in the Ozarks; I didn't know where I was but I knew that *Ozarks* wasn't a state) sponsored something called Red and Black, when the camp was divided into two teams that competed for points. Why this rivalry? And I couldn't grasp why we were graded on how well we made our beds and swept our cabins. I didn't realize that there is something militaristic about even the most benign summer camps.

My so-called best friend used to make fun of my noisy breathing as we climbed the slope to the mess hall. My second summer there I took prednisone, which caused me to get my period twice. In those days that meant no swimming. That summer an older camper, a lifer, went to Town with a counselor for a dental appointment. There was a car accident and she died. She had been sitting in the passenger seat, which other campers called the *death seat*. The camp closed after that summer.

I now understand why children love camp. It seems like a no-brainer: Who wouldn't love getting away from the city and living in a cabin in nature, where you can make friends, swim, hike, canoe, sing, build campfires, fish, water-ski, ride horseback? (And make lanyards!) Only a kid who's wheezing and coughing (or bleeding) the whole time.

I thought that telling my parents I'd rather stay home would be a defeat, a failure to do my duty. I should have told them—because camp was a waste of my parents' money and my time and health. Going for those few summers made me feel that my life was more tenuous than before. I began to associate camp and the outdoors with impairment, danger, my mortality. What was in me, what was wrong with me, what made me vulnerable to the Nazis, came out in the outdoors. The only place I was free from danger was in the city, inside, with air conditioning filtering out the dangerous pollens and mold of nature.

SPY IN THE HOUSE OF GIRLS

My mother was president of her sorority at the University of Texas, and when I was a freshman at Northwestern in the mid-seventies she wanted very much for me to take part in sorority rush. I refused. *Elitist system,* I said. *Superficial. Not my kind of people.* I was afraid that the great intellectual enterprise of college would disintegrate into the system of classification we'd had in high school, where your social rank was more important than your mind. So even though I filled out the rush form before I left home, I never sent it in. I filled out another card that said I wanted to live in the coed dorm with single rooms. Ostensibly, this was because the building was new and air-conditioned, and thus easier on my allergies, but more specifically it was because I used a machine for asthma and figured I would never find a roommate who would put up with someone breathing in mist and coughing up phlegm for twenty minutes every morning and night.

That was that, but after I arrived on campus, I'd walk by the sorority quad on my way to classes and see those happy girls in clusters, wearing bright skirts and laughing, always in a patch of sunshine so that they seemed part of a magical closed world. I looked at these girls who seemed so rooted and was sure that I hated them even more than I envied them.

When I was twenty-nine, I found myself back at North-western, teaching journalism. I was on leave from a newspaper job, and I was either going to return there after six months or go to Nicaragua for an extended time. I'd taken the leave partly because I thought if I entered academe I would be allowed to write whatever I wanted and become a leftwing activist. But there wasn't much time for writing or politics.

That fall I had three friends and no acquaintances. I never went anywhere without two folders, one marked Graded and one To Be Graded. They were always full. I looked and dressed like my graduate students—actually, not as well as they did, once they started dressing up for suburban city council meetings. I felt like a student masquerading as a professor masquerading as a student. I don't know when the idea first hit me, but it seemed to make perfect sense when it did: as long as I was masquerading, I might as well do the one thing I'd never had the guts or desire to do as a real undergraduate. Three months before my thirtieth birthday, I went through Northwestern's sorority rush.

Now, I thought, I could take it. Maybe then I would have been awkward around young women blessed with supreme grace and accomplishments, but not now; I had proven myself on several fronts. The breathing machine had been replaced with pills and the hand-held inhalers you see basketball players endorsing on TV. I'd interviewed Rosalynn Carter and a death row convict (separately). I'd found my way to a refugee camp in San Salvador. I'd spent days on end speaking French with a Tunisian in Paris. I'd registered voters and worked in a food co-op and knew how to make miso soup and tofu quiche. I'd had proposals of marriage, though I didn't believe in the institution. During a ritual to bury cuteness, I'd written "cute" on a leaf in blood and rubbed it in the dirt.

Getting through a tea party at Beta Pi Acropolis would be a piece of cake.

I couldn't pass up the chance to take the road I had almost taken years before, to see if I could get past the border guards. Besides, I had a secret weapon: I was going to write about it. I would have the last word.

Orientation was in the university auditorium. It was packed with women in shorts and T-shirts, and they filled the place with a sort of languid chatter. No one stood up and shouted at me, *Impostor!* No one said anything to me at all. We sat in our seats and listened. The chair of Panhellenic spoke first. She was blond, had straight short hair, almost punk, was dressed for success in small-heeled pumps and a straight pink skirt and matching jacket with boxy junior exec's shoulders. She looked down at her notes and read that sorority women (and she and her cohorts were careful to say *women*, not *girls*), at least at Northwestern, were *serious, committed, and intelligent*. She must have gotten wind of criticisms. Indeed, the next speaker said Greek life was necessary to help balance out our lives at such a competitive school; in fact, 39 percent of female undergraduates at NU had opted for it. She showed slides of formals, parties, general wholesome togetherness.

But this is not, said the next speaker, *frivolous.*

Doth the ladies protest too much? I wondered. Were they a tad defensive? Wouldn't it have been a better marketing strategy to assume that the women who were there already had the requisite amount of enthusiasm?

Maybe not. *I'm just here out of curiosity,* said a fuzzy-haired woman behind me. *I don't have enough clothes.*

A woman down the row said to no one in particular, *You have to be yourself.... If they don't like you for what you are.*

Speeches ended; the rush counselors sat on the stage, smiling. They were wearing blue T-shirts with sunglasses emblazoned across the fronts along with the message: "We're watching out for you." Blues Brother turned Big Sister. Some wore buttons that said, "3–5: It's the law."

I thought it had something to do with the drinking age—maybe some sort of near-beer had been introduced without my knowing it.

We were divided into groups, geographically. The rush counselors held up signs with the names of dorms. Most of these signs were finely crafted, looking as if they'd been made carefully and lovingly the night before over fresh-baked sugar cookies

in the kitchen of one of those houses. I went to the counselor
holding up a half-hearted piece of notebook paper that said,
"Commuters."

There is always something dangerous, big city, worldly
about commuters. The bleached blond next to me said she
already knew she didn't want to live in a sorority. She'd been in
her apartment since August 1 and didn't plan to move until she
was married. She had furniture.

I'm just going to see what it's like, said a junior in ROTC.

Our leader was reassuring: *A lot of people go through just
to go through.*

I paid $10 to register, in cash, and filled out the rush card.
I became Cynthia Levinson, sophomore transfer student from
the University of Iowa (where in real life I'd been a graduate student). I, Cynthia, was a graduate of Scattergood Friends School,
a tiny Quaker boarding school in West Branch, Iowa. (It was
near the University of Iowa in Iowa City, and I knew some of
the Scattergood students and a teacher.) U of Iowa had been
too big, not intellectually demanding enough, Cynthia would
say. I'd liked it fine for grad school. Cynthia wanted to study art
history, she was interested in architecture, she wanted to come to
a big city. I had two confederates who agreed to play the role of
my parents. They let me use their phone number, address, and
bestow fake names. I planned to imply that I had a teenage sister
who had spent the summer hospitalized in Houston—nothing
like a terminal disease to redirect a conversation veering into
dangerous territory, to sanction an aura of mystery.

Remember and forget, I thought. Remember to erase the
commonplace experiences that were once adventures—going
grocery shopping alone, using a laundromat, finding my way on
the El, arranging my own vacations. Forget that I remember Ike,
President Kennedy's assassination, and Bobby's; the Beatles on
Ed Sullivan, the moon before man, the Twist, Twiggy. Say SAT
instead of GRE; forget what it's like to live alone, to go to baby
showers, to go out with men who have children.

The woman behind me looked familiar. I remembered
that her name was Jenny and she'd had a boyfriend named Peter
and one day she'd had a terrible headache or eye problem. It was

coming back to me. I'd taught her in a high school program at Northwestern three summers before. I thought she was trying to look at the form I was filling out but I covered it with my arm. Anderson, Anders, what was her name? And wouldn't she be a junior by now? I got up as soon as we were dismissed. Andries. At home I looked her up in an old student directory but she'd moved. She wasn't in directory assistance, wasn't listed yet with the journalism registrar.

A few days later when we commuters met again I corralled her. *We have to talk,* I said.

She told me she'd taken a year off to go to Sweden on a Rotary fellowship, was going through rush as a sophomore. I confessed everything. We came back to the group and she told everyone that we'd met in the spring during a campus visit when I'd stayed in her dorm, a residence hall for students interested in world affairs. So Cynthia became a person interested in foreign policy.

We were sitting in the commuter lounge of Norris, the student union. A short cute woman with a button nose and dark asymmetrically arranged crinkly hair said she was on a waiting list for campus housing and meanwhile living at the Orrington Hotel up the street. She worried about telling sorority women where she lived. *They'll think I'm the maid,* she said.

Your mom's the maid, your father's the bellboy, someone said. This was humor.

Someone else worried about holes in her blouse and other problems: *They'll say, "She sweats."*

Orrington was worried they'd notice her mustache. She was worried she was dressed like a schoolgirl. She was wearing a skirt and sweater.

Silly girl, I thought, though I was worried about my shoes, my sweat, my mustache. Despite myself. Even though I had struggled for years not to judge by appearances, not to worry about my own, had resented the way I was raised—wishing in retrospect

I'd devoured the *New York Times* or even *Newsweek* instead of
Ingenue and *Seventeen,* that I'd become adept at pitching soft-
balls instead of buying and applying eye shadow. I'd had the
first real synthesis of all my loose thoughts during my junior
year abroad in Paris. I'd read Germaine Greer and Kate Millett
and agreed fervently—yes, yes, women have been raised to be
cute and sweet and hairless, to be things for men to look at and
play with, and any discomfort I'd felt in being tall and smart
and, yes, hairy, had been caused by the system. The system was
conspiring to keep women in their places, to keep them competitive with one another, trivial. Feminism was a religion and
I adopted it, absorbed it into me, so I could barely articulate it
anymore. Years later in Iowa City I'd come into pacifism and
feminism full flower. I'd left my legs unshaven, trained people in
civil disobedience, and tried to be peaceful and strong. Still, I was
hooked on romance. When my heart was broken, it hurt no less
because the perpetrator was a high-minded draft resister. But I
was working toward something, trying to figure out where politics
figured in with writing, believing in the hundredth monkey, that
my own pacifism could spread and grow and actually change
the world. Being a reporter in Miami for two years had taken
the edge off my belief. Still I believed—in what? In the Left, in
feminism. That equality for all was an ideal way to fashion the
world. After the revolution, no one would be judged according
to how closely she resembled models in *Vogue.*

Yet there I was in the commuter lounge wearing navy
pants, a white jacket, a sleeveless, diagonally striped pink, navy,
and white blouse. I was conscious that I was not stylish and it
bothered me. My hair was very short and I had a braided tail
in back—I would have fit in perfectly at the Michigan Womyn's
Music Festival, but my face was not as beautiful as my friend the
wood nymph's in Miami, who had a crew cut and was the inspi-
ration for my hairdo. The night was hot and I was sweaty. I was
passable. As I write this, I wonder why I didn't wear my sleeveless
blue-and-green sweater and coordinated culotte skirt instead.
I think I must have been saving the outfit for the next round.

We learned we'd be given name tags. Someone said to put
your name tag on the right side so the sorority members could
read them while shaking our hands.

Our leader, who'd done an economic research project in India, passed out hard candy. She led us across campus.

From other buildings, other well-dressed nervous young women streamed out into the dying light.

And so we began the winnowing process. The plan was for us to visit, traveling in our pack, thirteen sororities in two nights. A few days later we'd find out which seven (or fewer) wanted to see us again, and then we'd visit them, for longer stays. So they'd get to know us. And so on and so forth, through informal drop-in tea parties, the food and dress growing more and more lavish until we would choose and be chosen and spend the next four years bathed in light and laughter.

The goal, everyone said, was to find a place where we felt *comfortable*, a suitably polite word.

The system was carefully orchestrated. First, we would stand in front of the door of a sorority while the members sang at least three songs. General themes were the desirability of their sorority, the sisterhood, the dates, a few ditties about boys ("Every night they fight over me, tee-hee"), and general welcome. There was much jumping and clapping. In a mating dance, this would be the equivalent, I suppose, of a great waving of antennae or an expanding and bobbing of the dewlap. Then the singing would end and the door would open.

Our leader introduced us to the sorority officers at the door. They pinned on our ready-made name tags (a shock and a welcome to see "Cynthia Levinson" waiting for me, from one house to the next, carefully written and surrounded by black velvet or a cutout of a lion), and introduced us to the next person in line, repeating our names as often as possible—a mnemonic device that would stand them in good stead in the world of business and trade. Then we were each taken by one woman who talked to us for a little while, then passed us on to the next sorority member.

Each chat lasted three to five minutes. That was the special law that the T-shirts had referred to. *The rules are for tact,* someone in Alpha Epsilon Phi explained later. *So four girls won't talk to one girl while her roommate is still sitting there wondering, "Why aren't they talking to me?"*

They went to unbelievable lengths to be fair. I noticed that in house after house where the photos of the members were

displayed, there were pictures of movie stars such as Farrah
Fawcett and Brooke Shields taped over some of the faces. They
were covering the photos of rush counselors; we weren't supposed to know which sororities our leaders were in.

We had conversations on predictable topics: majors, home-
towns, families, reasons for coming to Northwestern, what we
thought of Northwestern, what we'd done that day, what we
hoped to find in a sorority, activities of the sorority.

We were brought punch, cookies, popcorn.

No one had ever been that polite to me except in a restaurant.

Some of the women were sincere. Some were nervous.
Some were fake and glib and chattery. Some stumbled. At least
one was manic. They all tried to give the illusion that, for those
few minutes, Cynthia Levinson was the most important person
in the world.

At Kappa Delta, a six-year medical student, very eager, very
fake, said she loved NU. *I'm from the South,* she said. *I didn't know
about snow.* She said she was from New Jersey, near Philadelphia.

We saw skits, which usually emphasized diversity (in
interests, not race; nearly all of us were white) and friendship. Kappa Kappa Gamma's skit featured women done up
in all sorts of student uniforms—showing that all types fit in.
Someone in my group was irate about lack of truth in advertising: *If you were dressed like that person in a Boy Scout shirt,
you'd be kicked out.*

At Pi Beta Phi, we sat on couches and chairs while the
members actually scooted on their knees from one of us to
the other. I was drawn to another woman who was tall (at
least from her knees up), had a long face and no makeup,
and reminded me of someone I had known in second grade.
Do we feel most comfortable with people who remind us of
ourselves and old friends?

Alpha Chi Omega was done up like a lounge. The women
were slinky and sensuous, very New Yorky, frankly trying to woo
us. They were intimidating with their thin lips and sophisticated
cocktail-party dresses. Their skit was polished, clever. It was
about a freshman with a terrible roommate—a Deadhead, who's
on her way to a *Dylan lip-sync contest.* I was annoyed they didn't

give Dylan due respect. The young heroine also has to choose among a dizzying array of phone-service choices, the wind-up for a dizzying array of sororities and fraternities.

I was beginning to notice a common theme in the skits. The writers knew that we were overwhelmed and that we thought the sororities were all alike. The more clever groups parodied this, to let us know: *We know it seems silly and confusing and like we're clones, but we're individuals.*

The woman I was paired with at A Chi O talked nonstop about her college visit to Bates. I wondered how they could get impressions of us if we didn't get a chance to speak. Or was that part of the test, to see if we would take hold of the conversation?

Outside, we traded impressions. Jenny was upset at first because she felt people didn't care about her; then she found someone at one house to speak Swedish with. There was a double edge to my conversations with her. I was afraid she resented me for playing at something that was important to everyone else. I would tell her my impressions, afraid to sound too convincing, to sound as if it mattered. The strain was getting to me. I wanted to surreptitiously probe our group for usable quotes but seem to be acting perfectly natural.

By Alpha Epsilon Phi, I was bored and worn. The women were singing hard, and some guys at the dorm next door leaned out their window and clapped their hands. I hoped they weren't making fun of them. I felt protective.

Some of the A E Phi women were in Hawaiian shirts and shorts. How reasonable, considering the weather, I thought. Then I realized they were wearing them for the skit. Afterward, someone in my group said she thought their outfits were so tacky.

That was the house where I lost confidence in my self-confidence. I heard a junior transfer student in a purple sweater saying how fun it sounded to go to a boat-ride formal. I thought, She's so smooth. I'm choppy.

Then I realized the sorority members were nervous, too. A woman with small strained features and moving hands told me she was surprised no one had asked her before about the treble clef pin she was wearing. She was the song coordinator and explained her duties very seriously.

At Alpha Phi, I blanked out at the door. I forgot my name because the leader didn't introduce me. I said that I was taken aback because someone in another sorority had had on the same dress and I was experiencing déjà vu. (Which was true.) People kept jumping around. They kept saying, *I want you to meet so-and-so*, mentioning my name and the next person's.

I had no trouble passing for nineteen. At most of the houses people thought I was a freshman instead of a sophomore transfer. The sorority members looked old in their sophisticated, slinky dresses, and mascara.

At one house, someone asked which dorm I had lived in at U of Iowa. She had mentioned one called Stanley, so that was where I said I had lived. High rise? Um, yes. I hadn't planned for this at all. I thought, How terrible it must be to always lie, to be afraid.

When the rounds ended for the night, I thought: No mention of Central America, lesbian separatism, First Amendment rights, South Africa. No politics of any kind, in fact. No real or raw emotion, either. No one had been passionate. None of them really cared about me. They didn't really want to know the real Cynthia. A few had been interested. None had been interesting.

No one seemed clever. Was it just because they were unformed?

I didn't feel much camaraderie with my rush group. They seemed so—young. I felt the women were giving me the cold shoulder. Did they sense I was different? Had they discovered I was a spy?

I knew you could never dip twice into the river at the same place. I wondered how different the houses, and I, had been eleven years before. Did my nervousness at my disguise equal the nervousness I would have felt if I were actually being judged? But I was being judged, even though the points would eventually be disqualified.

If I had been in a sorority in 1974, I would have had a particular home and place and perhaps fifteen minutes a night of gossip allotted to me and my doings and non-doings. Instead, I was constantly unhoused, uprooted. Now I was even more transient. I was subletting a room in a three-bedroom apartment near campus. A few days before, I'd gone to look at an apartment on Orrington Avenue, across from that coed dorm I'd lived in freshman and sophomore years. I'd watched a load of energetic upperclassmen (as they were called then) in purple T-shirts help the bewildered out of airport buses, unpack their duffel bags and stereos and suitcases. There were banners and music, parents. I felt replaced. Students were all interchangeable parts. Our purpose hadn't been to make our marks, or for our professors to remember us and make us feel special. We had been there to draw from the stream, not to make our impressions on it. It reflected our faces only when we came near enough.

As I watched kids trail into the Foster-Walker Undergraduate Housing Complex, I thought of all the stereos and posters and telephones that had gone in and out of there in the past years, of the streams of people who'd called my room home. I understood why I had put up little sayings all over my faculty office at Medill; why I spread my clothes all over the floor in the apartment, the way a dog spreads its scent over the base of a tree to make known that it's the owner.

I felt like a displaced person. That was what I really wanted to talk about, but there was no way to explain this to the students that Cynthia was meeting, except cloaked in metaphor. I'd told the Orrington Hotel woman in our group that it must be terrible to be so unsettled. She looked at me strangely. *No,* she said.

When the first night's activities ended I stopped into my office on campus and read the bios of my new graduate students. Internships at the *Boston Globe, Rolling Stone.* Graduates of Yale, Columbia. One said he hoped to cover Congress for the *Washington Post.* Sounded like he wanted to do this right away. I couldn't tell if he was kidding.

I stopped in to see a colleague—one of my three friends—who usually stayed late in his office. *You're getting into this,* he said. *I know you are. You're going to go all the way through and bump off some nice woman who otherwise would have gotten in and you'll say, "I'm sorry, I didn't mean it. It was a mistake."*

Meanwhile, for the next few days I wouldn't eat lunch in the student union with the other instructors. I didn't want anyone to see us and wonder.

My apartment mates took great interest in the project. They were undergraduates; one of them was sure I was going to get my comeuppance. *The computers will get you,* he said. Few groups had access to the computer records, and Panhellenic was one of them. *You'll have to explain why you're not listed.*

The other thought my project was great—however much I could muck up the system, the better, even if I took someone else's place. *That would be wonderful. Save some young thing from years of triviality,* he said. His girlfriend had spent most of senior year in his apartment, and her Kappa Alpha Theta sisters had disapproved.

As the days wore on, I began to spot sorority members as I walked through town into campus. They were at Marshall Field's in white turtlenecks, on the street, on campus, in pairs. I saw one working at the checkout counter in the library wearing a button: "I love KD." If I'm asked back there, I thought, I'll have to avoid her. I gave her my faculty ID anyway. I thought, I'm getting careless. I'll have to stay in East Berlin forever.

The second night offered more of the same. I visited Kappa, which had censured my apartment mate's girlfriend. One of the top three houses, I'd heard, full of blondes. One of them asked me about Iowa and I talked about an institution there I really admired, the Catholic Worker movement. How could they not be interested?

That was Friday. Saturday night I went to a going-away party for a friend from grad school. In the living room, I sat next to a stranger who was talking about gentrification. I started to talk about changing neighborhoods in Miami, but the conversation was off and running somewhere else.

After dinner, I was talking to a professor in the kitchen who was expounding on his dissertation and how it had been published. I asked if he knew a friend of mine at his university. But he was tired of talking about writing. *I don't want to keep talking about this,* he said. *Let's talk about something else. Where do you live?*

For a moment I longed for the steady, rule-bound world of rush. No one would have been that abrupt there. I would have known everyone's name by now, and major.

Sunday night we gathered for primary results. *I'm going to have
a heart attack,* said Orrington. *Does anyone know CPR?*

A shy woman from Libertyville, a far suburb, was telling
me about how she'd helped a friend at Loyola University with
a descriptive paper about the guards at Buckingham Palace;
they'd gone to England together that summer. They were trying
to remember the color of the buttons on the uniforms. I wanted
to say, Why bother with that? She should look out the window
and describe Sheridan Road. But Cynthia wouldn't have had
much experience or credence.

I found out that six sororities wanted me, including one of
the top three, Delta Delta Delta. That was the place, I thought,
where I'd talked about the artwork I'd done (in real life) with
hair and bones. Be yourself. The advice had worked. The place
where I'd had a most pleasant conversation with someone with
a 4.0 average, who'd told me a story about getting into a concert
in Kansas City after losing tickets, did not want me. (I saw her
on the street later and she gave me a big *Hi, Cynthia!* Hypocrite,
I thought.) I was not wanted at the fancy KAT or at the place
where I'd forgotten my name. The slinky women of the A Chi O
lounge evidently had concluded that I didn't fit in with the decor.

But somebody wanted me. Somebody thought I was cute
enough and interesting enough to see again. They thought they'd
be comfortable with me. I had passed phase 1. I was pleased
enough, but some of the women in my group were disappointed.
One transfer student had only been asked back to five. I wondered if I had displaced her.

We began the rounds again: more skits, more refresh-
ments, more time. I couldn't imagine doing this for two days
in a row so I got special permission to "split"—to visit all six in
one night instead of three and three. But it lasted long enough.
As I sat through a skit with a *Wizard of Oz* theme, I wondered at
the silliness of it, amazed that these people had spent their time

practicing these songs with such short shelf lives, and decorating
sheets, making green castles to put in a hallway, buying crepe
paper, affixing foil to walls for a disco effect, covering black paper
with initials. *We work for a common goal,* one of the women told
me. *We work together toward rush.*

As I watched the *Wizard* skit, I scolded myself: You're the
one who had the quote on your desk at work for years, "Fun is
the absence of anxiety." Do you begrudge these people their fun?
You, the same person who once gave her boss a box containing
a lizard from her backyard for Christmas, with an endless loop
tape inside the box that said, *Hello, Doug, my name is Sammy.
I'm a Carolina anole?*

Yes, I did. And the same person who once believed that
protests would change the world, who hid her derision as someone in the newly revived Kappa Delta told the history of the
sorority: *KD was one of the top but in the sixties and seventies—you
know, "Hair" and "Godspell"—sororities and fraternities were down.*
(Thumbs-down sign accompanied this.) *It was one of the top and
because it was looking for quality girls, it didn't have enough, with
the movement.*

They remembered me at Tri Delt, saying at the door, *You're
interested in art, aren't you?*

They were Italian-Americans in black dresses. Three were
very excited because they'd realized that all three sets of parents
had gone to Venice on their honeymoons. I wondered if I should
mention my trip to Venice during my junior year abroad or the
oral histories I'd conducted with Italians in Chicago. I didn't. This
was the first place I'd felt something familiar: informality. We
were standing in someone's room and talking about boyfriends
with red hair, and there was some confusion about which sorority
woman was assigned to which of us and whose turn it was to
take us to the food. The general feeling was it didn't really matter.
I talked about a certain Larry who'd get all these *Red!* remarks
from people he didn't know. For some reason people needed to
lean out of car windows and point out his red hair. They knew
just what I meant; it had happened to their boyfriends, too.

In passing, I said I was a vegetarian and someone told
me several vegetarians lived in the house. Someone else told

me about the creative writing major. I wanted to know details. I wanted to know if she'd had the same instructor I'd had in 1977 but I didn't ask.

As we left someone said, *It was so excellent. I had the best time.* I agreed. I would fit in. I would feel comfortable. It would be fun.

The evening got better, perhaps because I was bolstered by knowing that however wide they had cast their net, these people had made a decision to see me again. At Alpha Gamma Delta I talked to someone about getting lost in art and music. She said she got carried away at symphonies. I felt we really bonded. I wondered if beneath the deception there could be honesty. Can a connection with another person be half honest? Half true?

Then I talked to someone who spoke incredibly fast, was very thin, talking about her father's birthday and a tie everyone denied was theirs but they gave it to her father in a box and so I asked if he'd worn the tie. *He hasn't bought it yet,* she said. I must have missed something.

In between houses someone said she was ready, she wanted to go out and work, that these were supposed to be the best years of her life and they weren't. I said, *I know I want to go back to school, to graduate school.*

At A E Phi, they took us up to their rooms. A blond journalism major talked about the fall formal, winter formal, philanthropy in Oklahoma and Israel, the Brownie troop they used to sponsor on the South Side. She asked, *What do you want in a sorority?*

Another rushee answered, *One that does a lot.*

She talked about exchanges, guys coming over, cocktail parties.

I walked downstairs with a woman who talked about having lived in Israel for ten years and having to decide whether to go into the army. I liked her. She made up for the woman who kind of hedged when asked if the sorority was mostly Jewish.

At Chi O the woman I was paired with didn't seem to want to make an effort. The skit was built around songs adapted from *Cabaret* ("Maybe this time, I'll be lucky, / maybe this time, they'll see me") and I felt with the singer: Do they see the real me? ("Pledge Perky, Pledge Perfect, that's not what I'm to be.")

I finished early, when the sorority quad was still humming with entering and exiting crowds. I stood there in the dark and felt a part of it all. I knew what was going on in those houses.

For the next few days I taught my classes, graded papers, dodged sorority women, and, heart pounding, checked out books at the library with my faculty ID. I waited for the next meeting, where we'd find out which few houses, if any, wanted us.

One night the phone rang at 11:30. It was my pretend mother. Seems a Cynthia Pratt had called, saying extremely perkily that she was a friend of Cynthia Levinson's from Iowa, and was passing through Chicago after a year abroad and had heard Cynthia was there.

Of course she was lying, but my mythical mother obviously was in no position to call this alleged Cynthia Pratt on the carpet for her impossible claim that she had been a friend of Cynthia's in Iowa.

I told her we were asleep and it was 11:30 but she was so pushy, said my faux mother. *She said, "Well, what is she doing there? Is she in school, is she a graduate student?"*

Bad sign.

I told my roommates. *How sneaky,* one said.

We couldn't decide whether the call was from a particular house or Panhellenic. I imagined a group of women lounging on soft carpeting, maybe eating popcorn and drinking diet soda, piles of unfolded computer printouts on the floor, making phone calls up and down the U.S. to get the scoop on various of us shady characters. Giggling: *Your turn, your turn. I was Cynthia Pratt last time.*

I waited for my rush counselor to call and demand an explanation. She didn't.

A few days later our rush group met in the commuter lounge for the results of the latest narrowing-down. Everyone was in jeans. *We look so different,* someone said. I saw a sheaf of papers with schedules of parties and dues. I started copying them down.

Orrington was talking about that night being the end of Yom Kippur, the Jewish Day of Atonement, explaining she couldn't eat until 7:45. I started to say something, but was afraid of betraying Cynthia's half-Quaker heritage. (No one had asked me about religion yet or for any details about my Quaker high school, but I was ready.)

The leader called each of us to a corner when she delivered the news. Some were elated, others subdued. My turn came.

Cynthia, she said, and I think I detected a slight bemused smile. *There's a problem. Are you registered as an* undergraduate?

I hedged. *Well, I talked to some professors.* I was trying to imply that I was auditing, on a waiting list, on my way in.

She asked again, relentless but kind. Had I succeeded in making her think I was a poor fool who'd come here on the strength of a place on the waiting list and a promise of something turning up? I could tell she wanted to know my status but I wouldn't give an inch.

If registration's worked out in the spring, can I go through then?

She said, *Yes, some houses have openings. . . . Did you register? Do you have a yellow slip?*

No. Then, she said, I must drop out of rush.

I said OK.

That was it. No torture sessions in which I was beaten to confess. No tearful accusations, no confrontation with "Cynthia Pratt." There was a striking absence of vitriol. It was all polite, low-key—just like all my dealings with the sororities had been, ever since the first party at the first house.

I took my backpack and walked out of the student union. I told Jenny I'd been found out.

On the way to my office I imagined Cynthia as a chrysalis, my imposed burden of studenthood, falling off me, drifting into the night. Now I can be a full adult again, I thought. I wanted to do something adultlike. All I could think of was drinking alcohol. But I was still fasting. It was the Day of Atonement.

They say that some criminals really want to be caught. If I had really been serious, I might have thought of some foolproof system. I could have found a freshman willing to change identities—but what about the people who knew her? Or I could have done a fake registration. I'd talked to the journalism registrar but she'd told me that such tricks were serious business, to be discussed with the dean. My quest seemed seemed too frivolous to involve the administration. Deception is permissible, I thought, to bust corrupt landlords or officials. But to rat on defenseless girls? I was too ashamed to ask.

And in the back of my mind, I began plotting: Maybe next year I could plan ahead, get a new name.

As the months went by, I grew out my hair and thought, It's at least twice as long as it was in September; looks much better, too. Next year, I thought, maybe I'll get asked back to all three of the top houses.

Why do we—and I speak in the plural because of the reaction I've gotten when I talk about this (my office mate, a successful journalist in her forties, told me she'd have tried the same thing if she thought she could pass)—why, two decades after the publication of *The Feminine Mystique*, do we long to be judged on personality and looks and charm and perceived ability to attract the right kind of males? Are we still so tied to that definition of success and role? Are we that bereft of identity? Why are we still begging on the sorority house porch: *Tell us where we fit in and we will tell you who we are?* And I know there are some of you out there who will argue, *It's not that at all. The sorority sisters are merely looking for a group of women with whom they feel comfortable. Seeking community. Sisterhood.*

Right.

I told the story of my rush attempt to a friend who's a public interest lawyer. He said, *Why didn't you just say, "Yeah, you caught me, I'm a writer"?*

I'm not sure why. Maybe I didn't want to give them the upper hand. I was in the middle of their game, on their turf.

And deep down, I still wanted them to like me.
I still wanted to be Queen of the Prom.

During the school year, I spent considerable time on campus—
teaching four days a week in the fall, and then, when I left NU in
the spring and was teaching two courses at the School of the Art
Institute of Chicago downtown, coming back to borrow books
from the library or pick up mail. I'd left the sublet and was living
alone in an apartment a mile from campus. Once in the fall I saw
the blonde from A E Phi in the journalism building but she gave
no sign of recognition. In the spring I saw Orrington and another
woman from my rush group in downtown Evanston collecting
money for Easter Seals, but they didn't even blink.

I'd see Jenny at the laundromat, in the journalism building, on the El platform, and when I asked about her sorority
life, I sensed hesitation, the fear of a woman modeling a hat to
someone who thinks hats are ridiculous. She'd tell me about
her journalism class, and once I got my professor friend to lend
her a copy of a Swedish newspaper he'd found at a convention.
I felt I owed her some recompense in exchange for playing at
something that mattered to her.

I didn't write about rush that year. I told myself it was
because I'd been caught so soon, but it could have been the
sheer volume of work that came just as the quarter was beginning, or, then again, perhaps a queasiness about the deception.
I would tell the stories at parties and I'd always talk about my
rush leader who'd interviewed Indira Gandhi—*They're not all
dips, you know.* I was fair and civil and noncondemning. *Who am I,*
I asked, *to judge them?*

So it was strange that months later I found myself getting
angry. I was at an artists' colony in upstate New York, being fed
and housed for a month on a berry farm once owned by Edna
St. Vincent Millay. It was the first time since graduate school I'd
had time to write all day, every day. When I wrote about rush I
found the anger stirring, despite the tranquility of the woods and
meadows, the yellow- and red-winged birds, and the scurrying

of deer and chipmunks. Who are they, I began thinking, to have judged poor Cynthia, or anybody else? I was angry because they seemed so limited. You care about the wrong things, I wanted to say. Don't sing songs about Daddy or boyfriends or being popular. Sing songs that mean something. You should perform charity because you believe in the common good, not because the group does it. You should know people you don't necessarily feel comfortable with, who don't understand your taste, whose mother isn't like yours. Examine the things that made you. Perform for a larger audience, a larger purpose than luring someone into your selective little rooming house with Greek letters out front. Don't you want individuality? Don't you want to be truly "serious, intelligent, and committed"? I know about your types. Back-stabbing, gossiping pseudo-virgins, getting together only for group vomits. I heard a terrible secret about how you let one of the sisters quietly die in the guest room, let her lie three days until someone found her. I know about you, minds filled with crepe paper and visions of boat-ride formals.

Oh, the conscience pricked, they were all different, they were sweet, they cared about water pollution and symphonies and Sweden. They put their arms around each other. They were young.

Why didn't I confess at the end that I was an impostor?

Because I—

Because, deep down, goddammit, I wanted all of it. I wanted to believe I was Cynthia Levinson and could be nineteen years old and wow them in the top three houses. I wanted to be perceived as funny and cute and wry and energetic and an asset to a house. I wanted to get dates with guys from the good fraternities and marry one of them. I wanted the creative writing major at Tri Delt to read my stories. I want to buy my first long black dress and drive in someone's car down to Chicago, where the pattern of glittering lights isn't familiar and let someone else worry about parking the car and how far we should go and where we're going for dinner. I want years and years of promise and sisterhood, people who are bound to me by friendship and circumstance and who'll love me and leave me folded notes with my name on them on the door handles in the library and greet me in the library lounge at the nine o'clock break. For once, goddammit, may I feel comfortable in that gloomy smoke-grimed black-and-gray lounge and back at the house they'll make up songs with me and say I'm clever for it and get me boyfriends who'll get me flowers that I'll press in some heavy book, even if I have to borrow it and I hope I won't forget to take it out when I leave for the summer.

Oh, dammit, I thought, give me a house mother to sneak out on and girls to drink hot chocolate with, who'll slip *Cathy* comic strips under my door and never forget my birthday. Dammit, all I remember from college is crying after being a guinea pig in a psychological experiment on guilt and writing angry journal entries about my boyfriend and wandering in the Shakespeare Garden and writing papers on Salome and Milton and *Middletown* and Isherwood and reading *And Quiet Flows the Don*, and none of it ever fitting together. Oh, dammit, I have voted and had driver's licenses in four different states and my mail arrives covered with yellow Inform Sender of New Address tabs. My friends are married and jumping from Minneapolis to Baltimore, New York to New Jersey, St. Louis to Jacksonville to San Antonio to New Orleans, are fixing up houses I've never seen, are having babies, have spent the last two years cooking in New York City without telling me, have fallen in love and bought a house and finished a novel without telling me, and sometimes I can't remember my old roommates' last names and would die, absolutely die, if I ever had to sit and list all the phone numbers I've had in the last five years. Every week, my parents tell me, more of their friends are dying.

Cynthia Levinson was not quite clever enough.

I was not quite stupid enough.

Or vice versa.

Dammit and dammit again, I thought as I sat there in New York State in a converted barn that once belonged to a famous poet, I'm thirty and published and living where the Pulitzer Prize winner retreated from the city, and all my needs are taken care of. The cook has bought the food we want, even the tofu and olive oil, and Adele and Holly, painters, have driven Becky's car to Town and brought back designer ice cream for us and cones, they even thought to bring cones. I am sitting at my new computer and out the window the wind is blowing the edge of some frayed rope holding open the shutter, and when I turn out the lights I see the rope glowing like the moon; if I stayed here till dawn I'd catch the edge of the sunrise over the ring of trees around me. I am thirty and I know more than I think about architecture and politics and Jews and literature and the developing world and ethics and bending to the rhythm of friendship and I am almost ready to Settle Down and learn about love. I have been out in the country for four days among all sorts of allergens and I have assiduously nursed and sprayed my lungs so that they will remain clear. I do wall push-ups so I'll keep the tiny muscles I've started in my arms, proof that if you work at something, you'll see a result. I am writing and writing right now, even though a lump clutches at my throat, an unsettling, a doubt, an anger. In the autumn I will teach the artist's novel and take drawing. Someone has left two shells on the windowsill. Downstairs there are baskets of shells and a record album with a high-pitched professor emerita wildly declaiming poetry as if she were alone in a large room. There are books of poetry and old political magazines from England and obscure journals from 1979 I'll never see again because I'm sure they couldn't have lasted. Someone surely has started new ones.

They say radiation is in the milk in New York State. The atomic scientists say it's three minutes to midnight. Everyone will die. My niece just had her fifth birthday. Right now spies are stopping at pizza places to make pay-phone calls about secrets. It will blow over. I will learn to make copies on a floppy disk. I will go swimming at the Y. I will learn exactly what foods I'm allergic to. I will try making collages again. I will live by a schedule and break it and try again. I will go out marching into the streets again. Pass petitions, learn an issue wide and deep and slow the way you learn a person. I will meet a man on the El who will fall in love with me. Or not.

Tomorrow morning, I thought, there will be flowers, as always. We can wander in the garden full of phlox and jack-in-the-pulpits and poppies and irises and a hidden clump of asparagus and unfathomable memories. Saturday or Sunday we will have brunch at the old wooden bar that overlooks the square pool they've promised to clean out. We will try to figure out a name for the statue of Cupid. I will scoop up a clump of tiny black tadpoles from the culvert behind the barn. I will watch them grow.

And if I find I can't nourish them, I will take the tadpoles back outside and slide them back in their water so they can grow legs and arms and hope they will not mourn the slow loss of the tail that provides energy.

Soon, I thought, I will walk through the hidden meadow and unhook the latch of Edna's studio and then come back to the barn and find the place on the door frame that somebody wrote, under her own name: "I was happy here."

Later I will write mine.

And in the morning will be a letter from an old friend.

I will make a ritual, I thought. I will toast friendship and seasons.

I will bury the Queen of the Prom.

THE YEAR OF THE KNEE SOCK

It was 1967, the Year of the Knee Sock, according to the notebook I kept in the class I was taking at Neiman Marcus. I remember our lessons only because, through all my moves, from Houston, to the Midwest, to the East Coast, and back to Chicago, I've kept my official brown-and-beige Neiman Marcus notebook from that course. I wrote everything down, with the all the seriousness that a very serious eleven-year-old could muster. I dutifully recorded the information that leather was the Fabric of the Year, as well as this straight-faced prediction: Purses are getting bigger.

There is no trace of cynicism in those pages. When I look back, I'm disappointed that I didn't draw pictures of purses growing larger and larger with menacing scowls. There are no side comments to my friends, whom I'll call Lynn and Cheryl, who took the Beechnut 88 bus to downtown Houston with me every Saturday after services at Congregation Beth Yeshurun. In that notebook, at that time of my life, there was room only for the facts of fashion—no commentary. I believed what I was told by anyone who seemed knowledgeable about clothes, beauty, or boys. My friends and I studied all the how-tos in the pages of *Ingenue*, *American Girl*, and *Teen*—whether they pertained to hairdos for the oval-shaped face, waistlines for the small-breasted, or the clever use of striped fabric in clothing for tall girls. Though I had never dated, I absorbed the conversational tips I found in book-length guides to fashion and beauty we ordered through *Junior Scholastic*.

I sent off for a free booklet, probably produced by a snack company, called "Time Out for Sports!" It explained football and baseball to girls so that we would know what to ask if we found ourselves sitting in the stands with a boy. We didn't play sports ourselves, beyond volleyball and four-square during recess. There was no such class as gym. This was in the dark days before Title IX, before the notion of women's history or gender studies; we'd never heard of Babe Didrikson Zaharias, the world-famous Olympian from nearby Beaumont. And we didn't Question Authority, either. I think those bumper stickers hadn't been produced yet, or at least hadn't made their way down to Texas. So when the sleek, model-like, authority figure in the front of the class at Neiman's told us girls that leather was the new fabric, I bought a leather jumper with a V-neck and a lace-up front. During the class devoted to hairstyles, I happily volunteered my head of dark wavy hair and let an in-store beautician do with it what he would, for demonstration purposes. He gave me a short, sophisticated cut that I don't much remember, so it must not have been traumatic. When we sampled a very light "eye gloss" that came in a tiny lipsticky tube, I insisted to my mother later that the product was OK, it wasn't real makeup, and *the lady at Neiman's had recommended it*. I *needed* shiny, sparkly eyelids.

I believed that if I learned my lessons well, I would succeed—with boys. I would be popular. I would be pretty. I would know what to do. And even though I was dreadfully tall, had been taller than everyone else since I started pre-nursery school and now was taller than the boys—I would be so confident, I wouldn't care. I might even shrink. And maybe shoot up again when it came time to try out for Eileen Ford's famous modeling agency in New York City.

And I learned, or else I had an innate sense. As a teen I knew my colors before anyone was "doing" them. I was, in fact, the first person I knew to wear turquoise (T-shirt) with purple (shorts), as well as combine gray and red. I remember clearly the gray wool culottes that came with a matching gray vest. I wore a long-sleeved red blouse under the vest, or wore the gray culottes with a white silky blouse with long full sleeves under a crocheted red vest with a navy blue apple in the middle. I also had a very cute navy blue vest with white piping—and I used words like *piping*. That vest had a picture in the middle, in white outlines, of the sailor boy from the Cracker Jack box. I bought the vest at—Neiman's. Of course.

We trusted Neiman's—that's how we referred to it, not by the formal *Neiman Marcus* or the scoffers' *Neiman Markup*. My mother grew up in South Dallas, not far from the umbilicus mundi, the flagship store on Main Street. She and her sisters shopped with their mother on Dollar Days, took part in First and Last Calls, and lunched in the famed Zodiac Room, home of an (untrue) urban legend about a $300 cookie recipe. My mother bought the cookbooks written by the Zodiac's Helen Corbitt. My mother liked to tell us that Neiman's salespeople were trained to be courteous to everyone in the store; you never knew if the mud-covered cowboy looking at jewelry was a newly made oil millionaire. Good manners were good business. My mother knew this from reading a book by Stanley Marcus. NM was like us, Jewish and Texan and established.

In 1967, in the days before there were middle schools, I was a sixth grader at Kolter Elementary in Meyerland, a Jewish neighborhood—the only Jewish neighborhood—in Houston. My bat mitzvah was the next year, but I don't remember preparing for it in 1967, beyond my attempt to figure out what to wear. (For the record: I did study Hebrew intensely the next year.) My bat mitzvah dresses in late November 1968 were a gray velvet and a turquoise taffeta; each outfit featured big puffy sleeves, influenced by the costumes of Franco Zeffirelli's Juliet. We girls needed a lot of fancy or *nice* dresses in sixth and seventh grades, the years of heavy bar/bat mitzvah attendance. If we were lucky, boys would ask us to be servers—junior hostesses—an honor which meant we would wear wrist corsages and serve punch at the receptions after services on Friday night and Saturday morning. Girls could ask us to be servers as well, and marchers—sort of like bridesmaids. The marchers would accompany the bat mitzvah girl down the aisle on Friday night.

I remember sixth grade rather clearly. There was a Black girl in our class, Bernice, who had taken advantage of "freedom of choice"—a ruse that was popular in southern school districts, developed to circumvent real integration. Anyone could choose to attend classes anywhere in the district. And she chose Kolter, even if it meant being the only African American in the entire school. No wonder she was so shy! She told me years later that she was glad her integration had been so peaceful. She said she felt more welcome at Kolter than later at MIT.

Every few years I might happen to tell someone that our class had visited the Alabama-Coushatta Reservation. I might mention the tortilla factory we'd toured, or the day the Spanish teacher accidentally cut her finger off in the school office. Once a decade I might think to mention the day the word *fairy* came up in class and our teacher told us if we wanted to know its definition (not the one from the Brothers Grimm) she would inform us privately after class. I didn't stay to ask, of course, because I knew what fairies were: those white puffy things (seeds) that float out of spent dandelions. At eleven and twelve I knew my fabrics but was not so wise in the ways of the world. As an adult I might tell friends about the outrageous girl who was rumored to have broken into a classroom one weekend and to have shat on the teacher's desk. She later became adept at radio communications. Then there are smaller memories that surface that I hardly ever mention—the international dinner we made and served, the too-childish rhymes we memorized, "Pop pop pop goes the popcorn in the pan," and Edwin Markham's short morality tale in verse about an outcast that ends "We drew a circle that took him in!" There was the mimeographed packet of our poems that had a typo; Andy Engler's began, "There was an old boy." He meant "There was an old man"; we hadn't heard of old-boy networks then. I'll never forget "old boy." Someday I'll be in the nursing home without any teeth, and I'll think: There was an old boy. Andy, according to our teacher, was going to be president of the United States.

For the record: He hasn't. So far. And he doesn't remember the poem.

I remember, too, that Señora Vela retrieved her finger. She wore a large bandage for weeks or months, and then it healed. For years I was afraid of paper cutters and told people that my Spanish teacher's finger had jumped into the trash can and she'd had to find it. That's where danger lies: in that long razor-edged arm.

One sixth-grade memory that I hardly ever mention is of a boy I'll call Tom. The silence is not because our encounter was traumatic but because it seemed unimportant. The boy himself was unremarkable—with a white crew cut and a thick rectangular face, a boy describable by *st* words: *stocky, stolid, stoic*. Blank-faced. No one who would draw you into conversation. I have no idea what his last name was. I don't even know for sure what his name was. I may be thinking of the crew-cut boy in my first-grade class who asked me to his birthday party, apparently not realizing that first-grade girls no longer attended coed parties. Boy-girl parties had become passé after kindergarten, only beginning again with fifth-grade dance parties.

Tom might have been as tall as I was; a few of the boys were. I was almost five feet, but irrationally proud that I wasn't the tallest in the class. Tallness was a moral failing. There was one ostrichy girl who was taller. She had a dumb laugh and frosty-framed glasses and was at least five-foot-one. Her height was something terrible, her own fault.

Lynn was the perfect height, four-foot-six, as short as all the boys, and Cheryl wasn't much taller. Cheryl had a laugh that sounded like she was pretending to be incredulous. Twice a week the Spanish teacher came to our classroom. (I'd like to think that I remember her because she was pleasant and truly taught us to speak Spanish in her three years of visits, and not just because of the falling finger.)

Another two days a week, the music teacher appeared. One day, any day, a Thursday, maybe, it was my turn to return the music instruments to the music closet in the school hallway. Tom walked into the closet and closed the door behind him.

The feeling is like being in a bank vault. The walls are opaque pale green, like every other painted surface of the school, but they have a metallic cast because the shelves are metal. A starkness. The walls are concrete block under the paint. I crouch down to put the xylophone where it belongs, and wonder where I should set down the rubber-tipped mallets. How did the music teacher expect me to know where she keeps these things? And the boy Tom walks in and my first notion is surprise, Why would he walk in? Is there a message for me, that came to class during my three-minute absence, a message from President Johnson, for instance, that the man in the army that Lynn and I sent cookies and letters to has died in Vietnam? Tom will hand me a telegram, or maybe this Tom has brought instructions, a diagram that shows one how to place the musical instruments in their proper places, a map you wouldn't expect to exist, like the one that comes inside boxes of chocolate candy.

Tom closes the door, hands empty, and turns off the light. (I stand up, xylophone mallets still in my hands, xylophone still in my arms.) He kisses me before my eyes can adjust to the dark. I say, without thinking, Turn on the light. And he turns on the light and leaves.

I am eleven or twelve years old. I have never had a boyfriend, I have never gone steady, have never had a boy's ID bracelet confiscated from my desk by Mrs. Kestenberg, the way she took Ronnie's from Janie because the teacher thought they were too young for such things. The only boy to ask me to go steady is a tall man-boy who has a deep voice and recently joined our class. On the way from the lunchroom one day he offered me the ring from a flip-top can to wear on my finger. I think he was asking me to go steady. I refused his token. He is worse, and stranger, than this Tom who is not desirable, with nothing to say, an empty mind, an empty face, sweaty palms whenever he's my partner at square dancing on Friday afternoons in the lunchroom. Square dancing is required, part of our physical education. That class is called rhythms.

Turn the light on! I say to him in the closet without thinking and I don't say much without thinking.

I'm shaking. I say, Turn the lights on, and he does and leaves. I'm sweating. I put away the xylophone. I have put Tom away. He is outside. I am in the pale-green bank vault. Alone. The door clicks shut behind him.

The hall is empty. I go back to class. I listen to words. Walking home from school the next day with Lynn and Cheryl, I tell them that Tom followed me into the music closet and that he kissed me and I tell them what I said. They don't say anything. And from their silence I suddenly and surprisingly know that I was wrong. My indignation was wrong, I don't understand boys and am afraid of them, as my older sister says she is, and what is wrong with me has to do with telling him to turn on the light.

I have made some mistake. Vaguely I sense that the mistake was that I forgot that a girl should do whatever a boy wants. A girl should want to kiss a boy. (In junior high, I will learn that girls should set limits. In sixth grade, boys didn't want to do that much. At least not the boys I knew about.) Lynn and Cheryl and I have identical notebooks from Neiman's; we three have documented the elements of our wardrobes on the blank pages in the back, just a few pages following the Polaroid silhouettes of ourselves, in shorts, so you can clearly see our lousy postures. On the Beechnut 88 bus people often ask if we're sisters or cousins, because we three have dark hair and olive skin and there's a two-inch difference in our heights. Standing side by side, we make a logical alignment, but we are not aligned in this. They don't say a thing when I tell them about Tom. Maybe they exchange glances or roll their eyes. I am a brain. Lynn is a brain, and we are both embarrassed about our special relationship with Mrs. Kestenberg, who taught us the summer before in a noncredit class for the academically able, which nowadays I suppose would be called gifted. Mrs. Kestenberg dotes. It's as if our grandmother is teaching the sixth grade. I deserve the As and Es (for excellent conduct) on my report card. Lynn deliberately, calculatingly, chews gum every day so that she will be caught breaking a rule and will get her grade lowered from E to G, Good. She is better equipped than I am to pass for what everyone knows is the ideal for a girl: cute, short, dumb, and chatty. She is cute, short, smart, and quiet. If she can't be chatty in class, she can at least bear the mark of lower conduct on her report card, the grade that the talkative girls get, effortlessly, shrugging at the warnings to hush. Cheryl is a chatty girl, an average student. She is short, cute, spirited—nearly perfect

As they say, beware of what you wish for. I stopped growing in high school and quickly became short, cute, and dumb. In my first quarter of college Up North I began to doubt that my high school, Bellaire, was truly one of the top three in the country, as everyone—in Houston—always said. Or else all my college classmates had graduated from the top two schools, where they'd had experience in writing research papers that contained actual research and, what's more, had learned to organize their thoughts in a logical fashion. I have remained not-tall. I'm average-height-average-weight (presuming the average contains a wee bit of extra flesh). When I tell people I once took fashion classes at Neiman Marcus, they either laugh—taking in my hairdo, which is wild and wooly; my lack of makeup; my typical warm-weather outfit of baggy T-shirt, nondescript shorts, resoled Birkenstocks; the stubbly or fully grown-out leg hair; my lack of jewelry (except for dangly earrings and platinum wedding band); the jobbed nose that grew after the plastic surgery—or else they don't believe me.

I live in Chicago and write at home and teach at two universities. I put the T-shirts aside when I'm dressing for the classroom. I dress pretty much like my students—except that my clothes are not as au courant. Maybe my attitude changed in high school, starting with the purchase (for $6) of used cut-offs at a tiny store owned by a classmate's older brother. His next business was Tootsies, eventually a famous and exclusive boutique. And I quickly found out that modeling was not in the cards. I had one meeting with a visiting representative of the modeling industry when I was about fourteen. As she ran the palms of her hands along my sides over my dress, she said disapprovingly, *You're shaped like a Coke bottle.* She rejected me for the runway but recommended I enroll in her several-hundred-dollar class. Even I could tell that was a scam. The last time I was in Neiman Marcus was in the early 2000s, at the double bar mitzvah luncheon for my cousin's twins, in the Zodiac Room. I didn't shop afterward, though I watched my thin, beautiful, little niece try on a few outfits. The expensive pastel coat-dress looked lovely on her, though it seemed so retro, "Vaguely Reminiscent of the 60's," as the folksinger Charlie King titled one of his political songs. For all I know, Neiman's might have declared another Year of the Knee Sock.

I haven't seen Cheryl since high school. I see Lynn every few years. One time I visited her at her work, where she was engaged in something financial and important. I don't remember what she was wearing but I assume it was what women wear when they're in business and have two secretaries and a corner office: suit, hose, heels. We were in a high rise and she pointed out the old neighborhood somewhere in the distance, around some tiny trees. It didn't occur to me to ask if she remembered my telling her about Tom.

As for Tom, I lost track of him by junior high. Like me, he must be almost fifty. Maybe he has children. Perhaps he jokes with them: *I was so inept. I was awkward and shy around girls. I was thick and slow. I didn't have a girl I could ask to go steady, not until eighth grade, at least.* The wife will smile. Tom will muse about the word *inept.* He will say, *There is no such word as "ept."*

No. He is not the type to play with words. He was not a quiet wordsmith of a boy. He was a quiet, ordinary boy, shy around girls, an indifferent student. He wasn't dim in class, but his mind wasn't remarkably nimble. I imagine him with a beer, watching a ball game on TV. Relegate him to stereotype. He will say to his family, *I had a hard time with girls. I didn't know what to do. It took me a long time to learn.* His wife will smile.

A while back I took self-defense as part of a kung fu class. The instructor directed us in role play. We yelled at one another the way men yell at women on the street, and we practiced shouting back: *Stop! Go away! Hold it there. Leave me alone. Move.* I remembered Tom in the music closet. I hadn't mentioned him to anyone since that day in sixth grade. I told the class about him. He turned into a story. I told them how I said, *Turn on the light.* Angrily, evenly. Without thinking. Another student said, *I wish I'd been the kind of kid who'd said that.* I answered, *I was that kind and I knew from the way my friends reacted that I was wrong.* I still remember my friends' silence. And I remember the boys in high school and college I kissed just because they wanted to, guys I slept with later just to be polite, or because if I said no I'd lose their companionship, or because this one was cute and I should be attracted, because I didn't want to be a prude, because I really liked his roommate better but this was the one who asked me out, because we happened to be the last ones left at a party. This went beyond Texas courtesy. There were a number of gaps in my education it took me a long time to fill; sex education consisted of the Kotex movie and scary slides of chancres. The Neiman's class and the guidebooks and teen magazines told us how to dress and act; nowhere was there mention of desire. If you don't know how to say yes to pleasure, you're not going to know how to say no.

The kung fu teacher told the class, *Listen to your gut. Pay attention to your body.* In sixth grade I didn't know my body could speak. I was a mind, a tall skinny mind, and when I wasn't paying attention my body broke through, and my mouth said, like an angry schoolmarm, *Turn on the light.* And the boy Tom left. And I shook inside and I returned the xylophone to the lower shelf and I walked down the hall back to class and no one told me I was entitled to feel triumphant.

SEPARATE
VACATIONS

It is late March and you and I are on a train going from the middle of Costa Rica to the Caribbean coast. The ceiling is tin and the seats are old-fashioned, high-backed, and we have the special ones that face one another in the middle of each car. I am traveling east with you, whose idea this was, and Beverly, a woman we met in a little line of ocean-front *cabinas* a few days ago. She does something in national housing based in Washington and was in the Peace Corps in Nepal twenty-five years ago. A friend of hers planned this vacation for her; Bev didn't know her destination until she arrived at the airport with a suitcase of summer clothes. Across the aisle are two people who speak Spanish. You refer to the woman as the Oral Woman because as each vendor comes past, chanting his wares, she buys more food. She is not fat at all. Both she and her companion are dressed in traveler chic: khaki or some other substantial material, light brown hair. They are reading Voltaire and García Márquez.

The rest of the car's passengers are people who, we figure, are actually going somewhere they need to go. The train makes more than fifty stops and we have been told via the writings of Eugene Fodor and others that one can't know Costa Rica without taking this eight-hour ride. We are obedient, though Fodor has disappointed us; the wildlife areas are not as easy to get to as our

Fodor's guidebook suggests they should be, at least in our short amount of time. A boat ride he so cavalierly said that we could catch from a private carrier is $175.

We are here—ah, it is hard to say why we are here. I am here, I guess, because of romance or the idea of romance. You said in January you wanted to go away with me. Two things: you wanted to go away, and with me.

Why are we here? I began asking myself that the first night in San José, when we took a walk on that main street, mostly looking at shoes in the windows and the jeans and high heels of the women, finding Fodor wrong again—the women here are not exceptionally beautiful, and later I wonder if by "beautiful," he meant European, since most of the Indigenous people were murdered. Why are we here? I kept wondering. It wasn't a reporting assignment. I could probably write a travel piece about our trip, but why would I? So other people could come and ask themselves, *Why are we here?*

This is hard for you to comprehend, because though my questioning seems intellectual, something imposed on the natural order of things, for me it is purely emotional. You wanted some place warm and I thought Nicaragua or Jamaica or Haiti but Jamaica was too touristy for you, Nicaragua too unknown. You wanted to read more first. Costa Rica, we heard, was an ecological paradise, peaceful, relatively well off. I was won over by the descriptions of the monkeys and toucans and butterflies. Your idea? Maybe mine, too.

Now you are standing between the train cars, feeling the breeze, maybe thinking about the railroad and the Jamaicans who came to work on it, because they were supposedly immune to malaria, and stayed. And now you and Beverly are into her hyperboles, she composing tall tales to try on her friends at home: episodes of giant gorillas, lions, wings falling from planes. I am looking out the window, envious of your engagement. There are mountains and lush growth and a church I am reading about, where a miracle was wrought, and the train vendors, just like the book says, walking up and down, crying, *Maní, maní* ("Peanuts, peanuts"), in an endless, tireless search to scrape a living. You

loved our last two days at Manuel Antonio Beach, where we
went out of instinct, almost, because it was next to a national
park, where you hiked, and I thought about the futility of hiking
(actually felt before thinking, do you understand?); it's really just
outdoor window shopping, trees instead of shirts, and though I
enjoyed the scuttling of the land crabs, their shells like painted
clown faces, and took pictures of iguanas sunning themselves
on the almond tree roots, I kept hearing, like a chorus: Why
why why? Why are we here? What is our purpose? What is the
thing we do next? And why that? And do I write or should I
read (seems I could do both anywhere)? Can't work on my tan
because fear of skin cancer has made that démodé. I tried not
to let you know these thoughts because they are not vacation
thoughts. But the thoughts kept coming, and so I continued to
wander mournfully while you hiked (sounds so purposeful,
such a short, decisive-sounding word) and limned my mournful
thoughts and collected a few shells and sketched the tiny blue
lizards in the crotch of a tree.

  And it wasn't all desperate, only partly. There was the time
when we whirled in the ocean after sunset, singing "Hernando's
Hideaway," and when we had dinners with the other Americans,
talking of rabies and of health care in Haiti, the Bug Lady who
was there last year (the place like a boarding house, quick friendships and assessments), who would shout all day about the species she was missing in her collection, as if she believed that the
loudness of her need would bring the insects flying straight to
her. Those moments lifted me out of my funk but I was aware
early on that we were on separate vacations, you in a lush, sun-
drenched country on the cusp of the rainy season, and I as lost
as a stray piece of luggage, fallen into some dark, sludgy place,
a certain waxy glaze over everything. I felt as if I had fallen accidentally and was embarrassed, a traveler taking the wrong road,
unable to speak the right language to get the correct directions
to be lifted out. I did not know the proper tools, the special lift.
And so I pretended I was in your Costa Rica.

  And now we are on the train and I work up courage to
ask, in my simple Spanish, the little chattering girls in uniform
whether they are in public or private school, and when their

vacations are, and they are not curious or are not interested in talking, and I feel I'm wrenching them from their natural conversations. At one stop I venture to buy a whole fish in a greasy brown paper bag from a very old lady—expensive, compared to the other offerings, almost a dollar.

I look out the windows, see the houses with their corrugated roofs and wooden porches, even the rudest ones draped with plants and flowers, the blue light of the television, the antenna, signs of electricity. A woman cooking on her front porch stops to wave—impossibly Disney.

And then it hits me, that what we are seeing is not just another way of life, not just countryside, but this is poverty, the real thing, as real as the decrepit people near the city cathedral, hands spread for coins, as real as the homeless people on downtown sidewalks and park benches in any city in the U.S. This is how they live. We see inside their living rooms. It is poverty with mosquito netting, maybe, and television and bougainvillea but it is poverty all the same and it begins to seem invasive that we are taking this train not because we have somewhere to go but because this is our all-day amusement park ride. (And tomorrow we will take a plane back to San José.) We follow a path because we are looking to test the texture of the packed dirt, the slant of light in the sky, the fauna and not what's at the end.

And that is a metaphor for our lives; the struggle has gone out of it, for the most part, the basic struggle, of gathering our food and building our houses. Travel is a poor imitation of that struggle: we are temporarily homeless, searching for food and warmth.

But we are also looking for amusement and comfort, and our money eases the way. And these thoughts of picturesque poverty (so many faded colored walls in the capital, reminiscent of Rothko paintings) stab me and flow through me. They break that wall of ennui. Or maybe the protein of the fish transformed me, and everything is so much simpler, more basic than I thought, all a chemical reaction.

I am filled with remorse that is somehow sharp and clean because it is the first realization to pierce through my melancholia. I don't feel indifferent or confused. People here are in pain, in straits, in this Switzerland of Central America; this is somehow important, just as whether we get up at nine or noon, or eat shrimp or trout, or go to the east coast or the west, is not. The journey no longer seems pointless. Maybe my purpose was to begin to comprehend the inequality as it presents itself in living color. We have already learned that even though this is the shining democracy in Central America, there are gold miners out of work for a year, and though there is widespread education, it comes at great price (so that man told you at the park on our first day, the equivalent of $50 a semester, if we understood him correctly, a lot for him); and we've seen the dusty shacks and people begging.

A man in San José kept repeating to you, *Sticka, sticka,* and finally you communicated by pointing to lines in your traveler's book. We never figured out what he meant.

I realize now that *Sticka, sticka* is partly why we travel, too—for the mystery, for the simple joy of the mystery. And you haven't told me this, but even if you had, or if I'd read it in *Fodor's,* it wouldn't have meant a thing. I think I learn only with my heart, the dumbest organ but also the most sensitive.

And I realize I don't go on vacation so much to see a country, but to feel it.

When we arrive at the end of the line, Limón, we have trouble for the first time finding a hotel, and you are brazenly propositioned, both of which bring a certain charge to the air, some adversity, and finally we find a place to stay, our first with air conditioning. We listen to a fundamentalist preaching to a large crowd. (Later we learn that fundamentalism in Central America is a bona fide force.)

Did you write about Bev? you ask me now, and the sunburned guy we nicknamed the Alaskan King Crab, and the doctor on his way to Haiti, and monkeys and the gold miners? A little, but not the way you would write it. And you think my unease was caused by my writing, that I should have put down my pen, and just enjoyed—the mountains, the vineyards, the oceans, kids skating in the park. But the writing is part of the equation; as much as it catalogs the vicissitudes of my distress, it pulls my feelings from me, or pulls me toward them, illuminates my internal train ride through unknown landscapes.

In Costa Rica I thought we were so distant, our countries' separateness irreconcilable, but then in Limón I found that you, too, had had the same revelation about poverty, that in Spanish dress it is still poverty and we were like voyeurs in a moving fair. And for months more, that was enough, this memory of our shared revelation.

When I called Bev in order to fact-check this piece, she said she thought that during the trip I was trying to figure out if I wanted to stay with you. She was right. Still, I was devastated almost a year later when you broke up with me. Since you'd made the decision after spending time with your dying cousin, I imagined that your thinking went along these lines: Life is short. I don't want to spend it with this difficult girlfriend. She's not *the one*, after all.

I can render it poetically: We admitted we were living in different countries, speaking not only different languages, but words that scraped against one another because of their foreignness. In Costa Rice I wanted you to be different. You wanted me to be different. I wanted Costa Rica to be different. I wanted national prosperity and shabby beauty without poverty.

About eight years later, when I was thirty-nine, I started taking antidepressants; five months later I met my True Love. It took years to learn how to vacation with him and even longer to have an ecstatic experience during travel. I didn't know that was possible. I have been filled with joy, that's the only way I can say it, when exploring art nouveau, Gaudí-inspired apartment lobbies in Barcelona, extravagantly curly art nouveau facades in Paris (the twelfth arrondissement), the buildings of Louis Sullivan in Chicago and Buffalo, and wild, exuberantly mosaicked structures in Chartres and Philadelphia. I finally learned how to open my arms and senses, to stop and drink in experience as deeply as I can, and to wait in the stillness as the feeling grows.

YOUNGER MEN, OLDER MEN

Around younger men I feel less lost in the world. I lend them books and recommend others. It is not quite crucial what they are doing right now because their futures beckon on the horizon. They do not have to unlearn chauvinism; they know automatically to refer to me as woman" instead of "girl" (or maybe it is because they see me as old, though I'm in my early thirties). They lack the gloss of politeness. They do not annoy me by helping me on with my coat and arguing who pays for tickets (they are usually broke) but they also do not think to unlock my car door first so I will not have to stand in the cold. They are good if you do not want anything serious. They are too young to be taken seriously; they carry with them the magic of impossibility. They are too young to plan the future with. Their lives are filled with unknowns, a string of X factors. They are romantics. They will walk in new snow at midnight to make angels. Or to the beach at dark to wade. They will tell you their dreams, attaching an almost preternatural significance to them. They cast some spell of remembrance, awake something in you so that every time it snows new and wet and full, or you look at the water, black and rushing, you think of them. They may be flailing at life, like the miller's daughter alone with a roomful of flax and no Rumpelstiltskin to weave gold cloth. I am not Rumpelstiltskin. I have no magic formulae. I need the younger men, too. But their rough edges snag me, making small

scratches they aren't trained to discern. They have the ability to
bruise hearts but their own hearts are not bruised and weathered
enough to be wise. My heart still feels young, but buffeted. *My
heart is soft,* I say to a younger man. *I'm afraid to let it out alone
without a guide. It could get hurt.* The younger man says, *Yeah.*
Younger men examine my metaphors like quaint handcrafted
ornaments, or they do not quite understand them. Sometimes
I have to explain my jokes. Their older brothers (younger than
I am) laugh. The younger men are misers or spendthrifts with
language; youth makes everything extreme. The miser will flinch
at the word *love.* When I use it, he says, *Yeah.* Or *That's nice.* The
spendthrift believes too much in language, gets me lost in its
ocean. He crafts swirls of rococo, curves I let overwhelm me.
He cannot assay the deadweight heaviness of the words. He is a
boy who throws stones in the dark without thinking they could
hit a soft body hidden in shadow. He is drunk with the power of
Dad's new gas guzzler, barely under control. We say silly things
to each other about June bugs, quote *The Little Prince* in French
and English. Giddy and greedy, we drink the word *love* like chilled
champagne. He sends words I fall in love with, that I catch drunk-
enness from. Our timelessness ends. I begin to look ahead. The
spendthrift younger man chides me for breaking our pact to live
in the present. He is young enough to believe in each day as a
tabula rasa. Ad infinitum. No plans. I cannot live without plans. I
keep journals, write in my calendar, look in the mirror. My watch
has a second hand; I take my pulse after running. Time moves
differently for younger men.

My heart comes back to me with another bruise. If this
were an earlier century, I would be content to grow into an old-
maid schoolteacher, a nice great-aunt clutching mysterious
pictures to my heart, sighing when I dust them. But this is a
different age and women are not content with so little. A past is
not enough. We want futures. We are less willing to settle.

I lose my trust in words. They are dry and thin as leaves.
They are useless in the winter. You cannot stuff words into the
cracks of a cabin, cannot keep a strong fire going with them.
And then my heart, young and foolish, takes to more images. It
begins to fill up on thoughts of another younger man, thoughts

that take over like a tropical disease, impossible to rout. The image cannibalizes some crucial section in my brain, slowing my thinking processes by half. When we speak, finally, on the phone, his voice is small, rough, raspy. In person he is impatient, wearing the face of the Sphinx. He is not what I had ordered.

The next day I realize I am no longer addicted. Somehow his image has burned away. I try to conjure him up but cannot. The projection room that played his picture is boarded up. No trespassing. I realize that I am looking for one young man to save me, to sweep me from my life. As Jews, we do not believe in redemption offered by a man who bled for us and came down from the cross for us so that we could mourn and be cleansed. I'm not waiting for the coming of the messiah. But as women, that is the dogma we are raised on, that one man can sweep down and save us, from ourselves, from other men, from despair, can sweep us into his life, save us by his magic chanting of *I love you, I love you*. This is the stuff from which we spin our beliefs. We women are all spinners, that is what we are trained to do from the beginning. At birth we are given the skein and, later, our own lambs. We sacrifice them to our dreams. And I look up at yet another younger man, wondering whether I want to surf upon the waves of his energy, or if I want to contain it, the way my mother tried to capture mine and bottle it and bury it because the wind of it frightened her, the sparks of it frightened her, the direction of it frightened her; she was afraid it would take me away, her daughter lifted and departing in a strong wind. The one who might not come back. But in truth our own wings are removed when we are too young for the pain to do permanent damage (our elders suppose). We shy away from strong winds, yet a certain restlessness pervades when the tide is high, the moon, full. We belong in that dark sky. We see the younger man's silhouette against the moon.

Older men are amused by me. I become light, fey. I move faster, dance around their doubts and old-man worries. They become older, and I, younger. The canyon widens. They smile through their wrinkles. They feel each one; they have heard each wrinkle forming. They care about bedtimes, though some of them stay up all night—dinner at eleven, driving around to find an all-night restaurant—and then the staying up late is habit, the joy removed because it has become part of a *lifestyle*, something they label. They eat the same thing for breakfast each day: coffee, cereal. Sometimes they jog. If they do, they do it religiously, the way they listen to *Morning Edition* on National Public Radio and snap the string around the newspaper or release it from its blue plastic bag. They talk about the antiwar movement only remotely, but remind me, *I was there*. Close enough to see the action, while at the time I was still in junior high, passing notes to girlfriends about some boy in the third row in physical science. They no longer consider going back to school, but think about changing jobs. When they move, professionals, hired by the new company, do the moving. They are semi-valued employees. What depresses them are their children, the evaporation of promise in their ex-wives, the bounds of their imaginations. They have not returned to Europe in years. They are very serious about mortality, which has become as familiar as a dinner guest. Their opinions are deep and maybe fervent but not red-hot like those of the young activists who know everything—whom the older men, by the way, resent and do not understand. The older men say soft, diversionary things like *That is a different answer to the question*. They, too, can lapse into rhetoric, but the better ones catch themselves at it, smiling. They are no longer angry with their parents.

It can go either way with older men. They can hurt deeply and be hurt. Their hearts are scarred in battle, soft as berries in places they do not often expose. They are polite. They try to pay. There are fun ones and politically correct ones and those who encourage you, are beyond competing. They do not gulp at life. They have acquired a certain grace to their movements. They are at their best when they are laughing—as long as it is an easy laugh, not one that is frightened, conscious of itself as part of a finite supply, anxious about the next one; joy rarely arrives on schedule. Older men are not looking for saviors. They try, every day, to become existentialists. But when I look up at their faces and squint, I think I see in their eyes that same hungry look reflected from mine.

EXERCISING THE PAST

The winter I turned thirty I registered for an aerobics class at the Evanston Y. Even though I had taken aerobics in high school and had jogged in college, the idea of moving and jumping to music, of paying someone to lead us in these actions, seemed absurd. During the first few classes, I tried to imagine explaining what I was doing to my near-mythical nineteenth-century ancestors in their premodern villages in Eastern Europe. I carry these people in my imagination, as touchstones. I'm doing this for exercise, for health, not ritual, I tell the ghosts of Avrohm and Sidney and Solomon and Baeky, family names passed down.

I enrolled in the class because I'd begun to mourn the condition of my body—because it had changed so little since adolescence. It was still all potential. I thought of the dozen years since high school not spent in training or even aerobic dancing. I thought of the miles I hadn't run, the weights my girl-thin arms had not lifted, and I felt behind the place I had started.

I've always had asthma that becomes worse "upon exertion," so I was never much of an athlete until my mid-teens. Somehow in high school in Houston I became an above-average runner. In the heady days of early Title IX, I almost tried out for the running team. (Is that what it's called?)

Then I'd moved North (as we said in Texas) to the Chicago area for college, where I continued jogging, but, perhaps because of the cold, running outside became too much of a production, so much time taken up breathing into my proto-nebulizer before and after, so that I gave up running. In the years since, I would jog from time to time, and every so often would think about swimming more or taking an exercise class or trying to figure out how to work the weight machines. But in the back of my mind, I knew this: The body was not that important. The body was not what I had gone to college to groom and strengthen. The mind was royal, and so was the soul. We were descended, after all, my grandmother used to say with pride, from the Gaon of Vilna, the legendary rabbi. Surely he did not spend his time running up and down flights of stairs or lifting barbells. No, the saintly man coaxed great secrets from the holy books and built arguments to balance atop arguments atop other arguments created by rabbinical scholars in the near and distant past. As the public radio stations used to encourage, he exercised his mind.

And he used some of his energy to exhort against a new movement, Hasidism, whose adherents believed in using the body and voice to express their joy in the Lord. He accused them of pantheism. He was traditional. And an ascetic. The Hasids or Hasidim were populists. He was elite. He railed against them, then returned to his studies.

So there I was, 188 years after his demise, forty-four years after the destruction of Vilna as a Jewish center, wearing black leotards inside the gym of the Young Men's Christian Association, in the hometown of the Woman's Christian Temperance Union. In class sometimes I had trouble following the teacher. I was jerky when I tried to mimic. But when the energy flowed like a river and I turned into an unthinking mirror, I could keep up.

Pulse. Kick. Bend. Stretch. The mind wandered. It has come to this, I was silently explaining to my unknown shtetl ancestors. This is what we do because we have cars and computers and indoor plumbing, because we shirk the manual labor that we were made for, because we don't chop wood or climb hills to fetch pails of water. This is not ritual as you know it, but perhaps I am performing a ritual of the secular humanists we have become. Or maybe what I was doing was religious, a physical prayer to praise the heart's relentless pumping, the continual necessary moving of parts.

One day my aerobics teacher said that for five minutes we were free to move in any way we wanted. I jumped, swung my arms, clumped along flat-footed, thumping. It was then that I realized why people exercise—aside from the effort toward immortality, though that is the impetus; we don't want to die before (or even after) our time, aside from wanting to "shape" or "sculpt" our bodies into pleasing, popular shapes, aside from wanting to be healthier and to increase our stamina. But beyond all that: We do this because we want to be children again, regain the same wild freedom we (meaning not me but the kids who didn't have asthma) had when we played Horses at recess.

Did everyone feel the joy in the physical, except austere intellectuals and people with chronic ailments, impeded by fear and mistrust of the physical self?

And what did you do to keep your endorphin levels up? I asked these ghosts.

I pictured the Gaon of Vilna and other sages before and after him, men whose DNA I inherited, bent over their books and scrolls in small rooms illuminated by bits of candle. But the women? Why was I not considering the women, ancestors with bodies like my own? The women, after all, were the physical ones, scrubbing clothes and floors and children, living in the world—many of them running businesses to support the husbands who were ensconced and entranced in those small, close rooms. Some of these female ancestors might have been joyous, singing as they moved, despite privation and persecution, circumstances we can't imagine, happily imagining the cerebral cells drinking from the same trough as the ones located in baser regions. Humming and keeping their secrets, all kinds of physical pleasures left unrecorded for the next and next generations.

HALLOWEEN, CHICAGO

We didn't know anyone who was having a Halloween party, so we were driving north looking for a bar that might have a semblance of one. We'd gone to a performance in Old Town and afterward we'd walked along North Avenue stopping people in costume and asking them if they knew of any parties. They all said no.

I suspected they were lying.

So now we'd retrieved the car and were in Lincoln Park. Phil was driving; his girlfriend Niquie couldn't because her wig cut off her peripheral vision. All of our costumes were impromptu. The wig was one Niquie had bought to decorate a pumpkin once. It was long and black with a white streak. She was Susan Sontag or Just Dressed Up. Phil had on a beret and a coat that had been Niquie's grandfather's. With his mustache and beard he looked menacing. He became the Man with the Hat. My costume consisted of sequins and glitter attached to my nose and cheeks (with false-eyelash glue) and my hair pulled up high in pigtails. The pigtails looked like dog ears, Niquie had said, so I put a barrette around a tuft of hair in the middle and declared myself a show dog. I perceived myself as some sort of talking dog that traveled with the circus.

It must be a sign of age not to know anyone throwing a Halloween party. In my twenties everybody was always having parties and, in grad school, costume parties for no reason. We'd dress up as the Virgin/Whore Dichotomy or Free-Floating Anxiety. (Free-Floating Anxiety told me later that she would beat her head against walls, literally.) We even had a prom. I made a dance card and collected the signatures of my partners, sure at least a few of them would be famous someday.

I lost the card and I don't remember who I danced with, but I went to school with people you've heard of by now.

In Chicago a decade ago, when I was in my early thirties, my friends and I would dress up as Daylight Savings Time or a Stranger in These Here Parts and drive south to Joy Darrow's famous Halloween party in her big old house on Prairie Avenue. She was a well-known photographer and journalist and grand-niece of Clarence Darrow. At first we were sort of invited—by a friend of a friend of a friend; then it became clear it was open to anyone who'd pay the cover charge. The food and drink were spread among the rooms in her gallery downstairs. I remember a photographer who wore a tuxedo and was shooting people with a squirt gun. Unfortunately he startled my friend Frieda, who—I think I remember this right—threw lettuce on his head. I met a reporter there who was, for that night, Carmen Miranda, with fruit piled on her head. (I think there were a few Carmen Mirandas that night.) We later became friends. Those parties must have been a long time ago because I remember a guy whose costume consisted of miniature roads and cars. He was a highway that had collapsed during the L.A. earthquake.

The best costume belonged to someone dressed as John the Baptist, whose real head was covered somehow and who carried another head on a plate. Or maybe the costumed person was Salome. Time passes and we were drunk.

A couple of years ago I called about the party and Joy said it had become private. And then not long after she died.

I swear there was a time when my real friends had Halloween parties. I think. But at some point, your friends, instead of having Halloween parties, set out bowls of candy for neighborhood kids, then children of their own who dress up, and then, for example, a child who is too old and independent (tenth grade) to help his father carve a jack-o'-lantern, which he used to love to do. This last bit I heard on Halloween afternoon from a friend.

So I was dressed as a glittery show dog and riding in Lincoln Park. On Sheffield near Armitage a parking space appeared and it was such an unexpected and rare phenomenon that we took it. We started walking. We passed a three-flat where a few people sat on the stoop. Phil said, *Happy Halloween*, but the people just stared so we kept going.

We saw a bar on a corner with pink lights in the window arranged in a way that looked like a bra or rabbit. A loose knot of costumed people was milling in front on the sidewalk. The bar had no signs in front. It appeared this was a house, not a bar. There was a small note in the front window that said to go around back. I figured the note was for us. *Let's go,* I said to Niquie and Phil. It seemed the most natural thing in the world to follow two women around back and into the party proper. In fact, it felt very similar to an evening two weeks before when my boyfriend and I had rung the doorbell for a friend's office party and joked around with several other people waiting to be let in. In fact, the Halloween party was less anxiety-provoking. I didn't have to worry I wouldn't know enough people or have anyone to talk to. I didn't have to introduce myself.

How do I explain how natural it felt to squeeze our way into the party, to exchange pleasantries with an Elvis near the door? (Who informed us there were six other Elvises inside.) We wanted to dance and snaked past a bank of votive candles, past witches with pointed hats and French maids and a nun or two. There was a lot of that cottony spiderweb stuff, and while we danced a little we bumped against stuffed ravens near the fireplace. It was festive, like Christmas. Maybe I thought that because I saw a female Santa Claus.

Everyone seemed young and innocent and collegiate, sort of like the crowds at the parties I used to go to with my friend Jessica (aka Carmen Miranda)—non-costume parties thrown by very young people in apartments with big furniture and low ceilings and I'd think about the time I saw President Eisenhower in a parade. (It was 1960 in Houston and I was in kindergarten.)

Nothing makes you feel older and more alienated than being among skinny pretty women wearing more makeup than you wore in the entire 1980s and talking about celebrities you've never heard of. Here they seemed as young, but welcoming, well, accepting; we were invited to the same party, no? And we were all in costume. There were three Brownies, sashes and all, sitting together on a white couch, and nearby a woman all in red who said, in response to my question, that she was not the devil. She was something from an old animated film. *You're too young to remember,* she said, and I thought, I doubt it.

Someone told us it was great upstairs so we went up two flights, realizing this was a several-apartment party, and went past bloody gloves on a kitchen counter out to a porch.

We passed a wan young person in a pinkish blond wig, sitting in a wedding dress with blood on it, holding a bouquet of dried roses. Niquie recognized her as Carrie. We met a young woman in an orange gauzy outfit with a pumpkin top on her head. I asked if the pumpkin was real and if she was Peter Pumpkin Eater's wife. She said no, she was the Halloween fairy. Niquie asked if she could grant us wishes. We snaked from the porch to the deck and talked to a cow with a nipple ring through an udder; Mr. Kotter, with his fake mustache in his pocket; a plainclothes cop and one in uniform; a man in a long slim dress; and Harlem Globetrotters. By this time people were asking us what we were, and we didn't have good answers. Niquie said I was a poodle and she was my owner. But then what was Phil in his beret? Oh, we decided, we were all French, including me, the poodle.

We talked to Lake Michigan (Michigan T-shirt with beer can, plastic fish, seaweed, crabs safety-pinned to his shirt). He'd already gotten a lot of ribbing for the crab. I swear that someone dressed as Lake Michigan at a Prairie Avenue party. Lake Michigan told us that the party was given by the seven Elvises. He worked with one of them, who had paid $300 for his costume and $400 for decorations. He was clean-cut and looked like a lawyer but later Phil said he must be an accountant. I tried to find clues about our hosts from the walls and refrigerators, but all personal effects were taken over by the holiday decorations and the exigencies of party giving.

Later Niquie said she was surprised I was talking to all these strangers, but it seemed natural, because for me, this was not idle party chitchat. There were vital things I wanted to know. Like: Who are you supposed to be? How did you attach that beer can? All conversation was concentrated on the essentials: who we were, what we were, how we put our costumes together, how many Marv Alberts we'd seen. No one once asked us what we did for a living.

I got the hiccups, and Phil said boo a few times but it didn't help. We went downstairs to the kitchen for some water, but that didn't help, either.

Once outside, we found another party right away. The crowd seemed older (noncollegiate; people who were at least twenty-five, said Niquie) with framed black-and-white Famous Photography and a dartboard on the walls, and a disco ball circling on the ceiling sending out its dizzying flashes of white. We danced for a while until I got woozy from the lights and the warmth and my continued hiccupping. (By the way, none of us had anything to eat or drink at these parties except tap water. After all, there's a difference between a crasher and a moocher.) There were cheerleaders at this party and doctors in scrubs, and when we got back outside, we encountered a confused person in a wig, sunglasses, golf pants, and a bowling shirt, who broke down under intense questioning about his costume. There were people walking behind us and I turned to them and said we'd follow them to the next party but they said they were going to the 7-Eleven. We went too. I bought water for my hiccups, and saw one of those lovely tableaux you see only on Halloween. There were about six people in line, two in black-and-white stripes. I think they were prisoners. There was also a cat at the cash machine, with a nice sturdy black tail, which I envied.

As we were about to leave the store, we saw a guy buy a pack of Coors. He complained about the price. The civilian-dressed clerk said soberly, *No matter how much you pay for beer— it's worth it.* And everyone laughed.

Outside, Phil was buying a *Streetwise* from a real homeless person, who was much more garrulous than an ersatz one we'd tried to talk to at the party. The guy told Phil that he needed something, man, and he reached into his bag and retrieved just what Phil needed—plastic horns and cow ears. He told Phil to pick the price. Phil gave him a $5 bill and put on the adornments, which complemented his dark hat.

The rest of the evening pittered on. Other parties seemed too intimate to crash and it was getting late. Niquie mused that it's too bad people don't dress up their whole houses. I imagined apartment buildings with giant ears on them and elephant trunks.

Niquie and Phil had to get up at six the next morning to stand in line to reserve a Park District building for their wedding in June. We had planned, once we were back at their apartment, to carve a pumpkin, but instead Niquie put the uncut pumpkin in the window among some big plants and I left.

When I got home I started taking off my sequins and glitter. I used soap and water, oil, Vaseline, and finally a punctured vitamin E tablet. It took about thirty minutes and still I had pink ridges where the eyelash glue had been thick and where the pink glitter had faded into my skin. I imagined being marked like this, by Halloween, for the rest of my life, but figured most of it would be gone by the time I got up.

FRENCH YOGA

Her eyes are deep and dark, and at the end of each class she says softly (*en français*) that she hopes that in the coming week we will have peace in what we see, peace in what we say, peace in our hearts (moving her hands from prayer position, to *les yeux* to *la bouche* to *le coeur*). Once she spent the first ten minutes talking about the EU and how Europe does not understand how to integrate the Arabs. I wanted the yoga to start but I also wanted to keep hearing progressive opinions in French. She was born in Morocco and is a secular Muslim and dances with a Chicago troupe. She teaches dancing to kids in a housing project after school and in the summer. She is beautiful like a Mediterranean woman in a travel poster. You would believe it if she told you that in some other country she was a movie star.

The instruction is in French, and she alternates between naming the positions in Sanskrit and French, and when she thinks we don't understand she'll repeat in English. We do *le chien en bas* (downward-facing dog), and also upward dog or *le chien en haut*, we collapse into the position of *l'enfant*, we stand in tadasana, squat in *la grenouille*, balance and stretch out our arms in *l'arbre,* or tree. *Respire, expire*, she directs us, distribute your weight between *les phalanges* of your fingers and *les talons* of your feet. Sometimes we take deep ujjayi breaths, where you vibrate the back of your palate like a snorer. There is *le triangle* and *la chaise.* At the end we lie on our back in savasana, corpse pose, *le cadavre,* palms up, legs spread in a *V,* eyes closed, relaxing while concentrating on our breaths.

Once she referred to savasana as what sounded like *la position Maccabee* and I continued to lie in the pose silently and wonder, Maccabee? Like Judah Maccabee? Relax the body, make your limbs heavy, but Maccabee as in Chanukah? After class I asked her about the word and she said it was another name for corpse. I couldn't figure out why the French would name a corpse after a Jewish hero. Must be anti-Semitic, I said to myself. (I do not mean our teacher. I mean the French.) You would think, if anything, one of the warrior poses would be named for Judah Maccabee. Those poses are ripe for naming; in English they're merely Warrior I, II and III.

I looked up *la macchabée.* It's a casual word, slang but in general use, the equivalent of "a stiff," often referring to the body of a person who has drowned. Thus, one of the Goncourt brothers wrote in his journal in 1885 of having dinner with Guy de Maupassant, who spoke a long time about poking around in the Seine and looking at *les macchabées* because their original ugliness was covered up. And Blaise Cendrars wrote (in French) in 1948, "When I've had enough of . . . the *macchabées* in the [medical] amphitheaters, the sick people at the hospital . . ."

A French etymological dictionary says the word is probably an allusion to people in the danse macabre, which itself was named after the seven Maccabee brothers, who died, together.

In Sunday school we learned of Judah Maccabee, great leader against the occupying Greeks, his name meaning "hammer," who led the fight for Jewish independence and cleaned up the temple after it was defiled—altars destroyed, pigs let in to run through. He relit the temple lamp with oil only enough for a day or two, and it burned for eight days and thus we commemorate this miracle at Chanukah.

We did not learn that after he won that battle, he lost the war.

And in that losing, the seven brothers were killed and became Jewish martyrs. After that, they (or seven anonymous bodies who happened to be martyred around the same time,

according to some sources) were adopted as Christian martyrs. "As martyrs took a more prominent role in the beliefs and
practices of Christians, and Christians gained Imperial power,
Rabbinic leaders ceded claim to the Maccabean martyrs and were
forced to relinquish control of the Maccabean shrine," rabbi and
scholar Shira Lander writes. In other words, the rabbis weren't
so enamored of the Maccabees, who eventually capitulated to
the Greeks, and the Christians wanted more martyrs.

I relax into the pose of *la macchabée*. At peace like a martyr who
died for his cause. Prepare for your death by lying down like a
corpse. Prepare for your martyrdom by believing in your cause.
Have confidence. "Ride your bike with confidence," says the
safety booklet from the city. The answer to all. To walking on
streets at night by yourself as a woman, keys between fingers,
ready to counterattack. Relax into the Maccabee pose, the pose
of the Jews who became Christian after their deaths. They died
for their religion and were converted posthumously anyway.
The Christians claimed Jesus, son of Joseph, for themselves and
called him Christ; they went to Auschwitz and set up a convent
there. I am lying on my sticky mat inside a tiny slice of France
inside Chicago, palms relaxed, outward, holding nothing. Not
grasping. We are all corpses now, letting go. Nothing is ours
except for our breathing, which is life flowing through us. In
the past hour we have greeted the sun, stood as warriors; we
have been frogs and dogs and rabbits and camels, monkeys and
happy babies, and then *les cadavres*. And after savasana, we slowly
come back to ourselves and roll to the right (so that the heart is
open, exposed), in *la position du fœtus* and then push ourselves
up and around to sit up straight, crossing our legs as tailors do.
We say *namaste*—meaning, "hello," but interpreted lately, and
by some, lamentably, as "That which is sacred in me recognizes
that which is sacred in you." We return ourselves to ourselves,
we put on more clothes, we walk out the door, into America.

MIKVAH
That Which Will Not Stay Submerged

The Visit

Rub a dub dub, three Jewish women in a tub.

It is an Orthodox tub but we are not Orthodox. We are trying to pull the wool over the eyes of the Orthodox.

We are trying to be sheep in sheep's clothing, naked Jewish sheep in no clothing.

We wonder if we are not fooling anyone, if we stand guilty, like Adam and Eve, God's loud voice offstage, demanding Adam and Eve to admit what He already knows they did.

Each of us is as naked as the day she was born, at least, just about.

The three women are Sonia, Peggy, and me. The tub is not really a tub, it is a small indoor pool. In accordance with religious law, it contains a certain amount of water from a natural source. The pool is a *mikvah,* the Jewish ritual bath, mostly frequented by Orthodox Jewish women. We are Jewish and women but not Orthodox. There are mikvahs all over the world—Bangkok, Anchorage, Bogotá. This mikvah is on Touhy Avenue on the North Side of Chicago. Peggy and I are accompanying Sonia. She is getting married soon, and before the wedding she wants to go through the bride's traditional purification rite. At a friend's house she asked if anyone wanted to come with her. Peggy and I offered, imagining ourselves as handmaidens to the bride, though later Sonia will remember that she invited us reluctantly. That is part of the reason I'm calling her Sonia here, which is not her real name.

Human Understanding

A Jewish woman's three duties: light the candles on the Sabbath, observe the laws of ritual purity, and, when baking challah, pinch off a piece of dough and throw it into the fire to echo the sacrifices burned at the ancient temple. (It goes without saying that she must make challah every Friday.) The laws of the mikvah are in the category of those that defy human understanding, and must be followed on faith. Other examples are keeping kosher and refraining from mixing linen and wool.

I grew up lighting Shabbat candles. I've made challah once or twice, but had never gone to the mikvah. Before this night.

According to the Jewish laws of family purity, a woman is unclean during her period and for some time after, and then she goes to the mikvah. While you are unclean you may not touch a man. Or a man may not touch you; there is a slight difference. Having sex when you are ritually impure, according to the Mishnah (the written account of the oral law), can lead to giving birth to devilish children. Or death in childbirth. The first time a woman is supposed to immerse herself is before the wedding. Orthodox women say that the abstinence adds excitement to a marriage, so that the first night back with their husbands is like a honeymoon.

Muslims also observe what's known as "menstrual control," which means they have laws having to do with what a woman is allowed and not allowed to do during her period. Christians do not. Therefore, the menstrual laws were followed by Jews more strictly in Christian countries, to counter assimilation.

This traditional mikvah is nondescript, silent, does not announce itself. No neon lights or blinking arrows. Jewish women duck into mikvahs inconspicuously, emerging with wet hair and an appointment in the marital bed. Typically women usually go to the mikvah at night—under cover of darkness, and also because Jewish days begin and end at sunset. They slip back into their homes, not meeting their children's eyes.

You step down into the pool—toes, pelvis, torso. Dip past the crown of your head. Pull down the floating tips of your hair. Rise up three times, say the prayer each time. It is written on the wall of the pool.

No priest or rabbi is there to sanction, to bless. It is do-it-yourself, after you've passed the gatekeeper—in the person of the "mikvah lady," who acts as inspector, attendant, and, in some cases, confessor.

Symbolic

The mikvah building on Touhy Avenue was modest brick. Inside it was like a health club or hotel—all hallway and long bathrooms. Peggy and I shared a bathroom. We decided, rather condescendingly, that this was a holiday for Them, the capital O Orthodox women, their only time alone, relieved of their burdens; this was where they could relax, a respite from their dozen children and oppressive husbands.

The mikvah does not clean you; its function is merely symbolic. You are supposed to be clean all over before you immerse yourself. Purely naked, free of jewelry, clothing, hair ornaments. At the edge of the pool I was sent back because my fingernails were dirty. Then the mikvah lady tried to brush away hairs growing on my breasts; she thought they were stray. And then there was the piece of surgical tape on one breast, protecting the stitches from a recent operation. Technically, the tape should have been removed so that I would be entirely naked, but the adhesive was medically necessary. The mikvah lady made a call, to a rabbi presumably, to see if I could go in with the tape. Permission was granted. The surgery had been outpatient removal of some calcifications that had shown up on a mammogram. There was no cancer. I think the mikvah lady gave us a towel test, that she wiped a white towel between our legs to make sure we were clean. Or else she handed us each a towel.

Then, one at a time, we climbed into the pool and recited the prayer written on the wall, immersed ourselves, and climbed out.
So we were never three women in a tub at the same time.

After we got dressed we were fixing our hair at a communal mirror where a friendly woman was drying her hair. I felt like an imposter. At the time I was living with a non-Jewish man; Peggy, with a non-Jewish woman; Sonia, with a non-Jewish man whom she would marry in a Jewish ceremony. Were we desecrating the mikvah?

We were outlaws—making our own rules. I thought, We want to be part of the Jewish circle of history and ritual, but are not strong enough or bold enough to make our own mikvah, to seize the means of production of ritual.

I should not be saying *we*. We each had our own reasons, our own reactions. Peggy and I went out of curiosity. Peggy told me later that she had felt unsafe. *The mikvah lady had seemed very free with our bodies,* she said. *We were so physically exposed; if it became known that I was a lesbian, I couldn't just run out.* So Peggy felt unsafe. I felt sneaky. Sonia said that the experience was meaningful for her. I told Sonia, *We could have done a mikvah ritual of our own for you.* She said, *But I wanted to go there.* The water was not ordinary; it was, according to tradition and law, two hundred gallons of water from a natural source.

So we were three women in a tub but it was not the same tub.

Heroics

The mikvah is so important to traditional Jewish life that it is the first thing a Jewish community is supposed to build, even before laying the foundation stone of a synagogue. You can pray anywhere but a woman may become pure only in a mikvah or a natural source of water. You can easily find books and essays that detail the heroic exploits of Jewish women in the anti-religious, anti-Semitic Soviet Union: using axes to crack through frozen rivers, to get to their nature-made mikvahs. You can find, online and in museums, a beautiful photo exhibit, *The Mikvah Project,* which shows women in water, in shadow, accompanied by their words on using the mikvah. The black-and-white pictures are nice and dreamy, the quotes meaningful and modern. Some of these woman are traditional and some aren't—they're re-creating the mikvah in their own images—and some are models. You can also go to new community mikvahs open to Jews of all stripes, such as Mayyim Hayyim (Living Waters), which is in a converted Victorian house in suburban Boston. Women and men go there as part their conversion to Judaism, or to mark a passage (menopause, divorce, birthday, bar/bat mitzvah, end of chemotherapy, end of nursing, start of sobriety, end of a mourning period), or to heal (from rape, incest, domestic violence, illness, mastectomy). Non-Orthodox women are also returning to the "laws of ritual purity"—the practice of abstaining from sex during and just after their periods. These new uses are recognized as Good Things in the *New York Times* and the *Boston Globe,* so they must be so.

And a young woman I just met told me of a tradition she had participated in at Stanford: a female Jewish leader on campus arranged for a handful of female graduating seniors to meet at five in the morning on the beach. They said the special *Shehecheyanu* prayer of thanksgiving, reflected on their four years of college, then stripped and immersed in the ocean.

It was beautiful, she said, and her first experience of a mikvah. At the time, she said, she didn't know about the traditional use of the mikvah.

In the Land of the Orthodox

Orthodox Jews bring new dishes (if manufactured in non-kosher factories) to the mikvah to make them kosher. Men also use mikvahs. Some Hasidic men immerse themselves weekly on the Sabbath. Other religiously observant men go to the mikvah on their wedding day and before Yom Kippur.

My late father never used a mikvah. Nor did my mother. My mother keeps kosher: keeping kosher is part of her tradition, but going to the mikvah is not. The mikvah, she says, is old-fashioned, extreme—which illustrates the axiom that anyone more religious than oneself is a fanatic; anyone less religious, a heretic. Both of my parents grew up Orthodox—southern U.S. Orthodox, which is looser than northeastern or midwestern. My father used to say that he was Orthodox in belief, Conservative

in synagogue affiliation, and Reform in practice, which was more
or less accurate, but he never ate *traif*—shellfish or pork—even
when he was serving in the navy during the War. He would eat
non-kosher beef and chicken outside the home, which is typical
among many modern and postmodern Jews. Let not the fare of
Colonel Sanders darken my door, but when we are under his
striped roof, we may avail ourselves of the thigh, the breast, the
crispy, and the naked.

Flush

The tradition in Jewish and some other cultures is for the mother
to slap the daughter's cheek when she reaches menarche. Slap
her—either because the girl is pale from loss of blood, or because
you are making a preeminent strike against sluttishness, now
that your daughter is capable of becoming pregnant.

My mother didn't slap me when I started my period.
She did not say, *Today you are a woman.* I'd already said that six
months before, at my bat mitzvah. My mother did not sequester
the two of us in the bathroom, as she had with my older sister,
to fit the sanitary napkin and elastic belt (raise your hand if you
remember those) snugly in place. I figured out the arrangement
of the apparatus myself.

Why was there no substantial ritual in 1969 to welcome my
menses—the sea that connects me to all women, and all people
who once nestled, at first microscopically, in that necessary bed?
I've read one revisionist prayer, published in *Lifecycles*, an anthology of Jewish women's writing. In the book, ninth grader Elana
Rosenfeld Berkowitz and Rabbi Debra Orenstein present a small
introduction and a menarche prayer, noting that the mothers of
girls have displayed more interest in such rituals than the girls
themselves. It is important to have a ceremony that is "short,
unceremonious and unembarrassing," they write. The prayer
was initially written for women who had trouble conceiving,
and can become many things to many women—it can be said
at the beginning of every period, or to "celebrate a marriage, a
good grade in school . . . or it can offer comfort in the case of an
illness." They suggest, "May it be your will, Our God and God
of our mothers, Sarah, Rebecca, Rachel, and Leah, to renew our

lives in this coming month. May it be a month of goodness and blessing, healing and vitality, fruitfulness and abundance, joy and happiness, deliverance and consolation." The prayer seems rather general and . . . bloodless to me. Inoffensive and hopeful. The prayer does not address what is going on inside the woman's body. It does not acknowledge the change that has taken place, that she has undergone, that her body has decided she is ripe for, made her ripe for. We need a prayer for the bursting egg and for the follicle being used as a roadway for the first time, a prayer that addresses the implications. Or a more pragmatic prayer that will work as an amulet to guard against tampon and pad leakage, a prayer appealing to the gods of PMS, a prayer to obviate the necessity of washing underpants in cold water and of soaking stains, and a dreamy prayer that connects back to the curse of Eve and reinterprets it as a blessing, the magic of the woundless blood, that wishes for the tiny egg's journey when we do want to be joined to make a new life. Where is this gush and wonder and detail, the prayer that considers the monthly flow as the occasion for both sadness and joy? The sadness is that potential nourishment—our bodies the original MREs, meals ready to eat—is dissolving, seeping out, weeping out; our blood signals the failure of new life to form, and therefore is the hallmark, handmaiden, byproduct of death.

If indeed the absence of a thing is the same as the opposite of it.

And why not a ritual for all women delighted, relieved, at the sight of their blood—because they were not ready to accommodate another life in theirs, because the blood set them free? Or homage to the blood that brings with it the relief that we do not have to become providers; for another month at least we can be self-reflective, turned inward, body intact.

And let there be another prayer for the disappointed women, those for whom the stream of blood means failure, as E. M. Forster said in a different context, to connect.

Without Child

I know a writer who left Chicago for New York because she wanted to live in a place that was less family-oriented. Manhattan, she said, was full of productive, not reproductive, people. This was before every other gay couple started adopting, as well as before Manhattan became generally unaffordable. She was about forty then, and was disappointed that men no longer seemed to notice her on the street. I thought she was quite attractive. About a dozen years since her move east, she's still in New York. Publishing. Maybe happy.

Synagogue membership is always counted in families. Which seems like an imprecise way of keeping track. Perhaps the reason is fiscal: couples pay as one unit.

We three women in the tub are childless. We have not fed others from our salty or milky waters. We have not hired lactation consultants or weighed the ethics of videotaping our nannies. We have not debated paper versus cloth diapers or entered lotteries for magnet schools. I have two grown stepchildren. A few months after the marriage, one of them referred to me as his "mother-in-law or whatever," in a not unfriendly way.

I don't know if I'm fertile. Or if I ever was. My husband has seen to the snipping and sealing of his vas deferens. I usually believe myself when I say I never wanted children, though I get sad that I no longer have the option. I would like to experience birth. (I guess I have already; I mean experience *giving* birth.) I like to think that I would have been one of those women who just squats in the living room and pushes out a baby. Like that. And I know I don't want to take care of a baby. I could be a surrogate mother, I've thought, I've seen the ads for healthy Ashkenazi women. That's me! I think. Then I see the age range asked for: twenty-one to thirty. I'm forty-nine. My stepdaughter is thirty. She has said that she will let me into the delivery room, as long as I don't ask questions. I am known for asking a lot of questions. I ask, *Even between contractions?* I'm joking.

She has the desire for children but no money and no suitable father in mind.

No, not even between contractions, she says.

Marriage

Linc and I were married almost a year ago. We did not immerse ourselves in his 'n' her mikvahs. I did not have a party for naked women friends in the lesbian-owned neighborhood spa, as I had imagined I would want to do. It crossed my mind, barely. We did not jump into the lake, as my friends Niquie and Phil did, though we have showered together many times using lake/tap water. I don't know why we didn't, except that my fiancé didn't want the wedding to be a big deal. He didn't care what I did with friends, so what was the reason I didn't create my own mikvah ritual? All I can say is I did not feel the need. It did not seem necessary.

Mezuzah at the Door

Years ago I made a clay mezuzah for my friend Don to put up in his new condo. A mezuzah is that rectangle you see in the doorways of Jewish buildings. Inside are passages from Deuteronomy. The thin rectangular case is not supposed to be an amulet, but some people treat it as such. It's customary to touch the mezuzah upon coming and going and to then put your fingers to your lips, remotely kissing the mezuzah, in effect. Don didn't want the traditional scroll inside so I made up my own statement of wishes and bless- ings for his house. He had grown up with a mezuzah at the door but had never had one of his own. A Hebrew scribe is supposed to write on the scroll, without mistakes. After a run of bad luck, some traditional Jews might suspect that their mezuzah scrolls are not "kosher," and will hire an inspector to check them out. Others have the scrolls looked over periodically, just because it's the right thing to do. After Don sold his condo he didn't take the mezuzah with him, because of my inept engineering. The nails holding it up couldn't be removed without endangering the glazed clay.

I don't know what the new owner has done with my mezu- zah, if anything. Painted it over? Cracked it open like a fortune cookie or piñata?

How far can you go? How far can you push the religion until it breaks or stretches into another form entirely? How far can you go in changing a symbol or practice to make it relevant, before it's no longer Jewish?

And when it comes to family-purity laws, how can even the newest of a New Age feminist ritual make up for the historic misogyny of Jewish law? What is the new ritual to acknowledge the fact that the religion was not made for us, for me, that we have to manipulate it and change everything so that it's meaningful, and that that's a sorrowful and exhausting task?

Mortals

The rabbis—(Which rabbis? Not *my* rabbi, who married us in the upstairs room of a café called the Bourgeois Pig; whom we'd asked to create a ceremony without God or Hebrew, and who almost followed our wishes, I'm sure he meant to but forgot; and who earlier married my friend Jennifer and her non-Jewish but philo-Semitic husband, and then officiated at their baby's bris, the circumcision ceremony, except this was a bris without a circumcision, because Jennifer thinks the custom is barbaric. There were water and prayers and explanation of the baby's name, but no cutting. That is another story. Perhaps.)—*the* rabbis, those rabbis distant from us in belief, scholarship, practice, and time, say that there are controllable secretions and uncontrollable ones. The controllable are not impure. Controllable include urine, excrement, tears, mucus, and the blood from a (true) circumcision. Semi-controllable is semen. Uncontrollable, wild, undisciplined, mysterious, like a woman, are the impure: menstrual blood, vaginal and penile discharges, blood of childbirth.

Anyone with severe diarrhea or food poisoning or postnasal drip would not necessarily agree that shit, vomit, and mucus are controllable.

It seems to me that it would be the opposite: that the discharge you *can* control is impure. If you can't help the drip, then you're blameless, it's pure. Purely beyond your grasp.

After a woman gives birth to a boy, she is unclean for seven days. After the birth of a girl, for fourteen. One theory: An infant girl could have a uterine discharge, and, if so, her mother would become impure because of it. This theory, in my opinion, smacks of apologia; it does not hold water. I get angry whenever I think about these rabbis making pronouncements now and throughout the ages—they don't care about me or my ideas; they care about the tradition, and I am an affront to theirs (which is mine). And they are an affront to mine. Mine has less behind it than theirs, admittedly. It may not even exist.

The Mishnah introduced details about the color of a woman's discharge. If it is red, black, saffron, muddy, or the color of diluted wine (two parts wine to one part water), it is impure. If it's the color of soaked fenugreek or the juice of roasted meat, its purity is under contention.

My friend Margie once told me about an Orthodox friend of hers who happened to mention that she had to go send a package that day. The reason: she was Fed Exing a pair of underwear to her rabbi so that he could analyze the discharge and tell her if she could have sex.

There are men you send stained underwear to, and men that you don't. My artist friend Bev and her sister had a get-quick-rich scheme: they would sell their dirty underwear to prisoners who were deprived of women and the scent of women. But, the sisters finally decided, even if they operated out of a P.O. box, the enterprise might be too dangerous.

Scholar David Biale writes that fluids that come from the organs involved in procreation are powerful. And because they are so powerful, if they are not used to create a living being, they become impure. I extrapolate that it is an impure act that uses raw material for creation. You must develop the gifts you were born with.

Parable: The Seven Wise Men and the Menstruating Women

1. The blind man said, *The woman smells of rust and fermentation. She must be confined so that she does not wet and ruin our things.*

2. The proud man said, *The woman is flowing over; a river is flowing through her. There is no room for me. I can make no impression. Banish her.*

3. The young man said, *When she nurses my siblings she does not bleed. Therefore, when she bleeds she is selfish, not providing for others. Punish her for displaying her blood.*

4. The old man said, *She bleeds though she is not ill. Therefore, she is an affront to me, for when I bleed that copiously it will mean I am dying.*

5. The fastidious man said, *Sometimes there are clots; other days
    there are yellow discharges. We must classify them all, and mea-
    sure them, because they are foreign.*
6. The priest said, *We make animal sacrifices; we blood-let animals.
    The woman will see this and think herself superior because she
    bleeds and does not die. Therefore, keep her from the temple.*
7. The fearful man said, *If she bleeds from that place, and does
    not suffer from it, then she may imagine that if she unmans us,
    we will bleed also without harm. We must keep tools and sharp
    objects from her.*

Because the blood had nothing to do with them, because the
blood meant that the seed had been rejected, because she will
think herself powerful, that she can bleed without pain or wound,
so they must make her see that bleeding means she is incomplete.
When she is bleeding she is less likely to conceive, and so could
have sex with anyone, without consequences.

And they cannot abide the lack of consequences.

Paradise

God has no body, no bodily desires, no hungers, no decay; no
flesh, bone, blood. The more we are like him, the less we are
messy, dependent creatures, feeding constantly upon the fruits
and waters of the earth, needing air and sleep and warmth.

In the time to come, say the scholars, when the messiah
descends to earth, sex will be forbidden, because it will no longer be necessary, mortals will have become immortal, no one
will need to procreate because all the souls that had to be born
in order for the messiah to come are living and breathing. Or
else, sex will be encouraged, taboos broken, including the one
that forbids sex with a menstruating woman. Biale writes, "In
this interpretation, the boundaries between pure and impure,
permitted and forbidden, will be erased."

Which is paradise, boundless sex or perfect contentment? Which
means freedom from all desires?

Pre-, Peri-, Post-

My periods are beginning to become ever-so-slightly irregular. Not long ago, on the phone, I asked my mother when she had begun menopause. Mid- to late-fifties. *You can't be going through it,* she said. *You're too young.* My friends and I sit around now and talk about peri- and total menopauses. *Have you started yet? Started stopping? Night sweats? Thickening waists? Irregular periods?* Just like we did in fifth grade, saying to each other, *No, I haven't but my older sister has.*

I will miss my period when it ends. I like looking at the changes in the blood, at the clots. I imagine them as rubies, dropped from the mouth of the good daughter in a fairy tale. I said to my husband the other day, *This one's a gusher.* I was proud, though it was not anything of my own doing. I'm like the men in Gloria Steinem's famous essay "If Men Could Menstruate." I want to brag about my heavy periods, the six or seven days of it, the lushness of blood, the vigor of it. I overflow. I made all this stuff and I don't need it. I am multitudes of corpuscles. I think of Mary McCarthy's *The Group*, where she describes some of the young women as too thin, no longer as vital as they were in college. One of them, Kay, whose wedding and funeral frame the novel, is pale and nervous post-Vassar, but she was vibrant in college—as evidenced by her copious menstruation.

We were talking clots one evening at an art opening. Three women: me, the sculptor Bev of the unhatched underwear-to-prison scheme, and either Mary the poet or Polly the painter. Bev said that she liked looking at them. The moment felt sur-real. *We're talking about menstrual blood clots, right?* I asked, just to make sure the topic hadn't jumped the tracks when I wasn't looking. Year later, even more dubious that such a conversation could have taken place, I e-mailed Bev. *Yes,* she wrote back, she remembered: *clots.*

"I've tasted my menstrual blood!" cries the Mount Holyoke graduate in Wendy Wasserstein's play *Uncommon Women and Others*. How can she be relegated to mere photocopier duties when she has performed such a feminist feat?

In the mid-1980s, when I was in my twenties, I created a ritual to banish cuteness. I used a tampon (my own) to write "cuteness" on a leaf and buried it by a tree, with a few select witnesses. The point was to become womanly, not girlish; it was time to change.

The Passage

Imagine a new ritual. A public menstrual ritual. Performance art. Imagine a woman walking on stage. She is naked. She has inserted a parchment into her vagina—her dangerous passage—and it is bloody, not from ketchup, but from her, from her lack of children, her fruitlessness, her lover's spermless messages. And on the parchment there are words addressing the Jewish community, words of protest to the bearded rabbis who would condemn her, of course, once they heard about it. And she wants them to hear about it. She wants to be part of the discourse, to have her voice heard, her bloody words listened to, as bearded men and radical women buzz among themselves in books and articles and emails, about women and prayer and ritual. She wants in.

Carolee Schneeman, a performance artist who was not Jewish, said she had a dream image that she had to follow and that is why she performed *Interior Scroll* in the mid- seventies. She told an interviewer later: "I stood naked . . . extracted a paper scroll from my vagina and read a text on 'vulvic space'—about the abstraction of the female body and its loss of meanings." *Normally I am very shy,* she said at a talk at the School of the Art Institute of Chicago. It was the vision that made her do it.

Stronger than her shyness. Her particular muse that drives her
to explore the "sacred erotic."

So. See that woman on stage. She is naked and menstruating.
We have already mentioned the parchment she is bearing. She
stretches out her arms like the crucified Christ. She isn't Christ.
She is a mezuzah.

The woman is pale and hairy. She is pale because she
stays out of the sun. She stays out of the sun because she is more
educated than vain. She seeks to avoid sun cancer. She is hairy
because she does not shave her legs or wax anything. She is a
mezuzah. In Yiddish slang, a mezuzah is a girl who fools around,
lets everyone kiss her.

Non-Jewish girls were called "McKenzies" by Jewish boys
in Montreal. From the Yiddish *m'ken zi shtupn,* meaning, "she
can be screwed."

The paper the woman is extricating does not bear words
from Deuteronomy. This parchment asks a question in English,
which she reads aloud: *Isn't the birth canal as sacred as the door-
posts of your house? The religion says a bleeding woman is unclean,*
she says. *I want to reclaim the house of the female Jewish body,* she
says. Through bleeding a woman cleanses herself each month,
gets rid of the egg and nest she doesn't need. Are a nest and
unripe egg dirty?

A riddle, a Jewish riddle: When is something unused
dirty? And if it is used, it becomes no longer dirty, it becomes
holy, a human, a spark. Is it dirty because it is unused, the way
of spilled seed?

The vagina is, in fact, the doorpost of the house, the house
all of us come from. The vagina is, in fact, the true old country.

Then she pulls a long piece of thin filmy material from her
mouth. It is covered with very small handwriting. It is a list of
things Jews put in their mouths. She reads from it to the audience:

Men kiss their *tzitzit,* or *tzitzis,* the fringes of the *tallis*
or *tallit,* the Jewish prayer shawl. We kiss prayer books after
we accidentally drop them on the floor. And when they are
too worn to be used, we bury them. When the rabbi takes the
Torah from the ark and carries it aloft through the sanctuary,

we cluster at the aisle ends of the rows to reach and touch the Torah, kissing our fingers. We do not kiss the Torah or its fabric cover directly. We do not touch its letters directly even when reading from it, we use a pointer called a *yad*, "hand." It was customary, the first day a boy began to learn his Hebrew letters, to put honey on the slate where the Hebrew alphabet, *alef-bais*, was written, or make letters of honey or cookie for him to eat, to associate learning with sweetness. The letter comes alive, the letter nourishes you. We devour honey and sweetness, we kiss the Torah when it is paraded around. We kiss it by touching it with our prayer books or with the fringes of our prayer shawls and then kiss the book or tzitzit, the fringes of the shawl. Associative holiness. Holiness by association. We kiss the hand that touches the mezuzah.

She looks at the audience and says:

I am honey I am sweetness that goes with wisdom. What if a man had to kiss a woman before he could study Torah? What if you had to partake of the flesh before you went to sit at the table for pilpul, *the discussion-debate over the Talmud? What if before reading the holy tongue you had to perform the* pilpul *of yin yang in and out, me and him? Because you must remember the flesh, the body from which you came. Do not forget the body.*

The Inquisition was about souls. Jews could change the souls inside their bodies—send the Jewish souls underground, declare themselves Christians. I've heard that Spanish inquisitors tested the Jewish soul by offering the body a mix of traif *food—shrimp and clams and squid and pork, which they mixed with saffron rice and called paella; it became a national dish.* Oh. let's go have some paella this Friday night, that new Spanish restaurant; the portions are so big we can share; each of us can pick out what we want.

The religion is about the body, about cleansing, cutting, trimming, purifying. The Jewish soul not darkened by original sin but the body impure by its uncontrolled wastes.

The last century made famous for destroying Jewish bodies. Attacks on Jewish bodies. En masse. Tattoos marking the body. The shaving of the heads, the piles of hair. Shaving for hygienic reasons. And in order to strip identity. Same way the army does. In the camps the political prisoners, the ones arrested for what they'd done instead of what they were, intrinsically, could keep their hair.

In the developed world we wear our individuality. Two women cannot come to a party in identical dresses. We must be original, different.

Hasidic men don their ancestors' black gabardine, eighteenth-century-style suits and beaver hats. Most Orthodox and Conservative Jewish men in synagogues wear prayer shawls, regulation blue-and-white fringed, which they bring from home in a velvet tallis bag, or else they take one from the synagogue's communal box before they enter the sanctuary. The experimentalists tie-dye their tallisim, embroider their yarmulkes. Often these experimentalists are women. Wearing the clothes of their grandfathers.

I am not performing this in front of the mikvah, she says. *I am not here to expose the plain brown brick building. I am not here to "out" the women who visit the mikvah for immersion so they will be pure again for sex with their husbands. I am not standing out front, picket in hand announcing: "The women coming and going from here are going to have sex tonight." I am not like those fetus lovers who position themselves along the walkways of the abortion clinics.*

I am taking what is hidden and making it visible. I am turning the mikvah inside out. I know that water is powerful, that it represents the womb and the ocean and what we can die for lack of and what we can die from too much of. That is all cheap symbolism. I am asking questions. Isn't a Jew supposed to ask questions?

Well, isn't she?

The Written

It's as if the rabbis have been writing all over our bodies for centuries, crafting their arguments onto our skin, in Aramaic and Hebrew and Middle French and German, Yiddish and English. They have been examining women's drips and discharges and dispatches and holding them up to the light. Of course, the rabbis have also been inspecting chickens and making pronouncements about giving to charity and on stealing and stoning and on burial customs and about the pronouncements of their predecessors on law and Torah and what this or that word meant in this or that portion of the Bible, which was written by God Himself, of course. (And the gentile experts haven't exactly been slackers in giving their opinions on women, either.)

One day my skin will be covered with their words, so much so that the words will cover other words from centuries past, their interpretations will have canceled one another out, and my skin will be one wet dark blue-black shape under layers of ink.

Then, say the rabbis, *she'll be ready for the mikvah.*

No, then I will rest.

No, no, they insist, *you will clean yourself and then immerse. So that we can start writing all over again.*

And then they will come, an army of red-handed women, fingers stretched out, ready to paint over the skin and the beards and the crisp, white, creased shirts of these men. Their cry will shatter the heavens.

SOUTH FLORIDA, BEFORE

I regret that I never took pictures.

I remember old people rocking, rocking on the porches of South Beach. I remember them as near-ghosts. It seemed you couldn't go up and talk to them—they weren't substantial enough. If you could touch them, say, on the arm, your hand would slip through their lined, dry skin. Numbers were inked on some of the arms, definitely. The rocking chairs were lined up. As if waiting. The white-haired people came from New York and *shtetlach* that had been eradicated. Eviscerated. Yiddish, which was old and gray and wispy itself, was inside these elders. Eventually, after the old radicals' community center in South Beach closed, volunteers came to pack up the Yiddish books and sent them to the then-unknown Yiddish Book Center in Massachusetts. The people in the rockers had always been old, they'd come to the beach for the warmth and the sea breeze; it seemed that they would disintegrate in water. I see the men in white T-shirts and gray pants, though that's probably not what they wore. The retirees were so frail and vulnerable that police installed cameras on the street to deter muggers.

A few blocks west of the porches was a youth hostel. I took my parents there for lunch when they came to visit. Salads. We went to a bedding store on Lincoln Road, and they bought me a red velvet and white satin comforter and a white blanket. Maybe they ordered them for me and I picked them up later, after my parents had gone back home, to Houston. Those were my first, and only, made-to-order bedclothes.

When I was lonely, sorry for myself, I would drive from my studio apartment in Coconut Grove to South Beach—with its wrinkled faces, flabby bodies, loose plain dresses, baggy pants. There, among the long-retired, I was young, firm, beautiful.

I lived in Miami from 1983 to 1985, in my late twenties. It was the era of fast romances; it was after the invention of the Pill and reliable diaphragms. Abortion was legal, and AIDS was newly the province of homosexuals, hemophiliacs, and Haitians. Quick romances were punctuated by quickie breakups; after one, I thought, Now I can be with women.

I thought this because I had been attracted to my best friend when I lived in Chicago, and I had loved that we chastely slept together sometimes on weekends when it was too late or inconvenient for me to take the El home. I would borrow a nightgown. We would talk in the dark. A few other times in my life I'd been attracted to women who weren't available. I could fantasize about my cake and fantasize that I was eating it, too.

The reason old people are sentimental is because of time. They know they can't get it back. There's more and more time that they have seen, more and more past that has gone past.

Father Time carries a picture of the Grim Reaper on his back.

Stained pastel buildings, formerly handsome little hotels: wouldn't they be nice if they were spruced up? we thought. An art deco tour. Mirrors in the interior, framed in deco lines. The hotels were dark inside.

I had come in June 1983 to work for the *Miami Herald*. I was part of a swath of young people, one of the so-called *insecure overachievers* who populated the newsroom. I was more insecure than anyone else, I was sure.

One afternoon on Miami Beach, the Black photographer working with me said, *You go to the door.* He was wary of knocking on strangers'—white strangers'—doors. An old white couple, he said, would not welcome him. So I knocked first. The husband was a lean, tennis-playing, still-Stalinist in 1985. He'd been one of Julius Rosenberg's pall bearers. The wife had dementia.

The tennis player's son told me his father still maintained that Joe Stalin had been a nice guy. I wrote about the old leftists on the beach for the local Sunday magazine inside the daily newspaper, the leading Knight Ridder paper in the South; and the art director of the magazine, who was British, put a picture of two of the old people on the cover, with the word "REDS!" He did not understand that the cover would be inflammatory, while I could already imagine the outraged commentators on local Cuban-run radio stations: a magazine that featured Communists! The Sunday editor wrote in his column about the naïve and misguided old folks, patronizingly. Both the cover and the column embarrassed me. But by the time my cover story was published I was gone. I was back in Illinois.

A group of us would go to the Cordozo Hotel at night on South Beach, sit outside, listen to the predictions of the fortuneteller who was the wrinkled daughter of a rabbi. She'd never married. She would tell the artists they weren't artistic, the lovers they weren't

passionate, the explorers that they weren't wanderers. We'd feel
sorry for her and buy fruit plates for her, drive her home.

I hied myself to a lesbian support group. I was afraid that in
Dade County I might see women I knew, so I drove to another
county and joined the Broward Womyn's Group, which met in a
church in Fort Lauderdale. The members talked about harass-
ment at work, work in general, monogamy, depression, the male
standard of female beauty. A New Yorker named Janet told a
story about shoe shopping in a local mall with her unshaven
legs. The clerk assumed she was European. We talked a lot
about not shaving our legs and armpits. (No one even thought
of waxing pubic hair.) My feminist reading had convinced me
that ridding oneself of body hair was a way of conforming to
the male idea that women should be powerless and childlike.
In graduate school, hairiness had been the norm. At the *Miami
Herald*, it was not.

Sometimes the discussion would focus on lesbian-specific
concerns: coming out at work versus the Monday-morning pro-
noun switch, answering your gynecologist when he asked about
your birth control, coming out to parents and grandparents,
going to family gatherings with your lover. In these cases, I had
nothing to say. One night a few womyn stayed after to reassure
me that finding a female partner might take a while, that the
right woman was worth waiting for.

I invited some of these women to parties, especially a willowy
couple, gorgeous, both of them, who'd met at Bennington after
each had had the same boyfriend. A sportswriter friend of mine
referred to the two as the wood nymphs.

I had come to South Florida after two years at the Iowa
Writers' Workshop in a college town that supported a bustling
food co-op, a feminist bookstore and press, legions of radical

student organizations. And then, whoosh, I was in Miami, a town full of anti-Communists. To work at a newspaper that was just at that moment undergoing the shift that most papers in the country had already undergone—from being run by an idiosyncratic, strong-willed editor to being managed by a bland, approval-seeking, corporate-approved, fair-haired boy. The boy really was blond, and he was frightened of anyone or anything that seemed untamed, non-mainstream; in other words, me. At one point the feature staff was down to just two of us, and I found out that the fair-haired boy referred to our section as Freak of the Week.

The womyn were a bridge back to Iowa City—they were vegetarians, political activists, wiccans.

I wrote about the South Florida peace movement. I had been an activist in Iowa City; we mostly young socialists and pacifists and activists would meet on the university campus.

On South Beach, retirees in their minks protested for peace, at night, in winter. I remember white-haired members of the Women's International League for Peace and Freedom standing in the street, holding up homemade signs.

One night a group of us, reporters, was at a bar talking and talking. I thought we should always spend nights talking in bars, but we didn't. I don't know why not. No one had kids. Few had spouses. We were young, clever, loud, newspaper people. We didn't need much sleep.

In the newsroom we would stand in the evening by the big west windows, watching the sunset.

There were security guards downstairs, even back then. A female guard missed work and then told everyone she'd been kidnapped. She was found out.

My landlord in Coconut Grove had a boat and at the dock he somehow stepped on a cat and killed it, and there were kittens that he felt responsible for. He brought some kittens home and then suddenly I had a pet and there was a card for Sheba Wisenberg at the vet's. I took her in because my landlord ignored her. And then Sheba ran away, came back pregnant, gave birth to feral cats just as I was leaving town for good. I think I asked someone to take her kittens to a shelter. I thought of driving them to a rich neighborhood, leaving them on a street corner, I heard that people did that. It seemed irresponsible: let the rich take care of our problems.

Another reporter and I traveled to Nicaragua, Honduras, El Salvador, Guatemala, with a left-liberal group: radical lawyers, pacifist religious leaders, leftist activists. They asked us about the *Herald*'s stand on the Contras, the enemies of the victorious revolutionary Sandinistas. We didn't know. I couldn't believe we didn't know.

One morning in Guatemala City we smelled gunpowder and were sure there was a revolution. To show that we were neutral, we wrapped white socks around our arms. That was the only white clothing that we had. We started to walk down the stairs of the hotel, notebooks in hand.

It was a parade. Fireworks.

I'd interviewed the feminist Robin Morgan by phone about her new book *Sisterhood Is Global* but suddenly the story was off. The editor above my editor had come by my desk, seen the fist and female sign (circle with a plus sign underneath) on the cover,

and vowed I wouldn't be writing another feminist story. I didn't.
Even though Morgan did make news when county officials tried
to cancel her meeting because they disagreed with her politics.

People seek their own kind. Desperately. A Cornell graduate,
class of '78, planned a cocktail party for Ivy League graduates of
the past ten years. Ten dollars to cover costs and there was celery
and dip and cheese in ingenious places: baked into artichoke
hearts, stuffed into snow peas, set into ridges of specially cut car-
rots. Everyone there complained about South Florida. Everyone
there praised the same bookstore, Books & Books. Everyone
wondered why they hadn't run into everyone else before. They
said, *Do you ever go to readings there? Do you ever call the poetry
hotline? Did you see Susan Sontag when she came to town?*

They exchanged business cards. They said, *Let's go down
to the keys some time.*

Later they visited the deco hotels on South Beach and
danced wildly through the lobbies: *This is great.*

I was there even though I hadn't gone to an Ivy League
school. My undergraduate alma mater, Northwestern, was the
next tier. I met Robert (Harvard '74) at the party. He was new in
town, had come down to Miami to profess at the law school. Years
later he was still telling people that he'd been scared to death
when I took him to the beach. It was dark, maybe ten o'clock,
and I wasn't afraid. He was. South Beach was crime-filled, but
the victims were the old, not the young and nimble, us.

I think that night, before we waded on the dark beach,
we came across a dance, old couples taking the dancing seriously, half of them on the beach, spilling from a building near
it. Music, maybe live.

There seemed to be one young crowd and Ivy Leaguers were a
subset of it. The crowd was mostly white and liberal/sophisticated.

It went to the Friday-night gallery openings and the movies at the Beaumont Cinema and the parties at the museums and festivals with more art than food. It listened to the speakers at Florida International University and the book festival. There was a political faction that was on the peace mailing list and learned about meetings that weren't publicized in the paper, the ones at the Haitian cultural center. The crowd went to the health food restaurant on South Beach and the Coconut Grove farmer's market. It voted. It rode its bicycles across town on Sunday or to the Everglades. It belonged to the science museum and Fairchild Tropical Botanic Garden so it could take the semi-annual moonlight tours there, wander around in the dark while a woman in a white dress played a harp. There was always terrible punch.

It loved the avocado and lychee trees in its backyard and the great apartments you could slip in and out of, three-month leases, four-month leases, six. Everything was on a provisional basis. The group learned to peel mangoes and eat them with sour cream. It found decent bagels. It took pictures of the old faces on South Beach, the old men playing dominoes in Little Havana. It became proud to have learned its way around this city with streets of numbers and northeasts and southwests. It was proud as a pioneer to be in this hybrid city, to be a transplant. It was happy the way someone who always thinks of death is happy, the groom with his heel poised over the crystal goblet. *We don't belong here. Our minds are going under.* It said, *We have to leave.*

My friend was a reporter north of Palm Beach County. Her riddle:
What do you call a double homicide-suicide?
A Brevard County divorce.

In the mid-eighties Miami was still scared of itself, apprehensive about the TV crew in town to film a show called *Miami Vice.* The city was afraid that the show would keep tourists away. Someone

clever had taken a tourism slogan, "Miami: See It Like a Native,"
and put it on a bumper sticker, accompanied by a drawing of a
revolver pointing out.

It was a Miami that should have been ashamed of itself—of
the city council that did not recognize China, of the bomb threats
that erupted like clockwork whenever a semi-liberal was about
to make a speech, of the veterans of the Bay of Pigs who were
happy to make themselves available for interviews. They had no
shame. Same as the former Somocistas, who applied for political
asylum, claiming the Sandinistas were poised to attack them the
moment they returned to Managua.

Through the havurah, an informal Jewish group, I met Anna,
a short, freckled New Yorker with no-nonsense white hair and
a bite and spriteliness. She was divorced. Had been in love for
ten (married) years with her best friend. Now she had her own,
as she called her, Cha Cha Lady, a Cuban who wore high heels
and couldn't understand why Anna didn't believe in Jesus. Anna
was taking Spanish in night school.

I became friends with Anna's friend Debra, who was com-
pact, tanned, and pretty. She was a Sabra (an Israeli native) or else
from Mexico—depending on her mood. She let out little bits of
information about herself, like a government official floating trial
balloons. She referred to the time she was arrested for speeding and didn't call anyone and spent the night in jail. I couldn't
understand. Just for speeding? Weeks later she'd add something
about drunk driving, her destructive period, after a breakup.

Debra was strong enough to move a piano alone. She often
wore white, had even white teeth. She knew which school board
members were in marriages of convenience. She'd had an affair
with the wife of one of them. They'd go shopping for dresses
together for an event, dressing to please each other. She'd been a
teacher at some unspecified point. She and I would sit in the cafes
of Coconut Grove, on the sidewalk or in small, open-air, vertical
malls lush with greenery. She'd send a glass of champagne to her
hairdresser in the shop next to the café—carelessly extravagant.

Debra and Anna sought out women for me. One was a bilingual Cuban with eyes like a spaniel, deep pockets underneath. We sat on the beach at 21st Street, where Our Kind congregated, and she told me of a best friend, lost because she had declared her love. I liked her but wasn't drawn to her. There was Lora, with a moon-shaped face, heavy-lidded eyes, and perfect skin. An interior designer. She was soft-voiced, Jewish but raised by Catholics. (That's what Debra told me and I don't remember what it meant.) Once Lora and I went to a Thai restaurant out west somewhere. We sat on a balcony. A family sat next to us, teeming with children. She told me the story of her marriage. When she finally recognized her sexual preference, it seemed to push out of her; it was unmistakable. She felt it. Like firecrackers.

After a friendly good-night, I wondered about her breasts, her eyes. Did I want to touch her? Soon she and Debra were a couple.

There was a massage therapist with curly hair and an easy laugh who rubbed away a headache and gave me a copy of Christina Rossetti's *Goblin Market*. I liked her. And more? Not more. The ones I wanted, really wanted, were taken: like the golden, laughing, Jewish attorney who was already claimed by a glinty-eyed activist who wore heavy eye makeup and dark lipstick. The underlying question: Did I feel pulled toward her because she was unattainable?

One Saturday I went last minute to a havurah retreat on South Beach in one of the shabby art deco hotels. At late dusk everyone waded into the water, and the rabbi, wearing Indian-cotton whites, like holy pajamas, legs rolled up, led us in leaping toward the moon. The breeze and ocean were warm. The tide bathed our feet, our knees. It became dark and the stars looked down on us. Everything I have, I thought, is enough.

The Broward Womyn were part of a core group that was planning Southern LEAP—Lesbian Empowerment Something Something. Politics? One early February I found myself in the House, which was on the Land, which was a couple of hours from Miami. About two dozen LEAPers sat in a circle with our shirts off, going over the LEAP statement. A fellow Jew said that in the part where we listed our ethnicities, we should specify that we were Ashkenazi (European) Jews, instead of just Jews, because otherwise we would be implying that we thought we represented all Jews, and we didn't; there were no Sephardic (Spanish/Ottoman) or Mizrachi (Middle Eastern/North African) Jews in our midst. Everyone else was deferential, said, *Sure*. It took more than two hours for us to agree on the rest—such as our purpose (to unite southern lesbians and celebrate the earth and our spirit and to plan political actions). The group defined *lesbian* as any woman who considered herself a lesbian, and she could decide that she was one for political or spiritual reasons. If her main relationships were with women, she was welcome. My friends Kelly and Taylor, a couple, told me I qualified.

The House was big and comfortable, with huge paintings of poppies and sculpture made from driftwood and white birchbark, feathers, shells. While we were stirring spaghetti for dinner, someone started chanting. How natural that seems, I thought. After dinner Kelly and Taylor sprayed on Cutter and went to look at the stars, and I went to celebrate Candlemas, the ancient holiday that falls on Groundhog Day. We saluted the four winds and lit candles.

We slept in tents and in the morning my asthma dogged me. I was allergic to everything on the Land, and, I figured, the dust and mold in the House as well.

One weekend Kelly and Taylor came down from Palm Beach County to my neighborhood for the Coconut Grove Art Festival. We were walking down the street. Taylor was Greek-god-like, with sturdy muscles, brassy swimmer's hair with bandana headband, turned-up nose, gold-stud earrings, wearing khaki shorts that she and Kelly had both just bought at the festival. Taylor worked the greens at golf courses, taking social work classes at night. She was outraged because the guys at work said that a fellow worker, a Haitian woman, stank because she didn't use deodorant. Kelly was taller, more femme, streaks in her wavy brown hair. She talked about the hair on her legs like they were banners; she talked about suits and high heels and makeup from her stockbroker days. A car came by and people inside it yelled out the window, *Hey, dykes.* I felt fire in my forehead, across my hairline. I was wearing cutoffs, Bass sandals, tank top, big moon earrings. My hair was dark and short, curly. Were we touching? We didn't remember. Where did it show?

We noticed we were just outside a gay bar

There is an episode of *Sex and the City* in which Charlotte just loves loves loves hanging out with power lesbians. After a while, one of them asks point-blank, *Do you eat pussy?* and because she doesn't, all her gushing about the energy of women and power and sisterhood falls flat.

I met a boy. And he was a boy, nineteen to my twenty-nine. We walked down the streets of Coconut Grove, gesticulating, similarly exercised about a *New Republic* article we'd both read, an ill-conceived attack on the Sandinistas. Another night we met at Lester's Diner, the tacky site of Broward after-meeting meetings. When we finished our coffees, we walked out and immediately sat on top of a car in the parking lot. We talked for hours, watching the waitresses leave after their shifts. I felt electricity between us and in my entire body, that attraction that I hadn't felt with a woman. Finally our hands touched. With that semi-decisive gesture, we decided to drive to the beach. We walked along the shore, waded up to our knees. Kissed. It made sense to us for him to follow me home.

A couple of weeks later he left town, then I left town, and

in between he fell in love with someone else. He wrote me a few
wonderful letters that soon, too soon, turned to lecture, denial,
chastisement.

It ended the way many stories like this end: We are friends
on Facebook.

At some point I realized that though I liked womyn's politics
and conversation and music, it was men I was attracted to and with
whom I paired up, with whom I wanted to be with for the duration.

Before I left Miami, Amber Wildwoman, one of the Broward
Womyn, had a party for me. She and her lover and Kelly and
Taylor and a few others gathered in a circle in the couple's back-
yard in Hollywood. Was there a bonfire? They gave me a yellow
Indian medicine bag with stones and shells and feathers inside.

A few years later on a visit, we had brunch together,
again at Amber's. I found out that the wood nymphs had moved
together to California, then broken up. I stayed with Debra on
that visit, in a cottage she lived in alone, after Lora had turned
crazy, she said. I visited Anna's new place: small, simple, with
an Indian-print bedspread, like a kid's first apartment. I took
pictures of her in slow motion, halfway behind the front door,
stepping onto the porch. She looks like an enchanted being, all
white and gauzy from the slow shutter speed.

Ten years after I left Miami, in 1995, I encountered a man early
in the morning on a staircase at Northwestern, where I was
about to teach a non-credit class. I thought: I can imagine kissing him. And: I can imagine bringing him home to Houston for
Passover. We have been together ever since. After nine years,
we got married.

I don't wish that Linc's body were female.

I have been back to Miami a few times, but have never gone back to South Beach. I know that it has been glamorous for years. Filled with Euro-trash, movie stars, models. I don't want to replace the South Beach in my mind.

I used the velvet and satin comforter, the one my parents bought me in Miami Beach, for a bedspread in my first two Chicago apartments. It became faded and torn and I finally threw it out. I still have the white blanket, I think. At least I have a white blanket among many others, its hem unraveled, its satin edge hanging half off.

The six-story *Miami Herald* building was completely demolished by 2015, two years after the newspaper moved out. The boy I loved is now working for the *New York Times*. The other wisecracking young reporters have moved on to the *Times*, the *Boston Globe*, the *Washington Post*, academia; have authored books and won Pulitzers and other prizes; have retired. It's easy to follow reporters and writers online.

The editor who hired insecure overachievers is long dead. In 2016 I went to D.C. for a memorial for my beloved features editor Doug Balz, who taught me more about structure than I ever learned at the Iowa Writers' Workshop.

I loved my lesbian friends. I loved the circle of them, the circle they formed around me, I loved them and I wonder how I could have let them go, flying off like the four winds.

THE JEW IN THE BODY

I grew up in a religion in which my first prayers, when I was four, five, six, described experiences of the body. I memorized the Hebrew blessings recited upon seeing the light of the Sabbath candles, the blessings before eating bread and before drinking wine—or grape juice, as the case was. The nightly prayer my father taught me mentioned not the soul but the body, the senses. *Hear* is the first word. Hear. Listen. The prayer, the *Shema*, has to do with remembering the words of God by the signs on your arm and in front of your eyes. We are a literal people. Because of the words of this prayer my father would, during infrequent morning prayers, wrap the straps of his tefillin around his fingers and arm and around his head, in front of his eyes. The English translation of the word is "phylacteries," which doesn't help. The tefillin consist of a leather box that goes on the (male) arm so that we will remember that with a strong arm God took us out of Egypt. It is attached with the aforementioned straps. My father did not put on tefillin every weekday morning, like his grandfather (who had been a Hebrew teacher in the Old Country) did, or probably did, but my father knew how to *lay* tefillin, as it is said. And on Friday nights my father recited the full Shabbat *Kiddush* following the prayer over the wine, a familiar paragraph that includes *zecher litsiat mitzrayim,* in memory of our liberation from Egypt. We remembered *our* liberation from Egypt. And lest we thought that this liberation had happened to someone else—our ancestors, for example, back in the days of the pyramids—all we had to do was wait around for Passover, when we would be reminded over and over that we were celebrating our own deliverance from slavery. We defied the words of Heraclitus, who said that a person could not step into the same river twice. Every Passover we stepped into the Red Sea, and every year it parted.

Just to drive the point home once again, one Passover in the 1970s our enthusiastic rabbi started dressing in white and leading his troops along the concrete-sided Brays Bayou in Houston. He did it the next year and the next, so that each year his congregants were following in their own footsteps, repeating their journey, from their liberation from Egypt, millennia ago, as well as their previous marches from the synagogue.

When you think of Jews and body, maybe you think of circumcision, which derived from a bargain struck between God and Abraham. We are told. The latter followed God's directive to take his long-awaited son Isaac up to a mountain and to sacrifice him. At the last minute, an angel stayed his hand, and Abraham agreed to sacrifice instead a ram that had conveniently appeared, and to circumcise his son instead of killing him. Why could he not have agreed to simply cut Isaac's hair or clip his toenails or even make a small cut on his left or right arm or to administer the homemade tattoo that is now called stick-and-poke? Jewish boys are circumcised when they are eight days old. Muslim boys are traditionally and ritually circumcised, but there is no set age. The Muslim explanation for the practice is that Mohammed was born without a foreskin, and also that the removal contributes to cleanliness. Such things are done partly or wholly to differentiate one tribe from another. I think.

Female circumcision is rightly called mutilation, and the only Jewish group that engages in the practice is or was a subset of Ethiopian Jews. A study of these Jews who immigrated to Israel found that they readily gave up the practice in the Holy Land.

There is so much to say about circumcision that I won't say much more in order not to get lost in it.

It's true that all religions address the body. If you grew up with a crucifix in your bedroom or classroom, then you grew up in a religion of the body, perhaps more of the body than Judaism is. Furthermore, we're the ones who dismiss the body of Christ and all its torments and miraculous feats. Indeed, a standard Yiddish expression of skepticism is *Nisht geshtoygen, nisht gefloygen*—which means "didn't climb, didn't fly." The noun of the sentence, of course, is Jesus. Not the son of God; not, according to us, the lord made flesh.

You could argue—the ritual bath and circumcision aside—that we are the people of everything *but* the body, considering our biblical heroes who keep breaking idols, and Judaism's lack of statues, and, until recently, our lack of depiction of bodies on stained glass. We are, after all, called the people of the book, not of the body. It might be true that we're the ultimate dismissers of the body, and maybe that was true for a long time. Except.

And it may be that everything I've written so far is what my former and late editor Doug Balz used to call throat-clearing. Because the real point is coming up. Because the real point has to do not with tefillin or circumcision or the mikvah or the body of Christ or the Red Sea escape or prayer, but with recent history. With me.

In Sunday school, where we learned our history and occasionally talked about ethics, we talked about a different kind of Jewish body—not the one that recites a blessing on making light or on smelling sweet Havdalah spices or the one that feels in her bones the liberation of the Exodus, but the unmoving and disappeared Jewish bodies from another decade and another continent. Jews are enjoined from worshipping graven images, but that is what postwar American Jewry has done, worshiping at the shrine of Auschwitz, worshipping our second cousins twice removed, whom we never knew, who didn't get on the boat with our grandparents in 1910, and who couldn't get on a ship in 1939. Theirs was the road not taken; theirs was our true destiny—avoided. Our 6 million martyrs and saints. Unlike the Catholics we don't pray to our saints. Instead, we beg their forgiveness—

For living.

We weep for them.

We procreate for them.

We are grateful—because they gave us an essential ingredient in the American post–melting pot. They gave us victimhood.

And in the early 1960s, as a near-sighted eight-year-old girl who had had asthma since she was only a few days old, I knew that without my glasses and my asthma medicine, if, or when—it was just a matter of when—I was taken away to a concentration camp, I would die immediately.

As I was meant to.

Because of this, or concurrent with this, *this* being the communal burden of the Holocaust, and *this* being furthermore the personal burden of asthma, the burden of self-consciousness that was brought early to my breathing—which should be an unconscious, easy, untrammeled, and unnoisy practice—there has been a voice inside me since always. A voice from my body, a silent voice inside my body, since always, telling me, *You do not deserve to live.*

The voice says, *You wouldn't have survived the camps. If your parents hadn't been able to afford your medicine, if they hadn't been able to afford your intermittent positive pressure breathing machine, you would be dead. And why do you deserve the machine, the medicine? It is only money that keeps you alive and what did you do to deserve that money?* The voice says that the artificial, the manmade, is keeping me standing and breathing and seeing; that so much has been given over to keeping me alive; that it is unfair, it is simply too much, too much, that too much of the everything of the world is being used to keep me breathing.

The voice asks, *How do you justify all that has collected*

around you to keep you alive, except to devote your life to the care of others, to the welfare of others? You must sacrifice yourself, all of what makes you you because what you have you don't deserve. You will never deserve it—"it" being your life—so that the making of art is out of the question; its utility has not been proven. If what you deserve is to die, then you don't deserve to be a writer.

I know a woman who works with torture survivors. She says that trauma lodges in the spinal cord, is carried from generation to generation (in Hebrew, *l'dor v'dor*). So is this voice one that has traveled up and down the DNA ladders? Did this voice originate in our enemies, the Cossack and the priest and the czar? In the haters of Jews? Is this the self-hating Jewish voice? I am often too tired to fight this voice. The battle over the voice is a battle over my life, my writing life. The voice is strangling the muse. The voice is the muse.

To have something in you that seeks to destroy you. Like an autoimmune disease. Like asthma. Furthermore, for twenty-three years (starting in high school, ending with Prozac) I had a lump in my throat, a tightness around my neck. The only other person I've met who had this symptom said to me, sadly, slowly, matter-of-factly, *My grandmother tried to strangle me. That's why I feel this.* But I did not have such a grandmother or grandfather or such parents. This death's grip is metaphorical. And real. And from within. And without. It is as real as the fresh lamb's blood we painted on our doors in the slave quarters in Egypt so that the Angel of Death would pass over our houses. It is as stark and real as the identity cards that the French government required all its Jews to fill out in 1940.

Call it a dark star hiding in my blood. It leads me to contemplate other deaths—in El Salvador, Nicaragua, the U.S. South and throughout the world. In Auschwitz, Terezin. *Come see the wooden shelf that was your deserved bed.*

Before Dachau, before Buchenwald, before Kristallnacht, there was Kishinev, the site of a pogrom, a massacre in Moldova/Romania/Russia in 1903 that the authorities allowed, encouraged, did nothing to stop. Afterward, help was sent from around the world. Reports were gathered. Hands were wrung. My grandfather was a young child during the assault—the grandfather for whom I was named, who gave me the *S* and *L* of my first and middle names, and my last name. My name was born in a city that became famous for tragedy.

Sadness walks through my bones.

Abraham's son Isaac's son is Jacob. He wrestles with an angel, with himself. Afterward Jacob is renamed. He is too exhausted to do more than tell the story. He does not know if it is a good story or a bad story, a story for children or for angels or for the merchants of death.

The angel who wrestles with me is death and he comes every day, every hour. What the angel wants from me is bigger than death. He wants to be made to stop killing.

I am afraid that this voice will take me over. But all I have is this voice, all I am is this voice. I forget that I have the prayers, too, the blessings, to acknowledge the miracles: of light, of food, of wine. Of good company. The pleasures of the body. (I forget that I am an unbeliever.) I forget that the pleasures of the body can save me. That words can save me. That passion can move inside the body, from the body, about the body, through the body. That words can chart its movement. Past and present and present and *now*.

THE LAND OF ALLERGENS

I tried to subsist on theophylline—and the two spurts each of Alupent and Vanceril four times a day, carefully following directions to get the full distribution, to coat down to the alveoli. Yesterday the sky hung white, as flat as slate, and each breath was a deep bruise. I was oppressed. Wind blew the grasses like a sea. Night brought no relief. I swam upright in darkness. The pond shattered the half moon and its haze portended storm. We waited for thunder as the radio predicted wild release. I could not summon the faith to wait. Did not want to spend my days of summer retreat nursing bronchi with hot mint tea, stroking Tiger Balm on ribs and breasts, hoping it would seep down to lungs. We drove to town and bought thirteen cookies, three-and-one-fourth for each of us. I did not mention my difficult breathing; no one noticed. I took my share of cookies to my room, finished them off, and in my haste I mistook a beetle for a chocolate chip. I could not wait.

I took the one-night stand over patient evenings waiting alone. I took the bird in the hand and admired its sad eyes and pretended it could sing. I couldn't wait. I was the mob at the gates yelling for bread now, for shelter now, and schools, and I was the government meeting in closed session saying, *But this will make them dependent. They must pull themselves up by the bootstraps.* Health, like everything else, must trickle down. I unscrewed the cap on the prednisone while the wise men sat in careful counsel, the mob crashed through, demanded grain, looted the warehouses for the burlap sacks, lit their way with candles, left rice trickling down the cracks in the cobblestones for pigeons. In each house stew bubbled, cheeks shone bright. The mob was stilled.

And today the bruise is a mere murmur, an echo of small torture. A storm blew over the hills and birds sang in the meadow, trilling over themselves in an eagerness I'd never noticed. Tonight the moon was bright and cold. I sighed, my breath clear as a shout.

I have bought my freedom, wondering if I took the quick fix in a moment of weakness or strength, wondering where is the delicate knowing: when to stop, when to accede, when to bend, when to hold tight and tap inner reserves? I could not find them. I did not look for them. I looked in the drawer and found four blue pills and directions for taking twenty-six more. No refills. No lessons either, but the quick fix stops pain.

The mob is dispersed, content with its full stomachs and glowing fires. But I dream that I am the leader of the mob and I know we can't ravage a storehouse every night. And there is no way to get seeds that we can plant ourselves, or buy cows or sheep to tend. And I am an elder, too, saying, *We will never let them get out of hand again.* The blue tablets sit in a heap, a heap waiting to be diminished. I wonder if later I will mourn my rashness and ask myself, *What next, after the last resort?*

CREAM PUFFS

There is no cake at the friendly wedding, only acres and acres of cream puffs. Ones with thick cream and ones with cream and fresh strawberries tucked inside. Joel the suburban lawyer brings back one round, layered, puffy thing to the table and we say, *What about the rest of us?* He did not bring back any cream puffs but rather some sort of shell topped with raspberries. I venture forth, see bride and groom near the dessert trays, squeeze hands, make a beeline to the cream puffs. Load the plate. A small plate. Bring back a plate full of cream puffs. And a cake roll and a lemon square. Nearly bypass the bride and groom for a plateful of cream puffs, cream puffs they ordered, designated, directed be made. I am hailed as a hero at my table. The great provider. The queen of the cream puffs.

We cut everything in half, everything that we can, except a tall pastry with a little hard square of chocolate on top. We break cream puffs. We eat cream puffs. We pass the plate. Mike the patent lawyer and his blond friend go out for more. She raptures over the lemon boats. We lick cream from our fingertips. It is time for our toasts and we leave the cream puffs, a whole plateful of half-eaten, cut-up, damaged cream puffs. *Do you want more?* I ask Chuck, who is always the big eater. He says, *I don't like them.* Not like cream puffs? Chuck the big eater doesn't eat cream puffs?

We give the toast. We dance, go home, change clothes, reconvene at the house. On the kitchen table is a plate full of cream puffs; on the counters, a box of cream puffs, two layers high and a huge bag of popcorn brought by a neighbor on Friday.

Cream puffs. Women sit at the table, cream puffs and Diet
Coke. We talk electricity and solar and nuclear and coal-fired
power and eat cream puffs. The groom eats cream puffs, downs
them in one bite. Downs bite-sized cream puffs. Rich and sweet
and not even that good, a bit like cardboard, you could say, taste-
less, the wheat part, but please give me more cream puffs. What
is my allotment of cream puffs? I have known the groom for seven
or eight years, how many cream puffs do I deserve? I gave the
bride such nice earrings at the shower, how many cream puffs
does that equal? Chuck and I are ordering a lovely gift, do I get
his share of cream puffs? We make jokes about heart disease and
think of arteries closing but, quick, give me more cream puffs.

Everyone is full. The cream puffs beckon. Everyone suc-
cumbs. *This is a fire drill. everyone leave, just leave me here with these
cream puffs.* Howard eats cream puffs. Kathryn eats cream puffs.
Karen eats cream puffs. The nieces eat cream puffs, so does the
sister of the bride. Only the bride doesn't eat cream puffs, and that's
because she had emergency oral surgery two days in a row and can't
eat much. She does try the tall chocolate pastry, sideways. The rest
of us, we're all eating cream puffs. All eating air and fat and fruit.
The wedding party talks of birth and death and eats cream puffs
and popcorn and drinks Diet Coke with halfmoon-shaped ice.

The men go outside, toss a few hoops, come back in, play
the guitar, sing Steve Goodman and Tom Waits. I eat cream puffs.
Busy hands are happy hands, we eat cream puffs. They are not a
symbol. They are what they are. They are not the marriage, a portent of the future, a future that's rich and fat and obsessive. The
groom is thin, the bride is thin, she is oh-so-slender in her shiny
tea-length dress, with her faintly puffy upper lip. Everyone is now
in sweaters. Eating cream puffs or not eating cream puffs. I take
Chuck to the airport, leaving the cream puffs. At the ceremony,
the rabbi said, *Be joyous until you are all joy, dance until you are all
dance.* We eat cream puffs until we are all cream puffs, fat and
lazy and golden, round as little Pooh Bears, waiting, tempting,
cute, creamy little cream puffs, baby-bear cream puffs, waiting,
waiting, and wanting, transforming into soft yellow fat that we
hope won't show up in the pictures.

LATE NIGHT

I am nearing forty and I already, or still, have trouble sleeping. I don't mean that I have trouble getting to sleep. I have trouble getting to bed, doing what I have to do to prepare to give up, go under, put out the light. I have trouble trusting that the world won't forget me, fly off in its spinning, leave me dumbly unconscious, alone.

So I stay up late. Sometimes I do things I would never do in the afternoon. I'll sit at the kitchen table in a trance and read the real estate transactions in the newspaper, the ones in agate type. I'll sew on buttons, listen to call-in radio. I'll sing and look in the mirror and draw dark lines and shadows on my face to see how I'll look in fifteen years.

At two, three a.m., it doesn't matter what I do because no one's keeping score. The day is over. It's elastic time, acquired time, a gift. An extra pocket. It's quiet, but I don't feel alone—no one's ignoring me; everyone's just asleep.

Sometimes I do the necessary, what's been shoved to the end of the day, the edge of it. I pay bills. I grade papers. I write on deadline. I'm being dutiful, but at the wrong time—a sop to my rebellious spirit. I admit: I have a tendency to put things off; therefore, I have a tendency to finish things late at night.

Sometimes I stay up just because it's the best time of the day for me. I write fiction and get lost in it. At one, two, three in the morning, there's a certain settling, an end-of-the-day sigh. I can concentrate.

And it seems that because I'm lively at two a.m. I'll be lively forever. I can't imagine being sleepy later in the morning, after a few hours of rest.

For years, fighting sleep was my own private battle with my own personal demon. Aside from the group rituals of slumber parties, high school newspaper sessions, college all-nighters, and some late romantic evenings, staying up was my own one-woman show. And on the mornings after—because I rarely had time to sleep it off—I was irritable, distracted, and close to tears. I could go on: feeling like a snappy dog on a short leash, suffering from a raw headache that shouts, *Not enough!*, afflicted by profound weariness. In time, having these sensations became the norm. That's what I do, in my thirties. That's how I feel. That's how I am. That's how I always was.

Now I find that my weakness may be our society's characteristic affliction. And it's not just fun seekers who carouse the night away, as they always have, back to the time of Juvenal. (And before him, too—it's just that I recently saw a reference to the Roman poet chastising revelers for going to bed at the hour that generals decamped.) *The average American is chronically sleepy*, according to Dr. William Dement, head of the National Commission on Sleep Disorders. The *New York Times* says most Americans need an hour to an hour and a half more sleep a night. The sleepless administration is working itself to a frazzle, chides the *New Republic*, blaming "the politics of exhaustion" for presidential missteps. On public television doctors appear solemn-faced, parental, white-coated, urging us: *Sleep*. They call us a nation of zombies. Magazines and newspapers put tiredness on the front page, in the science section, in features. Some headlines: "Rat race turning half of us into 'walking zombies.'" "Cheating on Sleep: Modern Life Turns America into the Land of the Drowsy." "Lack of sleep can be dangerous to health at work." "Lack of Sleep a Danger to Time-Conscious Americans." Researchers blame lack of sleep for disasters from the Bhopal gas leak to the *Challenger* explosion. The problem, says Dement, is more serious than the national debt.

In a medieval European village, you had to have your own tallow if you wanted to stay awake (or at least see what you were doing). In the modern global village, the satellite never shuts off. If you want dark and quiet, you have to turn off, tune out, unplug—and the temptation is not to. As Dr. Wilse Webb, a pioneering sleep researcher, puts it: *most people in industrialized countries go to bed when they want to and get up when they have to.* Even children sleep less than they did two generations ago.

Though researchers are concerned about all nonsleepers, there are categories. There are the relatively blameless, whose schedules are determined by circumstance: new parents, truck drivers, pilots, medical interns, the 20 to 30 million shift workers in the U.S. In the same group I'd include some, but not all, of the 65 million who complained to Gallup pollsters about insomnia. (It's unclear how many insomniacs bring their troubles on themselves by disregarding sleep until they have to chase it down.) The experts save their fire for the truly willful among us, the people who could go to bed at a decent hour and don't. The ones who lean forward into temptation. Into the night. Who treat our sleeping time like disposable income and often spend it foolishly. Who are torn: We want to sleep. We don't want to sleep. We want to be well rested. We want to stay up. We want to relax our guard. We don't want to die.

I keep waiting for the rules to change. Someday, a fundamental reprieve for humankind: *Sleep was a mistake. Sorry about that. It is no longer required.*

In Eden no one slept. The animals held rowdy no-slumber parties, all-night galas, storytellings and songfests by the light of the always-full moon. Lion danced and lay with lamb—this was B.C., Before Carnivores. One midnight the glossy, glistening snake sidled up to Adam and Eve, saying, *Friends, are you not made impatient by this eternal vigilance? There is a magical realm called*

Sleep, which you could visit if you so desired. There are new worlds you could enter each and every night. You could sing in different languages, talk with creatures that do not exist, travel to exotic lands. All if you take only the smallest bite from the fruit of that tree.

The fruit had been forbidden but the couple, entranced, took a bite. They went to sleep and slept all night and all day. Soon they came to regret succumbing to the lure of the snake. The world of sleep was all that he had promised, but they couldn't leave it or control their dreams. And they couldn't stay awake like they used to.

God thundered down to the humans in his garden: *You had the power to sleep before, without the fruit, you only had to wish it. But now you have become slaves of the body. You are no longer pure and endless. Because of your disloyalty I will introduce Death, and you will never forget him. I will let you be awake for two-thirds of your life. During the day you will work and each night I will send down Death's slight brother Sleep to transform you. You will pray before Sleep that your soul will be returned to you in the morning. And you will awaken—but with the dry taste of death on your tongue, a memory and a portent. Yet without sleep, this small stingless death, you will surely die.*

Your descendants will suffer even more. Some will be assigned to night shifts; others will stay up all night fighting wars, engineering inventions, composing symphonies, comforting inconsolable infants, studying for exams, arguing my existence, weeping in loneliness and despair, memorizing dramatic roles, tapping out email messages, and being mesmerized by Veg-O-Matic commercials. In the morning and all day long they will be regretful, and they will be doomed the next night to repeat—through the end of time.

We have the technology to light up the night, but we don't have the bodies to stay up all night and day. We're like Prometheus, that old fire stealer, who was punished for taking what belonged to the gods.

It's hard to live in these irreconcilable worlds of now and

later, the way we won't see the connection between that piece of cheesecake and that inch of fat around our waists.

And if we can get our fat cut out, why can't we have sleep inserted?

That's not a frivolous question. Sleep researcher Webb confessed to *Psychology Today* that his original quest had been to find a way for people to sleep more efficiently and thus cut down on sleep time. It didn't work. He learned to accept sleep as a "fixed biological gift."

A friend who studies psychology says that people's first memories shift according to their moods. When they're happy, they recall good memories. When I'm cheerful, I say that this is my earliest memory:

I am two or three and not yet myopic. I've just made the transfer from my crib to a real bed across the room. From the bed I can see the mobile of birds that hangs above the crib: red cardinal, yellow bird, bluebird. The same ones that are mentioned on my record *Bozo and the Birds*. This is what happens my first night sleeping like a grown-up: I awake in the middle of the night to the birds coming alive. They flutter. They do not fly across the room, but hover above the crib, content. Perhaps they don't realize I'm just a few feet away. Or maybe they are giving me this opportunity to see them in their splendor, a farewell-to-the-crib gift.

I believe that this happened. Or: I believe that I believed in the awakened birds.

Is it any wonder that late night remains magical? That the lesson I take to heart is: Things happen at night; you must be awake to see them.

When I'm not so cheerful, this is what I remember:

I'm three and sitting with my mother in Dr. Janse's office on a couch between two big lamps waiting for him to call me in to lie on the table. He will stick thin tubes in my nose and siphon away mucus. He is an ear-nose-and-throat man, thin and gray. He is different from the benign allergist who gives me shots twice a week. During the day my breathing ranges from clear to wheezy. At night it gets worse. I listen to the whine of my lungs and imagine the little German villagers playing accordions inside my body. It seems like it's always been this way and always will be, this bruising of my chest, the hurt of it, which gets worse, won't let the air out.

Is it any wonder that the night always held mystery and promise and terror? Close your eyes, drop your vigil, and you could be overtaken, transformed, by an internal coup. The villagers could get out of control, looting and pillaging and stopping up my lungs.

There's at least one song about refusing naps, a defiant anthem by Jonathan Richman, called "Not Yet Three": *You think I should be tired now / But my body's all inspired now*. I remember not taking naps; I remember learning the word *cantankerous* even before I went to nursery school. That was what my mother called me.

A few times a year my family would take the train from Houston to Dallas. Even with a suitcase full of dolls, I was sullen. *Just tired,* my parents said, when we got to my grandparents'. I wasn't friendly like the girl cousins from Midland or wild but endearing like the boy-puppy cousins from Harlingen. Or shy and sweet like my older sister.

I was different. I needed medicine, was allergic to their Friday-night chicken, their occasional salmon patties, refused to eat their boiled peas. I had different habits. And I grew more and more different as time went on.

In high school I slept five hours a night, on weekdays. I was an editor of the twice-weekly school paper. Each afternoon before the paper came out I'd go home with the car pool and drive back after supper in my mother's car. The newspaper sponsor was long gone; it was just us, a handful of good kids with keys to the journalism shack, the permanent temporary building just outside the main brick building. Ostensibly we were there because we hadn't finished the paper during the day, but gathering at night became our tradition. We'd make puns and headlines, write manifestos. I'd do last-minute French homework. After eleven the other editor would arrive from his shift at Jack in the Box, still in uniform, and we'd get a second wind. We didn't have sex or smoke dope or drink. We didn't need to. Night was a place we could go to on our own. During the day we wandered the fringes of popularity. At night we cast a magic circle and for a few hours lived safely inside it.

When the paper was finished, we'd lock up and I'd drive the mile home. And stay up even later at the kitchen table eating frozen bagels and reading Dear Abby. The next morning I'd drag myself back to school, carrying a big Thermos of black coffee. It was a mark that I had been where others hadn't.

Besides coffee, I drank Tab and Diet Dr. Pepper and swallowed NoDoz tablets. I was irritable, had frequent headaches. (My mother took me to the eye doctor for the headaches. *Get more sleep,* he said.) I was also prone to energy spurts, got a certain giddy high, one that I don't recall seeing mentioned in the books and articles on sleep deprivation. Maybe the doctors are scared to tell us. You never see headlines like "Staying Up Makes People Laugh" or "Four of Five Americans Thrilled to Be Silly at Two A.M." All I can say is there's much to recommend the curious insulation, the fragile delight bordering on ecstasy.

In high school my mother gave me a red candle on Valentine's Day, with a card that said, "For Sandi who burns her candle at both ends." My parents wrung their hands over my late hours, but they never gave me a curfew: My work was important. I was a sleep-defying wonder.

I was a ghost in that house, slipping in, slipping out, occasionally taking human form to yell and accuse. Maybe I wanted to escape from their hovering concern: The year before I was hospitalized for asthma, I had pneumonia. I used that breathing machine twice a day. I didn't want my parents to worry about me. I wanted to stay away, out of their line of vision. I escaped by being out of sync.

I carved out my independence on my own body, shaving hours off my sleep time. It was a quiet, pre-feminist, mildly self-destructive way to rebel.

In my high school class there was a pretty, voluptuous girl who lost about twenty pounds—for a time—and became gorgeous and thin. Her fantasy, she told a friend who told me, was to spend all night in the grocery store, alone, with an oven, and eat whatever she wanted.

It sounded reasonable; we girls were all keeping our appetites reined in. And she chose for her secret fantasy theater a neighborhood place, familiar as the pink cans of Tab we drank

incessantly. She knew that at night the store became mysterious
and secret as only the everyday does.

Or was I living out the jackrabbit theory?

Hunter S. Thompson speculates in *Fear and Loathing: On
the Campaign Trail '72* that he wrote in marathon sessions without
food or sleep for the same reason that a jackrabbit will wait until
the last minute before he darts across a highway.

A rabbit's life is pretty boring, Thompson writes. Almost
getting run over is the only way for it to put some excitement
into its life. Even jackrabbits need cheap thrills.

Historically, doing without sleep has been a way of transcending
the world of the flesh. Around the world, doing without sleep has
been used in ritual, denying the needs of the body to join with
the Great Sleepless Being, something like fasting for purification.
The eighteenth-century mystic Novalis claimed, "The less sleep
we need, the more closely we approach perfection." On Shavuot,
a spring harvest festival that also celebrates the receiving of the
Torah, Jews customarily stay up reading portions of the books
of the Old Testament and Talmud. According to *The First Jewish
Catalog*, it is said that the heavens open at midnight, "making it a
propitious time for our prayers and thoughts to ascend."

Sleep has been seen by the more pragmatic and judg-
mental among us as a waste of time, an indication of sloth. Plato
said free men shouldn't sleep all night. An old saying: "Nature
requires five, custom gives seven, laziness takes nine, and wick-
edness eleven." Ben Franklin said there would be time enough
for sleeping in the grave. Exceptional people throughout history
have battled with sleep; they have too much to do and just one
lifetime. While a student, the scholar of religions Mircea Eliade
trained himself to sleep only four or five hours a night. (He went
on to write about sleep-deprivation rituals.) Eliade wrote in the
first volume of his autobiography, "The struggle against sleep,
like the struggle against normal modes of behavior, signified
for me a heroic attempt to transcend the human condition." He

tried to cut back further to emulate the naturalist Alexander von Humboldt, who slept only two hours a night. With enough coffee, Eliade found he could stay up for twenty-two hours, but he started sleeping more because he was afraid of ruining his eyesight.

Read any biography or profile of an exceptional (or even merely spotlighted) person and you're likely to find a testimonial to sleep deprivation couched in words describing hard work, dedication, energy. Just from a magazine at hand: "How Macy's dynamo fashion director sails through her twelve-hour workdays (and four-hours'-sleep nights)." The pantheon of famous short sleepers includes Virgil, Napoleon, Charles Darwin, Émilie du Châtelet, Leonardo da Vinci, George Bernard Shaw, Eleanor Roosevelt, Winston Churchill, Isaac Asimov, Edward R. Murrow, Donald Trump. The common message: They have too much to do. They can't be bothered. They live fast, are impatient with the demands of the body. Their waking lives are important. The same holds true for groups. If a legislature stays in session through the eleventh hour, its work must be essential. Even though it's obvious that the legislators are in a bind because they put off important decisions.

Short sleeping is good for the images of movers and shakers. How can we hate moguls and call them fat cats when they deprive themselves of sleep like old-time truth-seeking ascetics? They're not capitalist pigs; they don't have time to wallow. And how can we begrudge Congress another pay increase? They're all working overtime.

On the other hand, short sleeping isn't always so easy to verify among the ones who flaunt it. Legend has it that Thomas Edison needed only two hours of sleep a day. He said in 1924, *Lack of sleep never hurt anybody*. But he wrote in his diary that he slept four or five hours, admitting that he sometimes went back to sleep and that he took frequent naps. Sleep researchers, advocates that they are, are particularly gleeful when recounting this.

The nameless middle managers, bound to work by modems, appointments, and voice mail, work more, work scared. They come to work early, eat lunch at their desks, and leave late, fearing they won't be taken seriously otherwise. They struggle because it's expected, because no one suggests they work nine to five. They don't punch time clocks. They're upright, trustworthy, and, by God, they've got to get ahead.

Federal workers were the first in this country to get an eight-hour day, back during the Andrew Johnson administration. That explains the terrible word for those boring people who work nine to five because they lack the creativity to think of working longer: bureaucrat.

But the ambitious hard worker is a far cry from the hapless person who just doesn't sleep much. From time to time "ordinary" people appear who claim they need little sleep. Sometimes they're monitored in sleep labs and found to be impostors. The apparently legitimate cases seem pathetic. In his book *Sleep*, Harvard sleep researcher Dr. J. Allan Hobson writes an Englishwoman who sleeps forty minutes a day feels fine but is "rather bored." In *Wide Awake at 3:00 A.M.: By Choice or By Chance?*, psychologist Richard Coleman cites a Reuters story about a Cuban man unable to sleep after suffering a trauma during a botched childhood tonsillectomy. He had recurring nightmares of dying and became afraid to sleep. The man hadn't slept for forty years. He needed drugs and Transcendental Meditation in order to rest and even then was technically awake. He described himself as feeling drained. "It's a tragedy," he said.

So it's no wonder that sleep deprivation has been used as torture, often as a way to break a subject down before questioning. Sleep deprivation was used in medieval China and in England on suspected witches in the seventeenth century. On her fourth night without sleep, one woman gladly confessed and named names. Menachem Begin, former prime minister of Israel, was tortured by the Soviets in 1940. "Anyone who has experienced this desire [for sleep] knows that not even hunger or thirst are comparable with it," Begin writes in *White Nights: The Story of a Prisoner in Russia*. In the 1970s the British used sleep deprivation on suspected Northern Irish terrorists. After a complaint, the practice was deemed inhumane by the European Court of Human Rights. The CIA still uses the practice.

At 4:01 a.m. on December 2, 1987, the Chicago city council elected
Eugene Sawyer acting mayor of Chicago. The crowd that had
gathered to protest in the lobby of city hall at some point became
a group, a group doing an extraordinary thing together—staying
up all night in a public place. By around two a.m., people seemed
to have forgotten their lives outside city hall. We had shed our
identities and become a new minority—people in a public building in the middle of the night, on neutral turf. (By day, officialdom
lays claim to city hall. By night, it's up for grabs.) I remember the
feeling: We're all in this together.

The same thing happens when people line up all night
to wait for tickets for a ball game or concert. Community forms
nightly, routinely, says sociologist Murray Melbin in *Night as
Frontier,* where he compares nighttime on-the-street populations
to populations in the nineteenth-century American West. Only
the brave, the outcast, the desperate venture into this fringe territory. Most of its inhabitants are young single men.

In Melbin's experiments, people on the street at night
were more willing than daytime pedestrians to take the trouble
to return a lost key or give strangers directions (and less likely
to be pressed for time).

And just as the Wild West gave way to civilization, the
night is being tamed, more and more, by becoming less and
less strange.

The street at night, however, has never belonged to women.
Women organize rallies to take back the night. They check calen-
dars, get permits, make fliers, issue press releases, line up speakers,
set up sound systems, silk-screen T-shirts, photocopy song sheets,
gather noisemakers—in order to walk down the street at night.

The indoor night has terrors of its own, but children are
told to trust it: *Don't be afraid of the dark. Trust the shadows, there
is nothing in them. They are empty. That is not a monster but your
jacket draped over the rocking chair. Freud said you were not touched
and you only imagine that you were. It was the night. It was a dream.*

You are crazy. You didn't see a shadow. And if anyone touched you, it doesn't matter. Besides, it was only touch. It wasn't violent. That wasn't a hand under the covers when he came to kiss you good night. It was a dream. You'll forget in the morning. It never happened. It was a love pat. He was trying to kiss your heart. If you were awake, it wouldn't have happened. If it did. If you had been sitting in a chair. Reading. Doing homework. If you had kept awake.

And in the dusk of memory, women and men remember and forget, bring the pictures and the sounds into clarity and lose them in more shadow.

And as we age, we get lost and lost again. Forty percent of people over sixty have some kind of sleeping problem. In *Sleep Disorders: America's Hidden Nightmare,* business consultant Roger Fritz tells of a study showing that nursing-home patients don't sleep more than a full hour at a time; two-thirds of the residents suffer from sleep deprivation. Are these the wide-awake thoughts we can look forward to: Someone is coughing, someone is screaming, someone is thinking of screaming, someone is watching, someone is waiting to snatch my meager belongings. Someone is waiting to snatch me from myself, someone in the hallways, scratching, pacing, scuffing, someone is asking me, *What do you want? Why don't you sleep? Why don't you close your eyes?* Someone is waiting for me to drop off.

It's already day, it's not yet day, it's yesterday, a year ago I didn't have these side rails, a year ago I had a yard, there were children and snow and a helicopter overhead and cookies and card playing. I was looking for the ace of spades. I was avoiding the queen of hearts. The cookies were heart-shaped, they're burning. And the children call and then are silent. My mother's apron. Gone. Snatched from me in my sleep.

When I was young and looking to the far future for a love life I could barely imagine, I would read Dear Abby's advice to teens. She cautioned against "going all the way" to "prove your love." Nowadays sleep is the thing that's sacrificed.

And the beauty of the concept of giving up sleep to your sweetest is that it's low-cost and nonsexist. You sacrifice future alertness, make yet another withdrawal at the sleep bank.

So you find yourself, for example, driving down the highway in the heart of the late night, the white line between lanes thickened to a smudge, sleep pressing your eyelids. Your body wants to sleep but wants to merge, to hurry home with your lover, though it's already recklessly late on a weekday night.

Your unspoken gift: This is a measure of what you are worth. You are worth an eclipsing of duty. I will be inside a dumb stupor all day long, and in that small way I am giving a crumb of my career for you. To you. Full in our desires, aware of every nerve and nuance, we are outlaws, while the good burghers are slumbering in their close, double-bolted, narrow chambers, hemmed in by pitifully small dreams.

Though of course the good burghers are doing nothing of the kind.

We know we're not supposed to. Really we do. The data are accessible, the consequences plain: people who don't sleep enough become paranoid, lose concentration, do poorly on tests, can't do routine tasks. But—here's the rub—they often recover quickly. One of the first bona fide experiments on sleep deprivation was in 1896 at the University of Iowa. There three young men did without sleep for almost four days. They were miserable. One hallucinated.

But after they went to sleep, they were restored.

In 1965, a seventeen-year-old Californian stayed awake for 264 hours as a team of Stanford sleep experts and clinicians observed. He wasn't much good at routine tasks during the eleven days he didn't sleep, but he managed to win pinball games every time he played one of the researchers monitoring him. And he bounced back after a long sleep.

But it's common sense that deprivation as a way of life is not a good thing. The *New York Times* has reported a suspected link between weakened immune systems and inadequate sleep.

"And it is not a coincidence," as Martin C. Moore-Ede posits in *The Twenty-Four-Hour Society: Understanding Human Limits in a World That Never Stops*, "that the most notorious industrial accidents of our time ... all occurred in the middle of the night, when those with hands-on were dangerously fatigued." Moore-Ede, a Harvard Medical School professor and a workplace consultant, points out that the NASA officials who gave the *Challenger* the go-ahead had been working for twenty hours straight, after only a few hours of sleep the night before.

In reaction to more common and less horrific consequences of sleep deprivation and other aspects of workaholism, a countertrend developed called downshifting. From the people who brought you quality time and slow food: Downsize your ambition a few notches; wake up later and smell the flowers. Moderation. Sleep will be rediscovered along with its natural restorative powers. The paeans will flourish, in how-to books and interoffice memos. I can see it now: Be proactive. Go to sleep.

Public service announcements will proliferate. But the ads will have to prove that sleep has a tangible payoff. I imagine something like this on the radio:

Background noise of footsteps of people arriving in an office; sounds of phones ringing and being answered.

> *Joan* (slightly harried): *Hey, Mary, you look great, especially for a Monday morning. Did you go to some fancy retreat last weekend?*
>
> *Mary* (calm, secure): *No, Joan, just got my usual eight or nine hours, like I do every night.*
>
> *Joan: But doesn't sleeping take a lot of time?*
>
> *Mary: You know, Joan, I save time by sleeping. When I get enough sleep, I don't need an alarm clock. I wake up rested, I think more clearly and I'm more productive. You know that $10,000 bonus I got last week for the new ad campaign?*
>
> *Joan: I've been meaning to ask you where you got that idea. It was brilliant.*
>
> *Mary: You're not going to believe it, but it came to me in a dream. You know, lots of achievers get ideas in dreams. Let me tell you about this chemist*

who was trying to figure out the structure of
benzene ... (Fade out.)
Voiceover: Sleep, nature's labor-saving device. Get to
sleep. Sleep and grow rich.

This public service announcement may not be so far-fetched. The Japanese government runs campaigns to persuade workers to take time off. The slogan one year was "To Take a Vacation Is Proof of Your Competence."

A sleep researcher told me: Staying up late is like building a secret extra room over the garage. And then one day you wake up and find you have to pay taxes on it.

I know what he means. Sleep deprivation is finally taking its toll—in fact, it's hitting me over the head. Nowadays when I don't get enough sleep, I get—surprise, it didn't used to happen—run down. And when I do get myself to bed at a decent hour, I have trouble falling asleep. I've tried to give in to my night-owl proclivity—to set up my life so I can stay up till three, sleep until noon, but it's hard. I have more flexibility than most people because I freelance and teach. But things don't always go my way. Periodically I'm offered a class that starts at the crack of dawn—10:15 or so. And even if the trains don't run on time, at least they run more often during rush hour. It's safer to walk the streets in daylight. And when my friends go out to dinner they go at, well, dinnertime.

On my thirty-seventh birthday last year I had a few close friends over for brunch. I drew up my courage and whispered my resolution: I'm going to get adequate sleep.

I did, for maybe 20 percent of the time in the year that followed. And I learned that I need nine or ten hours of sleep to feel truly rested. Which explains some frustration in the past. I'd sleep for seven or eight hours and still feel tired. So I scaled down to five—if I was going to be tired anyway, I might as well allow myself more time to work.

In my quasi-reformed lifestyle, when I do get enough I take note of the calm, washed feeling from a full night's sleep. I become a pool of water in a bowl, a perfect, uncracked one. I can finish sentences, retrieve the right word. I can focus. But the cost: sleeping through those hallowed dark hours, the time when I feel most myself.

And the time it takes!

I'm most afraid, I think, of losing my sense of purpose. If you don't get enough sleep, it's always clear what you need to do—sleep. You can arrange your life around that struggle. It's like being an alcoholic and knowing you need to stop drinking. The need to sleep protects you, even as it strips you of a lining of comfort, prevents you from probing into what you really need to be doing, what you're really feeling. And what if I get enough sleep every night and my rough edges don't round off? I'll no longer be able to explain the general shortness, spaciness, brittleness. I'll have to say, *This is my real personality.* "I had never known what I was like until I stopped smoking, by which time there was hell to pay for it" begins the short story "Days" by Deborah Eisenberg. That sort of unmasking terrifies me.

And when I don't get enough sleep, the headaches, the sleepiness, they feel like the beginning of a conversation. At least I'm not wandering aimlessly on this darkened plain; there are walls to it, you see, something to push up against. If I were to get enough sleep and end the wanting, I'm afraid, really and truly, that I would feel alone, suspended in the universe, no point to it all, the end of call and response.

Adam and Eve say to the snake, *We want to return. We want vigilance, we want life without death, without end, without fear of the end. We don't want to grow old. We want this world and none other.*

The snake replies, *I didn't know it would turn out this way.*

God refuses to enter the conversation.

At this year's birthday gathering, a dinner just a few days ago, I recounted my shaky progress toward getting enough sleep. My friends, indulgent people that they are, said they were impressed. Satisfied with my efforts in the area of sleep, they asked about my plans for self-improvement in the coming year. *Exercise*, I said.

But before that conversation took place, we had a dramatic brush with danger. One guest strode into the apartment, declared that she smelled gas, and started opening windows. I hadn't noticed anything. I called the gas company, and two employees arrived, pulled the stove from the wall, and found a leak. Another friend reminded me that she'd said she'd smelled gas in the past, but I'd dismissed it because the burners were working.

I've been in the apartment for fifteen months. The Peoples Gas workers couldn't tell how long the valve had been open.

This is and is not a metaphor. You get used to what your life is like because that's what your life is like. I'm a person prone to headaches and spaciness. I'm a person who had a gas leak in my stove, perhaps for more than a year. I'm a person who often doesn't sleep enough. You do what you can. When it gets bad enough, you do something.

I'm constantly working with real people, says Stanford psychologist Richard Coleman, who takes a commonsense approach to helping people with sleeping disorders. *My idea is to simply ask how they're doing now*, he told me. He asks people how much sleep they get, how safe they are on the job, how effective they are. *To show a particular schedule, to say, here's the ideal thing to do, is a total fantasy. You as an individual decide if you want to make a few changes.*

Every night it's a struggle to remind myself that if I go to bed now, I'll be alert in the morning. I recall with such fondness those high school late nights—that urgency, the sense of time rushing forward while it stands still. I'm explaining this to a friend, pattering on about the decor of the journalism shack.

And then something hits me; I put my hand on my forehead, the lump rising in my throat. In high school I had the run of the place, but I couldn't breathe.

I had the keys to the house, my mother's car, the shack. My asthma has always been better when I'm awake, vertical, and I didn't have any trouble staying that way. (I wasn't surprised to read in *Sleep Disorders* that 70 percent of asthma deaths take place during sleeping hours.) Whatever time I got home, no matter what, I would have to spend twenty minutes on my breathing machine. I would park the car in the garage, then sit at the kitchen table till finally I could put it off no longer—the moment when I'd walk to my bedroom, measure out the millimeters of liquid medicine, clamp my teeth around the white plastic mouthpiece, and breathe in the mist that would clear out my lungs until morning. The machine couldn't help but remind me, my psyche, before I turned off the light and faced the darkness, that I was incomplete; not just mortal, but in danger.

And it didn't matter how many French verb tenses I knew or number of puns I could make about required English texts. For at least a couple of hours I would have to lie down and let the body take over. Completely. Nestle into it, really—not trusting it, not welcoming sleep, but accepting finally that that was all I had, all there was left to do.

And all I could do was fight it like hell.

UP AGAINST IT

Because I touched the caterpillar to see if it was still alive and it reared up. As if in pain.

Because I drowned the live frog in alcohol, knowing it wasn't for science.

Because it was for science but I was eight or ten and I was not a scientist, I was trying to be a scientist, I had read the directions for suffocating and pinning butterflies but didn't follow them.

Because I loved frogs. And butterflies and worms and what we called doodle bugs but you may call roly-polies or pill bugs or armadillo bugs. They are shiny, segmented, and primitive.

Because I didn't send the name of employees to be paid, didn't send the names in time.

Because I was scared I had the wrong names, not enough names, I felt as if I would never get the names right, I would leave someone out or include someone who shouldn't be paid. So I missed all of them, all of them missed a paycheck because of me. I paid them cash to make it up and only one fully reimbursed me. And I feel bad because it was my fault and the person in charge took me to an office where the person in charge there said my timing didn't make any difference. I'm sure I feel worse than the two who still owe me money.

Because I reported a lapse. I was a whistleblower.

Because I was in the right. But did it for the wrong reason—for revenge. I did it for revenge. You should not do anything for revenge unless you have power. I thought smartness or cleverness was the same as power. Power is more powerful. Which everyone knew but me. It was obvious.

Because I didn't have tenure. I didn't have a union or triple-year contract. The person in power still is. There will always be a honcho. One comes, one goes, like monarchs.

Because I tried to write about it anonymously but made so many changes to anonymize it that it was no longer me or the honcho or the ethical lapse, which it turned out he didn't understand.

Because it didn't matter that he didn't understand. It mattered that he was the one in charge.

Because I couldn't get the copier to work.

Because they closed up the office early but I did everything too late and by impulse.

Because I'd look up essays in the middle of class to read aloud.

Because I would grade last week's papers while the students wrote in class. Everything at the last minute, and the instructor in the next room graded that week's papers during class, handing them back at the end of class. She gathered up her notes and books and coat at the end of class, one smooth package.

Because she used to be my student.

Because years ago I didn't take the job of my friend, which was offered to me, because it would mean his losing the job.

Because he still has it.

Because I didn't apply for the full-time teaching job back then because I wanted part time.

Because I wanted to freelance. I believed in print, in print paying writers forever, in the thousands.

Because magazines used to pay in the thousands.

Because I haven't been paid thousands in decades.

Because I accused the dead.

Because I told one person about this accusation. Because this person has hated me since.

Because I thought it was true.

Because that person did not respect my truth.

Because I was too harsh in telling my truth.

Because at eighteen I enrolled in the wrong university. I should have gone to a college for clever, silly, political students instead of the safe bet. After college I should have moved to New York City.

Because I didn't spend time with the lively people at that university, the theater majors. Because I was a journalism major but didn't read newspapers. I stayed in journalism school because I would be guaranteed a job. There used to be jobs for the taking, small dailies everywhere.

Because I didn't stay in Massachusetts that time, either.

Because I stored my furniture all over town.

Because I love the Back Bay. The buildings. Trinity Church. The New England compactness of the city.

Because as a child I tried to teach the dachshund to ride a tricycle.

Because I still have dreams where I haven't fed the dog in days. He's run away searching for food and water.

Because he died. We didn't know he was sick.

Because complicated love can be so complicated it is no longer love.

Because he thought he understood me.

Because he knew my pain but not my anxiety or fear.

Because fear was what I was. What I had. What contained me.

Because I cried at the first job, mostly at lunchtime. I cried when people hung up on me, I cried when sources were harsh.

Because journalism offered a paycheck but also pain.

Because I didn't stick with Yiddish.

Because I didn't keep up my Spanish.

Because I bought her a blouse and champagne for her wedding even though I suspected she needed American dollars more and didn't drink.

Because in Latin America many Catholics have become non-drinking Protestants.

Because I want to name my impulses the devil's thrust.

Because I can't get myself to bed on time.

Because there is no time anymore. There is only Zoom.

Because I think I will tell such-and-such to my grandchildren or children and I already have stepchildren and grandchildren and they are far away. They used to be close, but that was before March 2020. And we don't have conversations like that, the ones that begin, *In my day* . . .

Because I met my husband when I was thirty-nine, just on the edge, perhaps, of fertility, and I didn't want children of my own but I wanted to make the decision myself.

Because I wouldn't mind being pregnant but I wouldn't want to take care of a baby or young child or pay attention to an older child.

Because I would like to experience giving birth. My stepdaughter let me hold her leg open in the delivery room. I saw the crowning. I saw my granddaughter before she was fully born. The top of her head.

Because I still think I am young, I think I could get pregnant. I feel the same as I did when I was twenty-five, thirty-five.

Because when I turned thirty I thought I was old.

Because I used to calculate the age of every author with a new book and tell myself, They are older than I am, my time will come. Now I note when an author was born after I graduated from high school. After I graduated from college. After I published my story in the famous magazine.

Because they are younger and younger.

Because I did not intend to have this life.

Because each time I work on journalism I am anxious every minute and spend too much time researching.

Because I make mistakes.

Because I am so skilled at finding others' mistakes.

Because I was supposed to be famous. By half my age.

Because at half my age I had a story accepted by the *New Yorker*. Before the story was published I was afraid I would be hit by a car while riding my bike. After, I was afraid people would take it the wrong way. Years after it came out I had to explain to a nice young podcaster interviewing me what the context was, what things were like among progressives in the 1980s and early 1990s. U.S. out of Central America. Reagan and Bush the elder. Iran-Contra. Protests against nuclear weapons. The old days.

Because I wasted my time on this earth.

Because I worry about my time left.

Because I ask myself, *If you had one month to live, two, five years, what would you work on? What would you do?* My friend said he wanted his tombstone to mention his friendships, not his work, and I am the opposite. But I do love my friends.

Because antidepressants and anti-anxiety meds make writing not as necessary as air.

Because who will produce my play.

Because who will read my work.

Because no one reads literary magazines these days except other writers. What is wrong with other writers? There are too many writers and not enough readers though the writers are the readers. I suppose I could think of them as readers who happen to be writers.

Because we keep producing more writers who become non-tenure-track teachers who have wobbly finances and no insurance.

Because everyone is selfish and hoping.

Because the race is not to the swift. The mediocre win and win and they are younger and younger.

Because my mind is my asset.

Because I am older than you.

Because from 2008 to 2016 I was older than the president.

Because I am afraid I will lose my mind. I am afraid my husband will lose his.

Because I am afraid I will look back and wonder why I didn't know that right now was the good time, despite Covid.

Because we are safe.

Because we have outdoor space and plants.

Because the pansies are still alive in August.

Because we have love and food and money.

Because we walk for two hours at night or ride our bikes, noting cast-iron columns and Italianate curlicues.

Because we have been together one-quarter of a century, married for seventeen years, and we are happy together. But I am afraid that the fear is clouding it all.

Because for decades we were in the streets and plazas protesting against U.S. policy and nuclear weapons and U.S. invasions and inequality and racism and climate damage, and for abortion rights, but we can't protest now because we don't want to get Covid. We are playing it safe.

Because we are playing it safe.

Because love is loss.

Because loss is not love.

Because the person in charge, the honcho, keeps his power.

Because we had one conversation, and he said, *So many things people don't know about each other.*

He seems satisfied, strong. I don't want him to deserve happiness. I can't shake off this hatred.

I hate the person who started it, the one with less power than the honcho, but more than I ever had. Everyone always had more.

I tell myself that living well is the best revenge. I tell myself. I tell myself that hatred, that rage, do nothing. That they turn inward, and corrode. I know all that. I do.

WE HAD PARIS

We met, at least as I remember it, in the basement of the Alliance Française school in Paris, registering for classes or looking for housing or something equally bureaucratic. He must have said something to me first, or maybe he looked at me first. I said something about the process, using the word *angoisse,* agony, which he didn't know, surprisingly, though he was fluent. That in itself should tell you everything: my state of mind, the difference between the two of us. When we went out the first night I brought along my portable breathing machine, which I used twice a day for asthma. In those days, before AIDS, before anyone even worried about herpes, and in Paris, where the Métro stopped running around midnight, you assumed you'd spend the night; you'd either have a one-night stand or the beginning of a Relationship. I remember that first time, he came too fast. I was twenty or twenty-one, on my junior year abroad. I suppose he was my age. He was from Tunisia. I remember tight white jeans, high cheekbones like Elvis's, and bright white teeth, and my stopping on the street to yell at him in French: *But I am very intelligent in English!* I was explaining the theory of national character that I'd read the year before at college, and he thought that was stereotyping, or else I was making a case for a feminist view that the hierarchy of the family replicated the patriarchal system. I had joined the English-language Paris Organization for Women and borrowed books by Kate Millett and Germaine Greer from a

POW member. They were personally inscribed, and I assumed my friend had a deep friendship with the authors; I didn't know then that authors inscribed books personally to strangers at readings. I didn't know much then. I thought I could stay on in Paris alone and make a living creating personalized collages (which I didn't even attempt). I thought I could cut myself off from my family, nuclear and extended, because they were the source of my *angoisse*. I thought my allergist in Texas would be eager to get my ten years of medical records translated into French so he could send them to a doctor in Paris. Did I think I was in love? Maybe. His name, he said, was Fetty, the word for *gros*, in French, and it took me a second to realize he meant Fatty. His name was actually Fethi, and he lived in a room without a shower, and he would sneak into a dorm at Cité Universitaire, a campus that provided housing and a cafeteria for the city's university students. We also ate in the cafeteria there and I remember one time he made lewd gestures with a banana. He was Muslim and I was Jewish, which we both thought was dangerous. We were both atheists, I think. I went to a party with him once at his brother's apartment. There were North African and French students, and a shelf filled with volumes by Marx, and everyone was speaking French, and I understood some but couldn't quite follow.

Fethi had had sex for the first time when he was young, in the back of his family's shoe store. (I think this is right.) He grew up under colonialism, and was punished in school for speaking Arabic.

We American girls in classes at the Alliance did not have the French prejudice against Arabs. One blond friend had a boyfriend from Algeria or Tunisia named Hammami; she thought that was his name for months, until it was revealed that this was his last name and his first was Azzedine. I remember that after *Guess Who's Coming to Dinner* was shown on TV, followed by a televised discussion, French people were polled and the majority said that they would prefer an African to an Arab next door. That was probably because there were fewer Africans around.

Months passed. Fethi criticized me for washing underwear and socks together in the sink, and then I wasn't as attracted to him anymore, and he went to a place I'd never heard of, Abu

Dhabi, to make money. He sent me postcards, at least one after I'd already returned to Texas. But before all that, I remember a foggy walk one night across Paris, and when we were crossing a bridge from Rive Droite to Rive Gauche, *sans* premeditation, we both started to pretend that it was years later, and that we happened to be on the same bridge, talking without recognizing one another. *I knew a boy,* I said, *when I was twenty or twenty-one, and we would walk on this bridge, and I don't know what happened to him.* He said, *Ah,* oui, *I once knew a girl here in Paris, many years ago, an* Américaine—and in the late night, in that gray city in the mist it seemed like we were floating above our so very young (it seems now) selves and listening to our older selves, whom, we thought, couldn't have much to do with us now if they had so impossibly forgotten this.

LUCK
In the Valley

*A story is entirely determined by what portion of time it chooses
to narrate.*

—Joan Silber

Clara could speak and sing in six languages. She was trained as
an opera singer and her mother was a concert pianist. Clara was
born and raised in Pinsk, in Minsk Province. She met Sam there
in 1924, when Pinsk was ruled by Poland. This was during peacetime, after a relatively small war between Poland and the Soviet
Union. During that small war, Polish soldiers captured thirty-
five unarmed Jews in Pinsk who were holding a meeting—and
murdered them. The world was so innocent then that the Pinsk
murders created an international outcry, and Henry Morgenthau
was dispatched to investigate. No one could imagine that twenty-
two years later, 18,000 Jews would be massacred in the village of
Dobrovalia, just outside of Pinsk.

In 1924, Clara was nineteen and Sam was twenty-four when
they met in Pinsk. This was Sam's first time back home after
eleven years in America, he'd returned to see his parents before
they died, and to find a Jewish wife. He came to town in his
light-colored suit that stood out from the long dark clothes of

his family. Maybe Clara was only seventeen. It came out later
that she'd lied about her age. Her family and his were already
connected—her sister was married to his brother, or maybe
her brother was married to his sister. The two were introduced.
They married. It is unknown how much time they spent together
during Sam's visit to Pinsk, whether they married early or late
into Sam's two-month stay. We know that he returned to Victoria,
Texas, buying and selling auto parts and scrap metal to earn his
new bride's passage from Europe.

Clara set off from Pinsk, probably first by rail to Hamburg,
maybe accompanied by family, if they could afford such a thing.
Soon she was in a steamship traveling by herself. In New York,
Sam's uncle hosted her for a few days (concerts? parties? coffee
and rugelach with the women as they tried to explain how they
navigated the Lower East Side?) and then took her to the train
station. None of her six languages was English. The uncle got a
brown bag and wrote on it the six that she spoke: Russian, Polish,
German, French, Italian, Yiddish. He fastened the paper to the
front of her dress and led her to the conductor. Whenever the
train stopped to let more people on, the conductor would walk
through the cars, asking if anyone knew any of the six languages.
If they did, he would ask them to come and *ask the little lady if
there was anything she needed.*

In her new home in Victoria, Texas, there was a small
Jewish immigrant community. There wasn't one in Harlingen,
Texas, where Sam and Clara lived next and where both of them
are buried. Sam worked long hours in Harlingen, winding up as
the owner of a liquor store almost by chance. They had two sons,
Harry and Charley. Clara sang to them at bedtime, "Ave Maria,"
for example. Maybe that was also what she sang when she performed now and then for a local women's club. She spent much
of her time at home, cooking Ashkenazi dishes from scratch—
chopped liver, cabbage soup with meat, gefilte fish balls she
ground herself. There was no one like her in Harlingen. Her
husband had had about four years of schooling. She had a high
school diploma from Poland that was the equivalent of a college
degree, Charley said. His parents would joke that between them

they averaged a high school education. Every Sunday morning they would close the door to the kitchen and have coffee together. The sons couldn't intrude. It was the parents' time together.

Clara's sister Dina lived in Paris with her husband Aaron and son Gabriel. At the surrender of France in 1940, they evacuated from Paris along with everyone else, Dina giving birth to a daughter along the way to Marseille. Sam and Clara got them out, with the help of their congressman. That's what we say in the story American Jews tell of the War: *We got them out. We tried to get them out. We couldn't get them out.* Dina and Aaron and young Gabe and the baby Anne Marie spent the War in Harlingen, Texas. On Sunday afternoons Dina and Clara ate and drank with a French priest who was assigned to the local Catholic church. Dina baked French delicacies and the priest brought the underground publication of the Free French, produced by de Gaulle's group in London. Gabe graduated from Harlingen High at sixteen, valedictorian, and enrolled in the University of Texas. He earned his way through college by winning at gin rummy, penny ante.

After the War, of course, it was easier to *get them out.* Circumstances had changed and there were 6 million fewer to get visas for. Sam and Clara brought over a middle-aged cousin from Pinsk. His last name was Charney or Cherney or Czarney, her maiden name. In Harlingen the family gathered around him, *geschrei*-ing, yelling. Call and response: They would say the name of family member and he would report on the fate. It was all the same. *Geshtorben,* he may have said. Or *merderd.* As they had done in many other cities in the east, the Nazis rounded up the Jews of Pinsk and resettled them in an inadequately small, rundown area made into an instant ghetto. Some of the young Jews wanted to set the Pinsk ghetto afire, but the Judenrat, the Nazi-approved Jewish government, said, *We are too important in the War industry. They will not liquidate the ghetto.* The young people desisted, thinking also that they did not want to set off retribution. The ghetto was liquidated in 1942.

Dina and Aaron returned to Paris some time after the War. In 1976 or 1977 they invited me to their apartment one

Saturday afternoon during my junior year abroad. The table was filled with food, overwhelmingly so, because I hadn't realized we were going to eat a meal. I didn't know their history. I don't remember what we talked about or if I saw them again. Recently I found an old note inviting me to their apartment for Passover. Did I go? I know I didn't know about the history of the Jews of France. The government and the people of France were still lulling themselves into complacency by insisting that everyone had comported themselves heroically and had served in the Résistance. It was only in 1995 that the French government admitted the nation's role in rounding up French and foreign Jews. During my year there, I didn't see memorial plaques to commemorate the roundups, because there weren't any; the signs were relatively prominent some twenty years later, in the Marais district, which had been home to immigrant Jews before and during the War. And some twenty years after that, I noticed that at every public school I passed there was a black and gold plaque memorializing the Jewish students from the school and quarter who had been deported, "*victimes innocentes de la barbarie nazie et du gouvernement de Vichy.*"

Back when I was studying in Paris, I boarded with an elderly French lady who told me that the proper term for Jew was *Israelite*, not *Juif* or *Juive*; I didn't realize that this was because *Juif* had been sullied: because it was the word printed onto the yellow stars that Jews in France had had to sew onto their clothing. In 1977 I met a French Jew who was my age more or less whose family used a Christian last name in public and their original Jewish name among themselves. I thought they were paranoid.

After the War, when Clara and Sam's younger son Charley was stationed in Germany, he thought of traveling to Pinsk to see if he could find family. The Cold War had already begun and Poland had ceased to be a casual part of Europe. His intelligence officer warned him off: *Don't,* he said. *Your family there will be penalized by association with you. Anyone who talks to you will be targeted.*

Charley didn't think that there was any family left anyway.

Charley was married to my mother's sister. I met his mother Clara a few times when I visited my cousins in Harlingen. She

was my cousins' grandmother, not directly related to me. I
remember a short lady with an accent and dark frizzy hair. Her
husband died in 1953. She lived until 1972, lived to see her older
son Harry killed in a car accident when a train warning system
failed. Harry's family has been mired through the years in illness
and bad luck. Clara must have felt isolated, said her remaining
son and his wife—my uncle and aunt. Clara didn't get out much
or socialize. Sam had saved her life by taking her out of Poland,
and in that way ensured that their great-grandchildren would
be free to travel the world—one working each of his college
summers in Africa; another settling in in London after college.
The eldest great-grandson has returned to the faith of his great-
grandfathers with intensity—he is bearded and Yiddish-accented
though Texas-born, part of a strict Orthodox community in
South Florida. None of the family sings opera or plays the piano
but Charley was a local impresario, bringing performers and
Broadway shows down to his hometown of Harlingen in the
Rio Grande Valley. His older brother Harry had played clarinet,
saxophone, and piano by ear. As an army private Harry landed
in Normandy on D-Day. He collected German shrapnel in his
knee, but his wounds were less serious than those of his buddy
and lieutenant, as he wrote to his parents from a hospital bed in
England. There was an article about his letter in a local paper
in the Valley.

"I am almost well," he wrote. "It is only a period of days
before I leave the hospital, so don't worry. . . .

"So you see," he said, "I've been very lucky."

for Charley Feldman (1932–2017)

AUSCHWITZ
Like the Back of His Hand

I went to Auschwitz because it seemed the place had been with me always. But when I was there, I couldn't feel the weight of history. I couldn't bring what I knew of the genocide to the vast landscape of it. A few years later I had the chance to apply for a fellowship to study the Holocaust and visit camps. I had no interest. What would I learn?

It's been sixteen years since my visit to Auschwitz, and I continue to wonder about this vampire tourism. Like visiting a haunted house? Like the there-but-for-fortune-go-I frisson of danger? Auschwitz is our mecca, the place we must go to at least once in a lifetime. For me, once is enough.

I know Auschwitz like the back of my hand, Alan tells us. It's Christmas Day 1993 or so and he's eating tuna on whole wheat with sprouts at Coffee Chicago on the North Side. He was born in Chicago to a father born in Chicago. He started talking to us when he overheard me mention the Kraków ghetto. He's fifty-eight. My friend Mitch and I are a generation younger.

At home, he tells us, he has maps of the camp. He got one from the Polish government. *This big,* he says, stretching his arms wide, then up to the ceiling and floor. The map, he tells us, has a mark on it for every ghetto, work camp, concentration camp, extermination camp. He put it up at home and stuck pins into each place. *It's all covered with pins,* he says. *It's unbelievable.*

He's made a film. It's been shown in the Netherlands but he can't get it on PBS or sell it to the local Holocaust museum. It's about Auschwitz, about drawings made by Polish prisoners after the War. The pictures document every aspect of camp life, he says: eating, sleeping, crapping, standing in line. *But the Jews want it to be just their own Holocaust,* he says.

We want to hug it to our breasts: *ours, ours. Our struggle. Unser Kampf.*

He tells us that the two women in charge of the museum (one of them not a real survivor, he says—she spent the War passing as an Aryan) don't like his film because the voiceover includes a description of a Jewish woman at Auschwitz who abandons her child. The story is from a book by Tadeusz Borowski. He asks if we know Borowski.

That sparks recognition in some crevice in my brain. I say, *Yes, I think I have his book,* This Way for the Gas, Ladies and Gentlemen? I ask, *He killed himself, didn't he?*

Yes, in 1951, he put his head in his oven and turned on the gas, he says. He pauses to let the irony sink in.

This guy is crazy, obsessed, but so are we. Chicago Jews in a Chicago café, talking Holocaust.

Alan has been to Auschwitz five times. He knows it—well, you already know. Assuming familiarity with the camp, he says, *You know Block Eleven . . . ?* We don't know Block Eleven. Both Mitch and I have been to Auschwitz only once. Alan talks about his cache of drawings. Block Eleven was the site of executions and torture.

He found some Polish survivors, he says. Meaning non-Jewish, meaning Catholic. He interviewed them. He felt he wasn't getting much from them until they got him drunk and started telling him *cremo jokes.* Short for crematoria. He laughed. With them. An initiation of sorts. Then everything tumbled out of them. He's written about their experiences in a fictionalized memoir.

This was how it started: He saw a film when he was young, the same that's shown to the tourists, the one taken by the Soviet army who liberated the camp. He was very young when he saw the footage and he had nightmares. Afterward he was afraid each time his mother left the house. *You know that little girl in the film?* he asks, thinking he's found kindred souls with the same grooves of memory. We don't remember that particular image. He is one step further in than we are.

I had been telling Mitch—son of survivors—about the Jewish museum in Kraków, and how, just about closing time, on a summer day in 1992, this guy who looks like he's in his early forties thunders in with a line of teenagers behind him, from United Synagogue Youth.

    See that statue over there, kids, he said, *that was from before the War*. He had a New York accent. Rushing to the counter, he was told it was closing time. He protested: They're from the United States, they're in a hurry, they don't have much time, they're going to Auschwitz in the morning.

    The soft-hearted Poles who work in the museum let the New York Jews run through it for a few minutes.

Not long after our Christmas at Coffee Chicago, we were in my apartment. When my back was to him, Mitch turned on the radio. Jazz.

    I don't like jazz, I said. *But what other kind of music do you want: with words or without?*

    Without, he said. He looked at my tapes. *Enya is okay,* he said.

    Enya is music with words that aren't really words. It is sound lengthened and stretched and turned. Run around the gym to it or finish a conversation while it plays in the background. Then there were words: "How can I keep from singing?" We continued the conversation. I don't remember what it was about.

    Then: *I won't tell you where I got the Enya tape,* I said.

Where? he asked.

I wouldn't tell him. I felt it was shameful. I dashed onto another subject. He let it drop. He's a gentleman that way.

I got it at Auschwitz. Even I don't believe it but it's true. It was bad enough that they were selling bootleg tapes at outdoor tables in Auschwitz. Why did I have to hand over my zlotys for a tape? What is the meaning of buying music in Auschwitz? What does it mean that I was willing to buy a tape while at the extermination camp, that I was willing to turn my mind from the past, from the horrors, from the war against the Jews and Poles and Communists and *Mischlinge* for the sake of a bargain?

Kraków is a medieval city. When I was there, during the summer of 1992, there were nuns in black and small groups of tourists, not gaggles of them. There were barely any Jews on the street in the historically Jewish quarter, Kazimierz, only posters advertising a Jewish festival some weeks before. There were a few old Jews in the synagogue. One of them said he was old as old as Moses (or was it Methuselah?). And asked for dollars in exchange for a tour. The many Jews were underground in the synagogue's cemetery, which was overrun with large snails. In the Jewish quarter on a Sunday afternoon, mass was floating out of open windows from radios, drunken men were standing in doorways. Not leering, not as menacing as that, but close.

In postcards from the 1920s, Kazimierz is alive with commerce: chickens, children, rags, men in caftans, women in babushkas, tables of produce. Did I come to see where the Jews lived? Where they died? Where are the echoes of chants—those of the religious, in Hebrew, and those of the vendors, in Yiddish and Polish? Perhaps the same people chanted in all three languages, at different times of the day. Where are the feathers flying from ritually slaughtered geese, freshly killed? Where are the crumbs dropped from the bagel sellers? Where are the newspapers used to wrap fish? Those were the good old days, though they might not have seemed so at the time.

During the War this was not the Jewish ghetto—that was across the bridge, where Jews from all over Europe were crowded into unfamiliar tenements. The man I'd talked to at the Jewish library had been emphatic about this. *You have to cross the river to the* Umschlagplatz, *the gathering place, where Jews were rounded up.*

Where are the bloodstains, the echoes of shots and of families crying as they were torn asunder? (In Charleston, South Carolina, in the historic marketplace, where is the blood, where are the cries of slave families torn apart? In Charleston there are postcards and plaques. In Kraków there are postcards and guidebooks.) Come, come, dip your heart in it, this agony; that's why you've come here, isn't it, to relive the living nightmare?

The parks in Kraków seemed dusty, not as lush as the Jardin du Luxembourg in Paris. In the few restaurants in town the only fare for vegetarians was potato pierogis. Less than three years had passed since the Berlin Wall had come down, and Kraków was not yet Discovered—though the free tourist map was bordered with names of restaurants and hotels; very Chamber of Commerce. My hotel was small and plain, as if not yet aware of itself as a hotel, with a mournful, institutional-looking, beige restaurant downstairs. You could tell that someone with a certain taste had furnished it; someone had chosen the blue carpet and gold-flocked wallpaper, and then someone else had come along without the money or desire to keep it up.

I had the address of a professor, a friend of a friend of a friend, and showed up at his apartment. He told me I was following on the heels of Steven Spielberg, who'd just finished wandering the city, pacing out the boundaries of the ghetto and finding the work camp. Spielberg, who was working to remake the Holocaust in his image, or at least in his image of history. A friend who was in Kraków later, during the filming of *Schindler's List*, told me that Americans were hired as extras, to play the roles of Jews, and Poles were hired to be the Nazis.

"AUSCHWITZ," the paper fliers said, in black letters on pastel paper, taped on walls downtown. The writing was in Hebrew-influenced letters, the way *Zion* is spelled on salami. I took the bus to Auschwitz. Everyone on it seemed Polish except for a

young couple from America or Canada, he with yarmulke. I
wanted them to talk to me but they didn't. The very nominal
guide handed out hard fruit-flavored candy on the way. Free
with our 130,000-zloty fare (one way, about $11). I wanted to tell
someone, *Isn't this weird, the Polish people giving us hard candy at
ten in the morning as we make our way by bus to Auschwitz?*

At the extermination camp we sat in an auditorium and
watched a movie. Israelis were in front of me, boys and a father,
and the United Synagogue Youth from America as well. These
were the same Americans I'd seen the day before as I left the
Jewish museum at closing. The leader had said they were going
to Auschwitz in the morning, and he was as good as his word.

The United Synagogue Youth tour is called "From Darkness to Light." Students spend time in Eastern European cities,
observe the Sabbath, visit Jewish sites, and, after Hungary and
the Czech Republic and Poland, go to Israel. Just as you can enter
the darkness of the Holocaust Museum in Washington, D.C.,
and exit directly back into American sunshine. The camps reify
our victimhood and that's why we love them. *Look! They tried to
destroy us. In here! Right this way!*

It felt like we were all Jews in Sunday school together
watching the movie. It was our holy movie, our movie of martyrdom. Holy, holy, holy Auschwitz. The Nazi footage of their
own barbarity, the Soviet footage of soldiers liberating the camp
and witnessing atrocity. These are my people watching it with
me, I thought. I could reach out to any of them, find a common
ancestor or immigration story; we left here and came here, in my
family, in your family there was someone with a Yiddish cadence
in his voice. The children on film, huge images before us, black
and white, shown over and over for fifty years. Skeletal. Ghostly
ghastly smiles that weren't really smiles. The wizened people
who weren't old. The baseness of being human.

Now the small museum. Here are the famous mounds of
hair, the famous mounds of shoes, the famous mounds of eye-
glasses and suitcases in display cases. The museum staff doesn't
take such good care of its collections. They're dusty, the shoes,
and the glasses need a polish. The photos of the Polish martyrs.
Priest after priest. Since my visit Poland has recognized all of the

Jews who died there; there's more emphasis on the Jewish victims. After the controversy over a convent and a cross at Auschwitz, I suppose this is good news.

And outside? The emptiness. Mud, mud, acres of mud, plains of it, as people have written about. The North American couple was going to look up names in the library. I wanted to as well, but what names? My grandparents were safely in the United States long before World War I. The ones they left behind seemed so far away from us that we didn't know their names.

The bus was returning to Kraków but I decided to stay and take the train back. On the way to Kraków a few days before I'd noticed our train stopping at Oświęcim, which I knew was the Polish name for Auschwitz. An older woman met my eyes and I interpreted that as *I want you to know that I as a Pole recognize what this means.*

The visit to Auschwitz felt like a class field trip. It felt like a failure, a failure of imagination, projection. I didn't feel devastated. Or even mournful. I was not moved. It was not as vivid as a book. There were no people there, only tourists.

Would the people murdered there have wanted us to follow in their footsteps, cameras in hand, half a century later? Would I have wanted me to?

I am glad that Auschwitz was not paved over and turned into a mall or condominiums. The physical fact of it makes the Holocaust harder to forget or deny or dishonor. We are not the people who need to visit Auschwitz. It should be for deniers. But they stay home.

Germans are great at making Holocaust memorials. It must be the potent brew of guilt, resentment, and creativity. The best memorial I've ever seen is in the Bayerisches Viertel, Schöneberg, Berlin. On the first day the project's signs were installed, residents phoned the police to complain. They were outraged. This is why: The display, spread over many blocks, showed how Nazism affected the everyday life of Jews and the neighborhood. In front of a bakery was a sign attached to a lamp-post showing a stylized design of a cake. On the back was the summary of the 1942 law that required bakeries to put up signs forbidding Jews and Poles from purchasing cakes. Next to the post office, a sign that says postal workers who are married to Jews must retire. And so on, eighty signs in all. This neighborhood was once called Jewish Switzerland, a tranquil community where Jews of the professional class lived in comfort. Nothing bad could happen there.

The outraged citizens thought that anti-Semites had put up the signs. But it was art. A memorial, decentralized.

The snails in the Jewish cemetery in Kraków were big, like escargots. The dun color of their bodies smelled like moving decay. The cemetery was so dank that I imagined that the snails had crawled out of the sides of a well. The headstones were hundreds of years old and I didn't see any small stones on them, only snails. Leaving stones on a grave is a Jewish tradition.

The snails didn't mean anything. They were not symbolic. But the revulsion they caused, because it was unexpected, because they were unexpected, is the most visceral memory I've kept from that trip to Kraków and Auschwitz. I'm oddly grateful to the snails, because they made me feel *something*.

IN WROCŁAW, FORMERLY BRESLAU

I

The eighth International Bet Debora Conference of European Jewish Women, Activists, Academics, and Rabbis was not for women like me: those of us born and raised in the U.S., people whose bat mitzvahs were a given, who grew up with live grandparents and a great-grandmother, who do not have generational gaps on their family tree due to the Shoah. In short, women who haven't had to fight for their Judaism.

But this is why I went to my fourth Bet Debora conference in 2017: because the conference collapses time and space. In four days you can find out what it feels like to be a progressive Jew in Poland who fears the rightwing turn will never turn back. You learn in passing which American feminist classics were published in Poland. You meet the very young and sharp sole employee of the Jewish museum in Kishinev, where you come from, meaning: that's where your grandfather came from. You hear stories, of Communist fathers and of middle-aged women who didn't know what being Jewish meant until the Communists finally left. You hear that in Poland people buy photos of old rabbis and put a little money in front of them, an altar to prosperity, a shrine to economic success. Because you realize the myriad ways the Shoah and then the atheist state destroyed Jewish life in Central and Eastern Europe and the myriad ways it's coming back. Because by just being in the conference city—Wrocław, Poland, formerly known as Breslau, Germany—you learn a lot about the effects of the War. Once the home of the third-largest Jewish population in Germany, it now is home to about 350 Jews who have made themselves known.

Wrocław has huge public squares ringed by buildings that are baroque, or Soviet-bloc plain, or vaguely art nouveau. They look new despite their historical styles because much was leveled in the War and rebuilt after. The town is alive: restaurants, cafés, bars, windows open to the sidewalk where you can get *lody*, ice cream. Little English is heard on the street though there are English-language menus and that sign of western tourism: menus listing gluten-free options.

You learn at the 2015 meeting near London how the great Rabbi Leo Baeck's silence about the first female rabbi kept her dead, dead, dead for years. This year a room erupts in an argument about whether what you just heard on the screen was *real Yiddish* or merely German. It's a quick, hot debate and then it dies. You learn that a woman whose family was deported from Sighet, Elie Wiesel's home town, is sending Romanian Jewish women to Israel to study.

And you see a restored and newly scored Pola Negri silent film, *The Yellow Ticket*, about the limited options for an intellectual Jewish woman in prerevolutionary Russia. And a Serbian woman, Sonja Viličić, spoke in 2015 about the summer camp where kids learn about their Judaism while having fun, and about training teachers to lead Sunday school classes, and now she's leading a project to introduce non-Jews to Judaism.

This year there's a talk on Edith Stein, who grew up in Breslau and became a Carmelite nun and then a victim of the Shoah and now a saint. She was drawn to the Carmelites, says Rabbi James Baaden, and incidentally to Catholicism. And then on a university building you discover a plaque that says, in Polish, German, and Hebrew, that Edith Stein studied there.

An artist from Dresden shows slides of her montages and sculptures that keep bits of memory alive. You don't have to be embarrassed that you write about Jews and Jewish identity; that's normal among these people, not like it is at home. At the site of the Yiddish theater there's a plaque and a Polish theater, and nearby a mural showing Marek Edelman, a leader of the Warsaw ghetto uprising, who became a cardiologist, remained an anti-Zionist, a liberal who supported Solidarity and, later, the war in Iraq. Though it takes a while, a group of you finds the sign next to a parking lot commemorating the influential Jewish Theological Seminary destroyed in 1938 during Kristallnacht. And you get to spend time in the white and gilt and delicately stenciled White Stork Synagogue, restored thanks to the Bente Kahan Foundation, with no Torah on this bimah, because the sanctuary is used as much for cultural events as for religious ones. Kahan is a steady and pleased presence at the conference, and her foundation is one of the sponsors.

Did you really have to come this far to find your people? Perhaps.

A panel of Polish feminists notes that a lot of the feminists in their country and yours are Jewish, and ask, *What do you make of that?* And you hear criticism that the revival of Jewish studies and culture in Poland is *by non-Jews, for non-Jews, about the Jews,* says professor Marcin Wodzinski of the University of Wrocław, who also says that his students fall into these categories, broadly: New Christians who want to study Judaism as an early form of Christianity; children of *Fiddler on the Roof,* who see Jews as both exotic and close and tend to drop the major because it's not all Tevye and dancing; searchers who are looking for an alternate identity in a homogeneous Catholic country and who knows what exactly their grandfathers did in the War. The past hovers here sometimes, and roars at other times, and sometimes it hides and you have to coax it out.

II

The socialist revolutionary and political theorist Rosa Luxemburg was once imprisoned in Breslau. A group of us stood across from the former prison and I spoke about her. This was my open-air conference presentation. I said that Luxemburg wouldn't have come to our conference. The contradiction—we like Rosa Luxemburg because she was Jewish, but she shook off that ethnic mantle, trading it for humanism: "What do you want with this theme of the 'special suffering of the Jews'? I am just as much concerned with the poor victims on the rubber planta-tions of Putumayo, the Blacks in Africa with whose corpses the Europeans play catch. . . . I have no special place in my heart for the ghetto." She wrote this in a letter to her friend Mathilde Wurm (socialist, feminist), on February 16, 1917.

I probably first heard about Rosa Luxemburg in a class at North-western University in the 1970s. I was growing vaguely socialist, and anti-authoritarian. That was a quiet time, politically, on U.S. campuses, after the protests against the war in Vietnam, and years before students massed in solidarity with the anti-apartheid movement. During my first year at university I remember that I imagined having a boyfriend who would be a revolutionary. And then I could follow along.

It is hard for me to believe that, now.

We want to know what is hidden. Our heritage, Jewish and female, is buried in the backyard, the great Jewish backyard that is Europe. Ashes have settled over this yard. People have built houses on it, right over the history.

Who is *we*? I should only speak for myself. As a child, I followed historic Jewish women. Meaning: I lassoed them, the way a cow-boy wrangler loops his rope around a steer or calf. Growing up in Texas I went to rodeos, maybe at least to one prison rodeo— prisoners being especially willing to risk their lives and whole-ness of body for freedom to perform in danger and in public.

Rosa Luxemburg was born in 1871 into an assimilating family in Zamość, Poland. Educated at Zurich University, she moved to Berlin in 1898, the year after earning her PhD. In a speech in 1913 she called on German workers to refuse to fight against French workers in the event of war. While much of the socialist world was prowar, Rosa was against it. Because she spoke out, she was arrested. She was sentenced the next year and imprisoned in Berlin. After her release she was held in "protective custody" in Wronke, Germany (now Wronki, Poland), where she was free to move around the prison building. She found opportunity for nature study, reading, and writing political essays. In late July 1917 she was moved from Wronke to Breslau and imprisoned in the building across the street from us. There she had two rooms, but one or the other was locked at all times. She continued her work, amid potted plants and flowers. Every morning she watered the "little people" that made up her garden. She stayed there until November 8, 1918, when she was released during the German revolution.

Luxemburg displayed considerable empathy and interest in animals. In a letter from Wronke she wrote about large birds of prey that carried smaller songbirds on their backs while migrating—as if there were "a kind of God's truce, a general armistice." She wrote to socialist Sophie Liebknecht in December 1917 about "something sharply, terribly painful here" in Breslau. She was upset by the treatment of water buffalo that pulled military supply wagons into the prison courtyard. She witnessed a soldier beating one of them with the handle of his whip. "The attendant on duty indignantly took him to task, asking him: Had he no pity for the animals? 'No one has pity for us humans,' he answered with an evil smile, and started in again, beating them harder than ever. . . . During the unloading, all the animals stood there, quite still, exhausted and . . . one that was bleeding kept staring into the empty space in front of him with an expression on his black face and in his soft, black eyes like an abused child."

She imagined that the buffalo missed their native green fields of Romania, here in this "strange, ugly city.... Oh, my poor buffalo, my poor, beloved brother! We both stand here so powerless and mute, and are as one in our pain, impotence, and yearning."

She had a famous limp that marked her as much as Frida Kahlo's broken body. Kahlo was a Communist with Jewish lovers and associates; she claimed a Jewish heritage that turned out to be Lutheran. Rosa's body was damaged by a hip ailment at age five, Frida's caused by a traffic accident at age eighteen.

Luxemburg is known today as a humanist socialist, maybe the first Marxist with a human face? A woman's face. A Jewish woman's face.

When I first read about Luxemburg, I took special note of her Jewishness. We were Jewish together. Our Jewishness made it more likely that I could follow in her footsteps. I followed (in the form of reading biographies and other writings) Jewish and non-Jewish women who did things that the Jewish women around me in Houston did not do. The mothers of my friends did not fly airplanes (Amelia Earhart) or found organizations like the Red Cross (Clara Barton) or fight slavery (Lucretia P. Mott) or publish their teen diary (Anne Frank) or improve Black education (Mary McLeod Bethune) or organize settlement houses (Jane Addams, Lillian Wald). They had not married U.S. presidents or, for the most part, become doctors or lawyers or academicians or artists. They were mostly stay-at-home moms, wives of the so-called Greatest Generation, married to the men who had fought in World War II. They were similar to the women described in

Betty Friedan's 1963 book *The Feminine Mystique*—at least demo-
graphically. They were middle-class college graduates. Unlike
the women in Friedan's book, they seemed fairly happy. But what
did I know? They may or may not have been frustrated by their
lives spent tending the roost in detached houses with front and
back yards. Many of our mothers did not work *outside the home*;
they went door to door collecting for the March of Dimes and
Easterseals, arranged Hadassah meetings, collected pledges for
the Houston Jewish Federation, organized synagogue Sisterhood
luncheons and fashion shows, volunteered to lead Girl Scout
troops, led PTA meetings, collected signatures for progressive
school board candidates. They drove us to after-school art, ballet,
Hebrew, and science lessons. They took us to museums and the
theater and we traveled to family weddings and bar mitzvahs
and occasionally to Israel. Later, when we were in high school,
they went (back) to work.

   I followed the lives of far-off heroines for identification, for
indication that there was a wider world out there. Waiting for me.

I read Anne Frank's diary when I was eight. I saw my life in hers.
She had an older sister; so did I. She was a writer; so was I. She was
hiding from the Nazis—well, we might have to someday. It could
happen. Just in case, I had a getaway bag and my sister and I would
sit in our pink-carpeted, walk-in closets and pretend we were par-
tisans in the forest—though we didn't know the word "partisan."

After a general strike and uprising in January 1919, the fragile
Weimar government of Friedrich Ebert sent rightwing paramil-
itaries to kill the two leaders of the revolt, Karl Liebknecht and
Luxemburg. They were interrogated, tortured, and shot. Her
body was thrown into the Landwehr Canal in Berlin and recov-
ered five months later and buried near Liebknecht's in Berlin's
Friedrichsfelde Cemetery.

In 2009 a pathologist claimed that Luxemburg's body had not been thrown into the canal but hidden in the cellar of a hospital. Liebnecht's body was taken directly to the city morgue, so it seems more definite that he is buried in his own marked grave. Still, people pay homage to Luxemburg at her marked gravesite.

In the Jewish cemetery in the former East Berlin, I've seen headstones that obviously don't have bodies beneath them. The place and date of birth are given, and then the place of death: Auschwitz. I remember seeing, next to the extermination camp's name, a phrase that I remember as "God only knows why." If the person had died in peacetime, the body would have been buried there. The point is memory. The stone marks the life and death of the person who once lived in Berlin. The *Stolpersteine* serve the same purpose. They are "stumbling stones" in Germany and Austria set in the pavement next to buildings where Jews had lived before they were deported. Each cube of stone has a brass plaque on top; it provides the bare facts of a Jewish person's life. Each is witness, each is part of a decentralized memorial.

From the prison in Breslau, in a letter heady with optimism after the Bolshevik Revolution, Rosa wrote to Sophie Liebknecht: "The time of pogroms has passed once and for all. The strength of the workers and of socialism there is much too strong for that. The revolution has cleared the air so much of the miasmas and stuffy atmosphere of reaction that a new Kishinev has become forever passé. I can sooner imagine—pogroms against Jews here in Germany."

Loyal German Jews couldn't imagine such pogroms either, which is why many of them did not leave in the 1930s.

Luxemburg was referring to the famous 1903 pogrom in Kishinev.

Even in the U.S., now, historians discuss whether Luxemburg was a self-hating Jew.

In the U.S., some Jewish children, as a ploy to keep from having to go to Hebrew school, would tell their parents they didn't feel Jewish. Some mothers would respond: *Hitler would have considered you Jewish.*

Which is not exactly the point.

I want Jews to remain Jews even if they don't want to. I'm angry with French philosopher Simone Weil for all but converting to Catholicism, and with German author Alfred Döblin, who did convert once he left the Old World for the New.

The enemies of the Jews won't let them *not* be Jewish. More than a century before the rise of the Third Reich, the political writer and essayist Ludwig Boerne, born Judah Loew (or Loeb) Baruch, converted and later regretted it. "Baptized Jews soon found themselves in a no-man's land," Ruth Gay writes in *The Jews of Germany: A Historical Portrait.* In 1836 Boerne lamented that he'd paid a minister three louis d'or to baptize him. "It doesn't help me," he wrote after he'd been a Christian, at least technically, for eighteen years. Anti-Semites still attacked him as a Jew. He wrote, "Three louis d'or for a little place in the German madhouse! It was pure waste!"

Both of Karl Marx's grandparents were rabbis. His father had the whole family baptized when Karl was six. Leon Trotsky was born Leiba Bronstein; a rabbi famously noted, perhaps apocryphally, "It's the Trotskys who make the revolutions, and the Bronsteins who pay the price."

Rosa Luxemburg was never baptized. She was a nonparochial humanist. But who knows how her politics and identity would have evolved in a hundred years. And a Polish Jew was not the same in 2017 as in 1917 (or 1939 or 1945 or 1968 or 1989).

The world is at war. There's a war of the rich against the poor, of the religious against the secular and vice versa, of men against women, of humans against animal and plant life. The effects of getting and making and using fossil fuels are ruining the atmosphere, endangering life. Real (not just rumored) weapons of mass destruction are at the ready.

And still somewhere wasps burrow in the ground in the way that Luxemburg described while in the Wronke fortress. And wasps perhaps still fly inside of rooms in order to eat crumbs left for them, as Luxemburg did in prison.

And still the songbirds sing.

And still we don't know what they are saying

THE AMBIVALENCE OF THE ONE-BREASTED FEMINIST

Look at me.

If you were looking in 2007 you would have noticed first off that I was bald. On the top of my head you could read: "US OUT OF IRAQ," and you'd see drawings of grape leaves and little peace signs on the rest of my scalp.

Some people would look at me, grimace, and ask, *Didn't that hurt?* Drunken baseball fans in my Wrigleyville neighborhood would read my head and yell at me about pulling out. One night on the El a young woman with a suitcase glanced from my head to my chest and said, *Cancer?* She was in town for the wedding of her friend who had spent the past year in breast cancer treatment.

I had cancer surgery in early 2007 and went through chemo that spring and summer. My friends decorated my bare head with henna and a fruit-based ink called jagua. I had become one-breasted though it wasn't and isn't always apparent because my remaining breast is small and my clothes are often loose. On the left side I'm not completely flat because I got what's called in the business an SSM—a skin-sparing mastectomy. That way my skin can be stretched to encompass a container of saline if I decide to get reconstruction. I asked my breast surgeon whether she would counsel me to keep the remaining breast or not. She said it was up to me. There's a chance of the cancer forming in the other breast, but it's much less than 50 percent.

Look at me.

Friends and strangers have unbuttoned their blouses to show me their new breasts and new nipples, colored to look natural. They have invited me to touch their breasts. They've had the remaining breast perked up to match the new one, which was filled with silicone or saline or their own stomach fat. These breasts look "real." The nipples are pink and delicate; the breasts have an obvious or fading scar across them. The breasts feel real: spongy, not hard.

I met with a plastic surgeon who put me in touch with a patient who'd had both breasts removed and restored, though she'd had cancer in only one. She praised the doctor and explained she hadn't wanted to worry with every mammogram.

Look at me.

In my forties I gained about twenty-five pounds. When I was fifty-one I was diagnosed with stage 2A estrogen-positive cancer. I wanted to lose that weight way before even considering reconstruction because otherwise my right breast would become smaller while the salt-filled one would remain the same. *But your breasts are different sizes now,* a friend reminded me. Or, more accurately, I have one surviving breast and one absence.

For years I did not lose that weight. Was I punishing myself by not getting a new breast?

Look at me.

My hair was just past the marine corps stage. I was sitting behind a table, overseeing community workshops led by my students at the university. Unexpectedly I had to fill in for one of them. I went to the front of a classroom wearing my hot pink clingy knit shirt. The workshoppers could clearly see my one breast with its always-sticking-out nipple. I thought: Am I obscene? Am I making people uncomfortable? Am I throwing cancer in their faces?

Other times I've felt defiant in my solo-breastedness: *Here's what a one-breasted woman looks like. Fuck you, I'm one-breasted, I'm shouting inside.*

But who am I swearing at? The person on the street didn't cause me to get cancer, not personally; he's no more guilty than the rest of us who tolerate air and water pollution and pesticides, who overly enthusiastically embraced X rays and radiation treatments.

Or maybe the tumor came because I've never been pregnant. Or was caused by a gene mutation that hasn't been discovered yet. Or—blame the victim—that ring of fat around my waist that could have set off a round of estrogen through my body. (And, yes, I could get that fat shaved off and turned into a breast, which would shrink as I lost weight—but the operation is so complicated, so scarring.)

The women who wear wigs, who stuff their bras with prostheses or pads or have surgical reconstruction, they're easier to look at. They look as if nothing happened. They look as if they are not part of an epidemic.

Look at me.

If I eschew reconstruction, but camouflage the lack of breast by covering up with a sweater or jacket or scarf, what am I saying?

A meeting with the assistant dean and another professor. If I wear a tank top (hot flashes keep me sweating year-round) do I make them uncomfortable?

In the 1980s I stopped shaving my armpits and legs because of politics. The feminists had explained that women had been lying all these years with our bodies, trying to make our skin hairless like a baby's when in reality we had hair. Wild sweaty clumps, for example, under our arms. It was easy for the thin-haired blondes to disavow shaving. It was the swarthy sisters who stood out in polite society.

Look at me.

For a time I wouldn't read anything by women who'd died of breast cancer, so I avoided Audre Lorde's *The Cancer Journals,* published in 1980, until a couple of years after diagnosis. Lorde writes of waiting for her first post-surgery appointment with her doctor. The nurse admonished her, saying that her one-breastedness was "'bad for the morale' of the office." Prostheses, Lorde points out, are usually functional: "Artificial limbs perform specific tasks. . . . Dentures allow us to chew our food. Only false breasts are designed for appearance only." In other words, no matter how you fill your bra cup, you still won't be able to feed a baby. And the skin will stay numb.

Nobody tells Moshe Dayan to throw off his eyepatch and "to go get a glass eye, or that he is bad for the morale of the office," Lorde writes. "The world sees him as a warrior with an honorable wound, and a loss of a piece of himself which he has marked, and mourned, and moved beyond." So, too, are women whose breasts were amputated because of cancer. "For me, my scars are an honorable reminder that I may be a casualty in the cosmic war against radiation, animal fat, air pollution, McDonald's hamburgers and Red Dye No. 2."

Yes, yes, I cheer silently. I am your walking wounded, the symbol of post-modernity's stripping and defilement of nature. I am a direct victim of the Military-Industrial Complex. I am a martyr. I withstand the stares of the curious passersby because I am political.

Which is not entirely true. Most people don't notice.

Look at me?

I've read many breast cancer memoirs and blogs. The balance of the writer-survivors assumed they would get their breast (or two) rebuilt or get a measured for a prosthesis. They do not share Lorde's attitude. I have bought a prosthesis, which is a biggish squishy triangle that fits inside a special pocket in a special bra. Insurance paid for the prosthesis, but I had to cough up the dough for the nipple. I wear the prosthetic breast on special occasions such as weddings and other events where my mother is in attendance.

Canadian professor and blogger Mary Bryson noted strangers' reaction to the results of her double mastectomy without reconstruction: "When I catch people looking, they are scanning from the chest to the face and back again," she wrote. "I guess they are trying to figure it out. Hmmmmm. Looks like a woman's face, but no boobs. So they look at the face again, maybe the buzz-cut short hair is another distractor, then back down to the washboard chest."

Look at me.

During the pandemic my True Love and I started walking four to five miles a night. I lost thirteen pounds in the first year and I've kept them off, yet I haven't been tempted to reconstruct. I've heard of reconstruction problems and keep hearing more: saline implants that never became comfortable; lumps that formed under implants that turned out, too late, to be cancer; second surgeries that were needed to even out the first implants; and more. More reasons to stay "natural." The weird thing is that many people say they never noticed my one-breastedness until I mentioned it in (relevant, I swear) conversation. Do people really not notice?

Look at me.

I was wearing long cargo shorts and a T-shirt. My young Orthodox first-cousin-twice-removed asked, *Are you a boy or a girl?* I wanted to respond, *Why does it matter?* But it does matter, very much, in a world with strict adherence to gender roles and traditions. Here I was, an unfamiliar relative as old as her grandfather, not wearing a wig or a skirt, with half a bosom. I answered, *Girl,* and let it go at that.

There must be others who notice but say nothing. I'm afraid that people are thinking: Poor girl, she's missing a breast. Somebody ought to tell her so that she can do something about it. *Yes,* I want to tell them, *I've noticed.*

I want people to see that an obvious cancer survivor can be healthy. I want them to think about the environmental causes of cancer. I want them to question their notions about gender. I want my unreconstructed breast to be my latest henna message.

But I wonder if I want the attention for myself, maybe for the same reason I became a writer: *Notice me.*

FLOOD, MEYERLAND

In the days since Hurricane Harvey I have been living in two places, the way you do when you're in the midst of reading a book and you have that second landscape tucked in your mind somewhere. One place is Chicago, where I live. We've been having a cool summer, a few sprinkles over the last couple of days. Someone mentions school starting and I almost say, *But it's starting late, because of the water*. The other place is my hometown, Houston.

School started here in Chicago on Tuesday. Some students have already walked out, to protest President Trump's decision on DACA.

In Houston an ABC13 newsman was broadcasting from a rescue boat and pointed out my old elementary school, Kolter, which had three feet of water, with a highwater mark two feet higher. The school was named, our teachers told us, for the principal of another school who died in a fire, after everyone else escaped, like a captain going down with the ship.

Who by fire and who by water.

Houstonians have lived through it, the water in biblical propor-
tions, rescues, deaths, homes devastated and spared, heroism
and bad judgment. Severely damaged public buildings. The
smell and eternal wetness. The knowledge that it will take tens
of billions of dollars and many years to recover.

ABC was in Meyerland, named for George Meyer, who developed
inherited land (some of it rice fields) into a subdivision in the
southwest part of the city. Vice President Richard Nixon cut the
ribbon at the dedication in 1955. Nixon praised one of the model
homes as well as an H-bomb shelter.

Meyerland was already hit hard by the Memorial Day flood of
2015 and the Tax Day flood of 2016. Turf (sodden) of the Jews. In
the 1960s and 1970s most of Houston's Jews lived thereabouts,
though Meyerland was not majority Jewish. The same with my
public high school, Bellaire, in the 1970s. Meyerland agitated
me and stifled me with its smallness and steadiness, one generation begetting another that stayed within its confines. There
was gossip and pecking order and few intellectuals, besides my
friend Paula who read the *New Yorker* and was on the debate

team. The friendly girls were popular. I was tongue-tied. You've
heard this story forever.

And there is comfort, too, in community and continuity.
My ballet recital when I was six was held in the downtown Music
Hall, where we went for High Holiday services because the old
Beth Yeshurun couldn't handle the crowd, and where we would
have our high school graduation, in our red robes that hid our
squirt guns.

There were only six congregations in Houston back then,
and one had such a low profile I didn't know about it. I felt I knew
someone from every Jewish family. And sometimes family secrets.

Now there are dozens of synagogues and any number of
Jewish neighborhoods.

The city's Jewish population is 63,700, and 71 percent of Jews
live where there was high flooding, an official from the Jewish
Federation of Greater Houston told the Jewish Telegraphic
Agency. Zip code 77096, Meyerland, contains the largest percent-
age of Jews of greater Houston, 14 percent, according to a 2016
federation study. Jews comprise less than 1 percent of the greater
Houston population, but some 9 percent of Jewish households
had some damage from the Memorial Day flood in 2015.

A 1976 study states that the high-density area (of Jews) was
generally in the Meyerland and adjacent areas. In this area, Jews
made up about one-fourth of the overall population. Houston
is the fourth-largest city in the country. It has the thirty-second-
largest Jewish community.

The state's first synagogue, Beth Israel, was founded in 1859 in
Houston by thirty-two young, mostly immigrant men. At least
six of the men owned slaves, "though most only owned one as
a house servant," according to the Institute for Southern Jewish
life. Just one. But still.

Beth Israel was Orthodox, then Reform. When I was growing up it seemed that everyone was more or less the same kind of Jewish, preparing for a double bar or bat mitzvah, boys bareheaded in school. No one was hippie-Jewish or Hasidic—just Jewish enough to use Hebrew letters to handwrite notes in code during public school classes. We did not think of ourselves as less-than Jews or faux Jews just because we were not in New York or Chicago or L.A. We were our own norm. We didn't know that they never imagined that we existed.

Where are you from? New York? an interviewer asked my cousin Josh Brener, who used to live across the street from us. Josh is an actor and a TV star. *No,* he said on video, *You'll never guess.*

In the early 1960s when my parents *built* our house, as it was said then, meaning that they worked with an architect, they chose gray and orange and white century-old brick for the outside and for an inside wall behind the gas fireplace. We called it a ranch house, though the official designation is midcentury modern, the style that dominates Meyerland. We were one street from South Braeswood and didn't expect nearby Brays Bayou would do anything other than stay wet and catch rainwater.

The husband of my friend Sonia calls the architectural style Jewish modern. For the last two high school reunion weekends the couple hosted a party at their long low white brick house. In 2004 their daughter and her friends, newly graduated from Bellaire, walked in. I talked to them and for a moment I felt that *we* were the ones who were eighteen with new diplomas, with a summer before us and then the rest of our lives.

At Bellaire in the early 1970s, there was an open campus for lunch, a smoking area, and a dress code that forbade two things: flip flops and bare midriffs. Maybe cutoffs were banned, too, but nothing else. Only a few years earlier, in junior high, girls weren't allowed to wear pants. Because the curriculum was not demanding we had time for other pursuits, such as spending all night putting out the *Three Penny Press*.

In the news video, Ehling pointed out the original ranch houses, which were inundated, and the newer elevated homes, which were dry.

My immediate family has been lucky. My mother was safe in a high rise where many of our former neighbors also live, Meyerland gone vertical. A building of grandmas, as my niece once said. My sister and her husband sold their twice-flooded Meyerland house and are living in a townhouse with excellent drainage. My mother, sister, and nieces went to a baby shower the Saturday before Harvey's deluge. In the flood the couple lost everything, including the shower gifts. Someone has started raising funds for them.

Hurricane Harvey flooded the homes of one in thirteen Jewish families, according to the *Houston Chronicle*. Three synagogues, the senior home, a Jewish school, and the Evelyn Rubenstein Jewish Community Center were damaged. *The communal infrastructure of Jewish Houston is situated on a body of water that has now flooded three times in three years*, historian Joshua Furman told me months later, at Rice University. He was showing me the Houston Jewish History Archive he founded. The collection grew from the realization during Harvey that tangible objects of Houston Jewish life were vulnerable. Furman experienced this viscerally, as he volunteered to dry out waterlogged documents after the flood. Houston Jews, he told me, were having to adapt, as Jews have always had to, to outside menaces. Only this time, he said, it's *not because of pogroms, not because of physical persecution. Now it's the weather that's doing the persecuting.*

The locally famous Allen brothers, who founded Houston in 1836, were hucksters who touted the climate, for one. The nascent city flooded twice in 1837, and still white settlers came. In 1858 Jacob de Cordova, a Sephardic Jew from Jamaica who amassed land in Houston and beyond, noted, "The principal objection to these lands is that in consequence of their extreme flatness they are often in the wet season covered with water."

In August 2015 I was in town and went to our old street, still suffering from the effects of the Memorial Day flood of that year. I met the mail carrier, who was calling for Tinkerbell. She was a cat who had stayed on after her people left, and the mailman was feeding her and other cats in her situation. It was like a ghost town there on this strip of Braesheather Drive between South Rice Avenue and Chimney Rock Road. When we lived there, one Catholic family lived two doors down and lit up their house outside every winter while we were inside ours lighting Chanukah candles. That day in August all or most of the houses were empty. Some windows were boarded up; others had building permits taped on. There were dumpsters in a couple of driveways. Construction trucks were parked in others and there was a big white storage trailer in the driveway of our old house.

Mail forwarding hadn't been working, the postman told me, so he advised his customers not to sign up for it, and instead to come by their ruined houses daily to pick up the mail. He walked down the deserted street, putting bills and letters and magazines in slots and boxes in the front of houses.

As I stood there, the new owner of my old home drove up. She offered me a tour of the house and its additions. It had sustained three feet of water and consequently had been stripped down to the studs.

Also in the Memorial Day flood, as was much reported, a couple in their eighties drowned when their rescue boat capsized. They were wearing life jackets but the current defeated them. I know the family. A double funeral was held at Beth Yeshurun.

I look up the history of Kolter School, and I find that Jennie Katharine Kolter was not a principal but a second-grade teacher at Edgar Allan Poe School. In 1959 a distraught parent set off a bomb on the playground and Kolter was "blown to bits." The bomber, his son, and two other boys also died, as well as the school custodian. Many were injured. No wonder they told us it was a fire.

There were other things we didn't know: that in town there was Emancipation Park, bought by ex-slaves; that Sam Houston owned slaves; that Reconstruction was a revolution to bring radical equality, and it was successful until it was quashed. We never learned about a Black-on-white race riot in Houston in 1917, set off by Jim Crow conditions and police brutality. It resulted in the largest mutiny trial in U.S. history and the hanging of nineteen Black soldiers.

My friend Paula the intellectual died a few years ago of ALS, at age fifty-seven. She was a political activist and fundraiser, and unfailingly optimistic. My friend Sonia, sixty, is newly gone, as is the light that seemed to surround her as she approached people and drew them in. Friends visited her new grave and stopped at my father's to say hello. Another person who died too soon, they said.

These friends and I wrote for the *Greyhound Gazette* at Johnston. Named for Confederate general and "Lost Cause" cult figure Albert Sidney Johnston, it is now Meyerland Performing and Visual Arts Middle School. It was a costly change for the

Houston school district, which caused grumbling, but I think a necessary one.

Even now, as the seas are warming, the air is more humid, arable land has become desert, and the weather has gone screwy, still there are people, in high places, decision-making places, who think climate change is a myth, think that none of Harvey's lakes of rain were caused by human activity.

"Yes, the newspapers were right" (as James Joyce wrote in "The Dead"). Endless rain "was general all over" the coast. "It was falling hard on every part" of the flooded streets and avenues, the skyscrapers, falling hard on the cemented-over wetlands, "upon all the living and the dead."

AMERICA
A Polemic

I saw you at the Capitol on video, wild, gleeful in your unthinking symbolism and window breaking.

I saw you on the steps and scaling the walls, your id on full display, your muscles on full display, your evil individual liberty and libertinism on full display.

I saw you, America, captured.

I saw you in your white skin and proud tattoos and I heard your taunts and war cries.

Centuries ago other white men were grateful to finally arrive in what they saw as a virgin, untouched area, naming it after its purity, knowing it was theirs to conquer, to own.

The land was their discovery; it was their duty to settle it, to civilize it, their duty as Europeans and adventurers. Their adventuring, their birthright: they owned the seas, they owned their restlessness, they had royalty behind them.

They were sea-drunk, dazed by the land and sky vastness, disdaining the Others who lived and worked the land in front of them. Savages.

Early settlers imported chained Africans, *won* in a fight at sea. They worked these darker humans because they were darker; darkness was evil, as the Bible said; darkness meant they were foreign, children of Ham, cursed. Later settlers bought more humans and they rode them hard. Because the settlers owned them. *As was proper*, they told themselves.

They, the white anointed ones, became Enlightened, filled with the light of thought, as they pushed further and further inland all that was not themselves, that were not the natural heirs as they were, born to receive this bounty, designated to fight for the bounty.

They slashed forests and massacred birds, flocks so vast they had made the sky dark. Everything was theirs in this Christian cornucopia.

And they looked and saw that it was good, everything was theirs.

An endless loop of deserving and obtaining and ruining. Transforming the land, civilizing it: streets and houses and churches on every corner, the stocks, sermons, and whips; and finally revolution because they wanted ownership, they deserved ownership.

The revolution was about ideas and theory; therefore, it was bold and brave.

When the Founding Fathers won, they knew that God had granted all to them.

They had to fight the unenlightened, the savages, the bleeding brainless women, the primitive, the landless poor.

This is America, this has always been America.

● ● ●

They say that you, America, are the city on the hill.

They say America is the land of equality. They say that America cares that everyone is housed and healthy.

Pursuing happiness.

They say America is a young democracy but where is there an older one? Greece, with its slaves and hidebound women?

America, you are not exceptional.

America allowed Jews sometimes. We were not (usually) considered Black. We were willing to throw off our old languages and customs and names; we were willing to go door to door selling knives and rags. In the South we were willing to befriend the whites who knew themselves to be superior; we were willing to go along, to get along; we were willing to join hands against the Blacks so that we could walk in and out of front doors.

We accepted the mantle of whiteness. We were willing to nod at the monuments to the Lost Cause as we stepped up to the courthouse for naturalization. We were willing to keep our heads down to get ahead. We wanted to live. To thrive.

The children, after all.

Me.

● ● ●

America, you are the worm in the apple.

America, you are the greed of the worm.

America, you are the sickness that causes the greed in the worm.

America, you are lying to your children. You are brutal to your children. You turn your back against your violent history. Your police carry guns, your police fought in wars, your terrorists have fought in wars, your terrorists are aggrieved. Your terrorists are benighted. Your terrorists fight against terrorists in uniform. Your police fight the curse in the sons of Ham.

America, you began with invasion and you will end with invasion. You were torn apart by those who named you. America, you are being torn apart by those who thought they deserved to inherit everything.

SOMETHING TO SELL

My husband came in the front door and said I needed to go out and amuse our neighbor, Sharon. She was trying to sell her parking space to Cubs fans and was getting bored. Her husband John had already tried his luck for about fifteen minutes.

Outside Sharon was leaning against a parked car with her sign for "E-Z Out Parking, $40." In a couple of hours game 4 of the World Series would begin. We're half a mile west of Wrigley Field. Down the street they were asking for $60, so Sharon was trying to undercut them. But the reason fans weren't stopping was because they were being driven. Most of the cars that passed were taxis and Ubers.

When the Cubs qualified for the series, I thought: I need to monetize the Cubs. I had never used that verb before. It is an ugly, Latinate, crass verb. But it seemed to be the right one for what I wanted to do: rent out our basement bedroom (bathroom en suite) and our driveway. When I lived in a condo I sold my parking space, but now that we have a house, we don't dare. Our driveway has a deck on top of it, kept aloft with wooden posts. My husband is afraid that a careless parker could run into one of the poles and bring havoc and ruin upon them and us. I don't disagree. We let our friends park there, for free.

When the Cubs made it to the series, I looked up prices on Airbnb. People were offering whole apartments for $150. Where were the rooms for $1,000 a night? How could we offer our little basement for more than $100?

My husband speculated: People who can afford the $2,000-plus (rooftop, obstructed view) and $10,000-plus (in-stadium seats) aren't looking for a cheap room in a house. They'll stay at fancy hotels downtown. Or they'll go back to their Chicago-area homes to sleep.

Suddenly I realized: My friend Jennifer was coming to stay with us. She needed to spend time with her ninety-five-year-old father and had asked for the basement room. She was driving in Wednesday and staying through Saturday. Well, I thought, Saturday night and Sunday night were rental possibilities.

Then my husband reminded me that his friend from work, who shares a season subscription, was parking in the driveway on Saturday night. We've come to enjoy the predictable ritual. After the games he comes to chat and if he's with his older precocious daughter, now ten, she makes a beeline to the bathroom, then fills up her water bottle. She knows President Obama personally, can run a 5K, and organized a third-grade summer book group.

We'd also promised the driveway on Saturday night to the guy my stepson became good friends with while they served in the army reserves in Kuwait. That wasn't a problem because we can fit two cars in our driveway if one is behind the other, and if the driver of the second one believes us when we say they won't get a ticket because the car blocks most of the sidewalk and sticks out into the street. The people in the back car leave their key with us. The army reserve guy brought us a bottle of wine. In the summer the other guy and his wife bring us homemade raspberry jam and other fruits of their garden labor.

Then Jennifer texted me to ask if the daughter of a former professor friend of hers could stay with us on Saturday night. The woman lives downstate and is a huge Cubs fan. Fine, we said, though my husband was grousing about the driveway, which absolutely cannot hold three cars. I told the woman that she'd have to find her own parking space. Oh, she said, she was taking the train. Smart woman.

Jennifer arrived on Wednesday night bearing gifts from the Indian/Pakistani neighborhood north of us—huge pomegranates, small cucumbers, a gigantic daikon radish, papadams (the brand with an inexplicable bunny on the package), asafoetida—as well as a pair of turquoise socks for me with dachshunds on them. Jennifer defected from Chicago more than a dozen years ago and we don't get to talk much. This visit, we had good conversations in the kitchen; then on Saturday morning she stripped her bed and put her linens into the wash, so they were clean and dry for her professor's daughter Jodie, who arrived with Cubs shirt, a heavy backpack, and plans to join her son and his roommate at a local bar, one that did not have a $250 cover charge. Later Jennifer told me that when Jodie found out she had a free place to stay, she cried.

Jodie left on Sunday morning, having written us a sweet note with an offer for us to stay at her house sometime in Lawrenceville, Illinois. Later on Sunday my husband was leaving town so I drove him to the El. On the way back I saw no parking spaces on the street, just people offering parking for $60. I parked in our driveway. I had nothing to sell.

Through Jennifer, we've hosted two Antioch College students who were interning in Chicago. We mentioned this to my step-daughter once and she said, *Oh, you're giving back.* My husband said, *Not really. We don't think of it that way.* We were lucky enough to be able to buy a house with room for the kids and grandkids to stay. The rest of the time, we have empty space. A semi-famous writer has slept in our basement, as well as my mother-in-law, two Swedish NATO protesters, a friend's nephew who was working for Al Gore, and out-of-town friends.

I grew used to this unofficial couch surfing when I was in graduate school and traveling around Iowa and the U.S. to protest just about everything Reagan was doing. I spent some nights with many other people, some of whom I knew, on the floor of a large beautiful apartment on Central Park West, owned by somebody I never met. In Des Moines for a protest, a bunch of us stayed at the Catholic Worker house of hospitality there. I remember how sweet it was when one of the residents came by to make sure I had a blanket. When I moved back to Chicago and lived in a one-bedroom apartment, my floor was always open for Iowa comrades traveling east. Through the National Writers Union, I've stayed with other writers in Portland, Oregon, and Oakland, California, during book tours. This spring when I was going to D.C. for a memorial gathering, I got in touch with someone I hadn't seen in twenty years but who had offered his house if I happened to come to town. It was beyond pleasant to stay in the basement and meet his family.

So when a friend's daughter was looking for places to stay in Dallas and Brownsville, I thought it would be a snap to help her, because I have a dozen relatives in Dallas and I knew somebody in Brownsville. Our friend's daughter was traveling to the two cities with her documentary film crew. I called my relatives in Dallas. Either they couldn't or were going out of town—and they weren't inclined to offer their empty pads to strangers. I called my mother in Houston and she suggested I contact a filmmaker she'd once hosted a fundraiser for. The woman lived in Dallas, and when I emailed her, she said she was going to be out of town. I emailed a colleague in Fort Worth. Her house was going to be full of grandchildren, and she mentioned a friend (the same filmmaker my mother had suggested). Finally, at my wit's end, I emailed an Episcopal priest in Fort Worth whom I'd interviewed once on the phone. Yes, she said, she had a couch and could find someone with the same. She had marched in Selma in 1965 and so had the filmmaker's grandfather. There's a nice circularity in that.

There are many things I came to understand when I read Lewis Hyde's *The Gift: Imagination and the Erotic Life of Property*. I came to see that I had grown up in a small stable Jewish village called Meyerland (located inside the sprawling, ever-changing city) where for generations my family and others had hosted one another's wedding brunches and showers; exchanged gifts for bar mitzvahs, engagements, weddings, anniversaries, landmark birthday parties, brisses, and naming ceremonies (for female babies); supplied food for receptions, parties, and shivas. These are all known as lifecycle events. I want to be clear that I'm not talking about a tightknit, black-hatted, and bewigged Orthodox community operating inside an *eruv,* a boundary that separates public from private. These are moderns who are more relaxed about the rules and attend Reform and Conservative synagogues.

I purposely left that community, though I sometimes long for its rootedness. Because of the constant exchange, we never keyed the price of a wedding gift to the cost of the provided wedding meal. (Crass, crass.) Before I learned that gifts create community, I would wonder why someone I barely knew was inviting me to a bar mitzvah or wedding. After reading, I knew: We were part of a weave made of the constant crisscrossing of give and take. It was just like a web made of colored yarn that I watched being created a long time ago at the Women's Pentagon Action, protesters tossing a ball of yarn from one person to another.

In Chicago, our own driveway-basement bedroom-crop exchange is informal. I never thought until now to count up the goods that our friends bring to our house. And I've long admired the Catholic Workers, who say they appreciate guests because they allow the Workers to provide hospitality. I could go on about the biblical mythical Abraham and Sarah entertaining angels unawares, but I won't.

The traditional cry of *trick or treat* has lost its meaning, but it once presented a threat: I'm going to play a trick on you—unless you give me a treat. The kids who climb up onto our front porch on Halloween are a delight to see, though grabby. I don't expect to retrieve my mini Snickers bars in the future. I guess I see the chocolate bars as payment for the glimpses of cuteness at my door.

Everyone else loves Uber and Lyft and Airbnb and Vrbo. Me, I have a bad rep on Airbnb because the host in Manhattan complained about us. Much of it stemmed from the fact that she kept texting us and we were technologically behind and didn't text yet. I've stayed in two Airbnbs that were adequate. One was corporate-owned, though it was advertised as belonging to a particular person with interests and hobbies, who was dying to find out mine. All of these nonregulated systems operate like the U.S. and Soviet Union during the Cold War. Back then, there was MAD: mutually assured destruction, a form of deterrence. We don't bomb them because they can bomb us. We don't say anything bad about the host or driver and they won't say anything bad about us (well, in most cases). It's a dance, and not a friendly one.

On Saturday night when the baseball game was over we went outside. Sharon and John were coming back from an outdoor dinner and a movie, using money from a guy who had parked his long van overnight in their parking place. (A great deal for $40.) They were happy with their commerce.

There is a time to every season, they say. There is, for instance, the season when you have something to sell, and the season when you don't.

A TRAVELER'S LEXICON

Hike: that which other people do on vacation, preferably not on yours; walking at an unfortunate and uncomfortable diagonal in order to see views (see *Views*)

Views: that which hikers say is part of the joy and purpose of hiking; seeing these cause them to exclaim passionately; also the subject of photos that hikers assume you will be passionate about

City: where to go on vacation (see *Nature*), and where you walk on vacation (see *Hike*)

Nature: that which stands between cities, often green but can be brown or sandy; more attractive and necessary than freeways or franchises; too much of it can provoke anxiety and asthma; redwood trees are an exception because they are people

Cappuccino: basic and frequent necessity on a vacation or any time

Ocean: nature that goes beyond itself; it speaks of the vastness of the planet and eternity in a rhythmic way that soothes instead of provoking anxiety

Mixed blessing: finding, then gathering beach glass and sand dollars, because isn't collecting a form of capitalist acquisition? (See elsewhere, Jason Goldsmith in *River Teeth*: "When birding becomes active pursuit rather than conscious observation, it is imbricated in the logic of capitalism. Species become commodities to be acquired, checked off a list. . . . There is always . . . another acquisition that holds in it the promise to make us whole.")

Conference: a civilized way to vacation; tax-deductible

Unexpected pleasure no. 1: remembering the word for "notebook" (*cuaderno*) in Spanish in a stationery shop in Barcelona

Unexpected pleasure no. 2: the Maison Picassiette, a local-bus ride away from the Chartres Cathedral; it is a house, garden, chapel, and more; indoor and outdoor surfaces covered in bits and pieces of broken glass, porcelain, broken dishes—every wall, every ceiling, every path, even furniture—causing you to feel overwhelmed with emotion and appreciation and to exclaim passionately and take photos you show to friends whom you hope react passionately

Unexpected pleasure no. 3: Philadelphia's Magic Gardens in South Philly, an exuberant so-called visionary mosaic environment by artist Isaiah Zagar, whose mosaic facades on South Street helped revitalize it; he turned to this work after a nervous breakdown; there is something about breaking hard materials and fitting the pieces together in a new way that can be healing; the art is inspired by his dreams and it dares to be blatantly whimsical

Weissensee Jewish Cemetery, (East) Berlin: where the caretaker is not as friendly as the one at Graceland Cemetery (Chicago) when he has to unlock the gates to let you out after closing; areas are overgrown because who was there to tend the graves?

Unexpected pleasure no. 4: running into Paula and her sister Cynthia when you're in Paris; they tried to meet up with their parents in London but their father liked checking into hotels using a made-up name; this was before hotel guests had to show their passports

Camping: that which causes asthma; you try to deconstruct it: isn't it just driving to nature and sleeping sort-of-outside and picnicking for every meal? (see *Hike*)

Karma, example of: Nazi headquarters that is now a Résistance museum, Lyon, France

Hype, things that live up to: Bayeux Tapestry (a 224-foot-long embroidered narrative), everything designed by Antoni Gaudí in Barcelona, mosques in Istanbul, Ed Galloway's Totem Pole Park northeast of Tulsa, Indian food and fish and chips in the U.K., any pastry in France, the Oregon coast (espresso huts along the highway from Portland)

Mosaics, rendered in outsider or visionary style: a reason to be alive

Vacationing at home: walking downtown and seeing family groups and noting the similarities of the faces; eating almond croissants with cappuccino at Leonidas Chocolate Cafe on Chicago Avenue; visiting the National Museum of Mexican Art for the Day of the Dead or any time; taking the human-operated elevator to the tenth floor of the Fine Arts Building to see the nineteenth-century murals

Ennui: when you're twenty and have a European rail pass and can travel anywhere but have no reason to go to one place over another on any particular day and are afraid you're not fun to travel with; when you're anywhere and don't know why you're there (see *Money*; see *Anxiety*)

Money: what you need in order to have a European rail pass in order to have ennui; what you need in order to travel (see *Anxiety*; see *Ennui*; see *Unexpected pleasures*)

Unexpected pleasure no. 5: near midnight when the sound of bells moves close as a flock of sheep passes your table at an outdoor café in Greece, where a tall waiter asks if you know the famous politician in America called *Goosall* (and you figure out who he means: Gus Hall, four-time presidential candidate, U.S. Communist Party)

Uncategorized insight: reading a prayer book in the Ashkenazi synagogue in Guatemala City and noticing that the prayers address God using the informal *tu*

Unexpected pleasure no. 6: chocolate chip cookies at Levain Bakery in Harlem

Unexpected pleasure no. 7: peacocks outside the Cathedral Church of St. John the Divine near Columbia University

Anxiety: what can ruin vacations; what stands in the way of pleasure (see *Guilt*; see *Unexpected pleasures*)

Atlas Obscura: magazine and website whose purpose, it seems, is to remove the chance of encountering the unexpected, but to be fair also leads you to the surprising

Unexpected pleasure no. 8: discussing dreams and second sight with three strangers in a sidewalk café in Montgomery, Alabama

Guilt: who said you were worthy of taking a vacation? Are you working hard enough?

Doing research at a destination: what can help justify traveling (see *Guilt*)

Unexpected pleasure no. 9: sculptures of Susan B. Anthony and Frederick Douglass having tea, Rochester, New York

Making history concrete: one of the reasons to travel, such as a visit to a slave cabin in Charleston, where you stand inside the place where enslaved people lived and slept, and your imagination and memory returns there when slavery is discussed; the injustice becomes not more blatant (because how could it be more blatant?), but more tangible

Taking pictures: an action that can feel ridiculous, especially of yourself or a fellow traveler in front of a landmark, but an action that you usually appreciate later; but then the photo sits there in your second brain, the phone, and you could look up a better picture of the landmark, but you wouldn't be in it, and what are you trying to prove, that you were there? Or do you take pictures when traveling to remind yourself that you existed for a moment on the same ground as this monument and maybe through the picture you can capture what you felt or wanted to feel? Does the picture help you forget that you didn't feel the way you wanted to—awed or happy—at that moment? What does a photo mean in this world where people order food for its photogenic rather than gustatory qualities? The experience you had that's photographed—it automatically becomes more important than the one you had that wasn't photographed; the latter one can fade into obscurity, almost as if it didn't happen. Or do you take the picture because you want some of the eternity of the landmark to rub off on you?

Unexpected pleasure no. 10: riding bikes in Buffalo and coming across an intricately decorated early skyscraper, almost like frozen lace, and realizing it's the Louis Sullivan you've been looking for

New York Times: where even Alabama natives learn about small southern festivals and lore

Unexpected pleasure no. 11: the European beauty of the sculpture, staircases, arches, floor, and ceiling of the Library of Congress, a public building with cathedral-like magnificence

People met while traveling: most too numerous and complex to fit into a lexicon

Best question you're asked after returning from vacation: *What's the worst thing that happened?*

THE ROMANCE OF THE SPIDERS

On warm nights when Linc and I walk around the neighborhood we always stop at the Spider House. That's what we call it. It has white siding and, by reflecting the streetlight and outside house lights, it attracts bugs to one outside wall, and the bugs attract spiders.

Sometimes we count them. Forty, fifty, all sizes and shapes. We'll look to see if anyone's about to lure a fly into her webby parlor, or if a moth is about to get stuck following its bright fatal goal. Our comments are general, even if they're personal: *Check out that egg sac she's carrying.* Or *Look at that giant.* Sometimes the lights and spider are positioned so that an arachnid the size of my pinky nail will cast a shadow as long as my thumb. We don't know the spiders well enough to recognizes species or individuals, in the way I heard a neighbor of mine recently address a pigeon. *Hello, Brownie,* she said nonchalantly to the bird who was bobbing on Sheffield Avenue south of Byron Street—his haunt, apparently.

It's often midnight when we stop and we'll be standing there, underneath screened-in windows that are open and might lead to a bedroom, and we're afraid that we're waking up the occupants, that they'll come after us in their pajamas with shotguns cocked. But that's never happened. We don't hear anyone stirring inside. So we stand and watch; and because this is Wrigleyville, the warm nights are full of pedestrians, often Cubs fans, in various stages of inebriation. Drunken strangers notice us standing and staring at a wall and ask us what we're looking at, and when we tell them, they don't seem interested. We can't imagine why.

My True Love and I have been together almost eleven years. I don't know when we first noticed the Spider House, but it seems like it's always been him, me, and the spiders; the last, depending on the season. We wait for them. After a few spring days we stop to see if anyone has shown up. After a cold fall day we stop to see if there's anybody left.

The other night we had dinner on Southport Avenue and started walking home, eastward. We were already hard into spring—almost two months into meteorological spring and more than a month after the vernal equinox—the crocuses already gone and lilacs blooming, yellow and red and pink tulips standing tall. It was high time for the spiders to return. (I know that most of them don't return. They're not swallows. Most of them die in the course of a year. Let's say they recycle.)

Let's go on Waveland, I said, heart quickening. We walked east on Waveland Avenue. One block. The second block has four stocky stucco houses in a row, usually with flowerpots on their front porches. The houses always seem friendly, in the midst of three-story brick apartment buildings. We passed the dark slate house, the yellow, the light gray, and the lighter slate house, and then reached the alley. We came to the Huge Hulk in Progress, an outrage of orange and red and gray brick walls that takes up a whole half-block.

We'd bet not long before about whether it was destined to be a single-family home or a condo building. I'd said single-family and won. We figured the developer was asking about $2 million. (I looked it up later. It's $2.199 million, to be exact.) A big sign on the corner announced that this would be an "incredible corner lot home" with an "incredible custom kitchen," heated garage and floors, five bedrooms, four full bathrooms and two half-baths, and "exquisite stone and marble finishes throughout."

The sign didn't have to say that when completed the building would be ugly and seem out of proportion to the rest of the block. We kept going. More apartment buildings, no more houses.

No spiders. We both knew it but didn't want to accept it—that the Hulk had replaced the Spider House. We'd passed the Hulk many times when we hadn't been thinking of spiders. Now it was abundantly clear that the Spider House had been flattened and carted away but we kept hoping that it was just ahead. We stopped at the brown brick building where I used to live and checked the names on the buzzers to see who was still there, then kept walking, across Clark Street alongside the new! improved! Wrigley Field, across Clifton and Seminary avenues and past the fire house that's my polling place, past Kenmore Avenue, then up the alley that leads to the back of our six-flat condo building. We have bright outdoor lights that our first-floor neighbor put in. We always get a few spiders along the wall, but nothing in comparison. *This is the Spider House*, my True Love said. And we looked at a few medium-small gals and their webs, and we went inside.

ACKNOWLEDGMENTS

These essays were written over a long period. I have many people to thank who were helpful at many different steps along the
way. First are the editors, especially Alison True and Michael
Lenehan at the *Chicago Reader*, which in pre-Internet days had
a huge "news hole," which was from time to time filled with my
work. And the *Reader* paid, too. Other editors have encouraged
and published work that appears in this book, notably Brian
Hieggelke at *Newcity*, Lisa Gray at the *Houston Chronicle*, the late
Rick Soll at the *Chicago Times*, Allison Joseph and the late Jon
Tribble at the *Crab Orchard Review*, and Rabbi Michael Lerner
at *Tikkun*.

I need groups. Many years ago Sharon Solwitz invited me
to join her writing group, formerly known as the Writer Gals,
which is now called the PerSisters. These talented women are
nurturing, critical, brilliant, and honest and have kept me going.
Current members are Rosellen Brown, Janet Burroway, Garnett
Kilberg Cohen, Tsivia Cohen, Maggie Kast, Peggy Shinner, and
Sharon. Weekly planning and kvetch sessions with the S/quad
have been indispensable to my writing, especially during the
pandemic: Thalia Mostow Bruehl, Galit Gottlieb, and Natania
Rosenfeld.

I love the National Endowment for the Humanities. Yes,
Humanities, not Arts, which I love too, though it's never given me
money. I've been lucky enough to be part of four NEH Summer
Seminars and Institutes, which have informed my thinking and
vastly increased my knowledge, introducing me to ideas and texts I
wouldn't have found otherwise. These four were led by Tony Kaes
(on the Weimar Republic; University of California, Berkeley), the
late James E. B. Breslin (modern biography; also UCB), Nathan
Bracher and Richard J. Golsan (legacy of European fascism; Texas
A&M, held in France), and Frances Jones-Sneed (African American
biography; Massachusetts College of Liberal Arts). I benefited
enormously from the lead professors and guest faculty and the

other participants. In 2013 then senator Jeff Sessions mocked these summer programs as providing mere "vacations," and criticized the subject matter. Thanks to him and other detractors, the budget was reduced and foreign programs ended.

A fellowship for a summer course at Central European University added to my understanding of modern Jewish history in Europe. Viktor Orbán is responsible for closing down the university (an act condemned as an "assault on academic freedom"—the *Atlantic*), which was founded and funded by George Soros. CEU has been reestablished in Vienna.

I am grateful to the Illinois Arts Council, which awarded me a fellowship that paid for travel in Europe. The trip deepened and expanded my knowledge of European Jews, past and present. I'm forever grateful for the friendships that began on that trip with Lara Dämmig and Jessica Jacoby. Through Lara, roommate and traveling companion, I have been a welcomed participant in Bet Debora conferences in Vienna, Sofia, Belgrade, Wrocław, and Hoddeston (England). There I met people who shared friendship and intellect, notably Rabbi Barbara Borts, Norli Lappin-Eppel, Anna Makówka-Kwapisiewicz, Tania Reytan-Marincheshka, Tanya Ury, Sonja Viličić, and others.

Another Illinois Arts Council grant funded part of my first Mississippi-Alabama trip. Michael Martone and the University of Alabama MFA writing program invited me to become Coal Royalty Chair in English for a semester, which provided me with a temporary home in Tuscaloosa while I traveled throughout the state. I plan to write more extensively about Selma in another book, as well as about other places in the South. In Selma, I was grateful for the welcome and time of Afriye Wekandodis, David Hurlbut and Bill Tomey at the Harmony Club, Robert Gordon of Gordon's Antiques, Mary Lynne Downie at Cheltenham Park Hall B&B, Doris Butler, Joanne Bland, Charlie Lucas/the Tin Man, everyone at the Selma–Dallas County Public Library, and Temple Mishkan Israel members Ronnie Leet, Hanna Berger, the late Steve Grossman (and widow Laura), and the late Ed Ember, who was my first contact at the temple.

I also benefited from a Holocaust Education Foundation fellowship for a seminar at Northwestern University led by Peter Hayes.

I am grateful to the Texas Jewish Historical Society for a travel grant to Houston and Austin, where I discovered a treasure trove of transcripts at the Dolph Briscoe Center for American History. Hollace Weiner of the Texas and Southern Jewish Historical Societies has been a source of support and knowledge.

The indefatigable family genealogist Lana Leavitt Rosenfeld has been more helpful than I can say.

It's hard to explain the magic when you enter an artists' colony. Somehow imposter syndrome falls away and your writing becomes the most important thing in the world, to yourself and to everyone else. I wish to thank the Ragdale Foundation for numerous residencies, as well as the Millay Colony for the Arts. The Fine Arts Work Center in Provincetown provided a creative home for seven months with a built-in community.

I am grateful to conference pals who have joined me at panels and dinners and discussions that have fed my writing: Jessica Handler, Tom Larson, Mimi Schwartz, the late Michael Steinberg, Simone Zelitch. To Bernice Narvaez' time and space.

For their friendship and ready willingness to read my work, I thank Jennifer Berman, Margie Smith Maidman, Irina Ruvinsky, Don Wiener. I send a general shout-out to steadfast friends over the years: Chuck Burack, Frieda Dean, Marv Hoffman, Dan Howell, Melissa Knox-Raab, Mitch Newman, Jessica Seigel, Barry Silesky, and Claudia Springer. And to Andy Cassel, thanks for the Yiddish advice.

I'm grateful to the folks at the University of Massachusetts Press, especially Courtney Andree, Rachael DeShano, and Juniper Prize judge David Toomey for his careful reading and appreciation. And to Dawn Potter, who dealt with my eccentric punctuation and use of italics.

And for everything else, I thank Linc Cohen.

A number of pieces in the book have appeared, in slightly different forms, in periodicals: "The Wandering Womb," *River Teeth*; "Notes on Camp," "A Traveler's Lexicon," "The Romance of the Spiders," *Newcity*; "Spy in the House of Girls," "Halloween, Chicago," "Late Night," "We Had Paris," *Chicago Reader*; "The Year of the Knee Sock," *Crab Orchard Review*; "Separate Vacations," *Sun* and *Chicago Reader*; "Younger Men, Older Men," *Whole Earth Review*; "Exercising the Past" and "Cream Puffs," *Chicago Times*; "Mikvah:

That Which Will Not Stay Submerged," *Fourth Genre*; "The Jew in the Body," *Ars Medica*; "Up against It," *Rupture*; "Auschwitz: Like the Back of His Hand," *Common Review*; "In Wrocław, Formerly Breslau," *Bet Deborah Journal*; "The Ambivalence of the One-Breasted Feminist," *Progressive*; "Flood, Meyerland," *Houston Press*; "America: A Polemic," *Killing the Buddha*; "Something to Sell," *Houston Chronicle* online and *Tikkun* online. "Female Protection" is forthcoming in *Stained: An Anthology of Writing about Menstruation*.

NOTES

THE WANDERING WOMB
Helen King, "Once upon a Text: Hysteria from Hippocrates," in the collection *Hysteria beyond Freud*.

GRANDMOTHER RUSSIA/SELMA
Cindy Gabriel, "On Loving America in a *Fiddler on the Roof* Kind of Way," *Buzz Magazines*, June 27, 2021. The article quotes Michael Newman on his grandmother's reaction in 1971.

NOTES ON CAMP
The title is from Susan Sontag's essay, which has nothing to do with this kind of camp.
The scholar is Marcie Cohen Ferris, who wrote, "God First, You Second, Me Third": "Quiet Jewishness" at Camp Wah-Kon-Dah," *Southern Cultures* (Spring 2012).
Echo Hill Ranch is now a camp for children of Gold Star families.

SPY IN THE HOUSE OF GIRLS
Jenny is not her real name.

THE YEAR OF THE KNEE SOCK
Names have been changed.

SEPARATE VACATIONS
Traveling is much easier and more meaningful when you're on antidepressants. Even when taking them, I like to have a goal to make the travel less aimless: meeting up with a Jewish writer in Florence, stopping in on an Italian outsider artist who lives in a suburb of a town too small to be on the map. He welcomed us, gave us bread and cheese, and spoke to us in Italian, which we didn't understand, and we replied English, which he didn't understand. We spent a fine time looking through art books together and pointing and trying to recognize words. It was a highlight of our trip.

FRENCH YOGA
To learn how the word "namaste" was transformed by westerners, listen to Kumari Devarajan, "How 'Namaste' Flew Away from Us," *Code Switch: Word Watch*, National Public Radio, January 17, 2020.

MIKVAH: THAT WHICH WILL NOT STAY SUBMERGED

I consulted David Biale, *Eros and the Jews: From Biblical Israel to Contemporary America*; Debra Orenstein, ed., *Lifecycles: Jewish Women on Life Passages and Personal Milestones*; Howard Eilberg-Schwartz, ed., *People of the Body: Jews and Judaism from an Embodied Perspective*; Hyam Maccoby, *Ritual and Morality: The Ritual Purity System and Its Place in Judaism*; Jacob Neusner, *Purity in Rabbinic Judaism: A Systematic Account: The Sources, Media, Effects, and Removal of Uncleanliness*; Rivkah Slonim, ed., *Total Immersion: A Mikvah Anthology*; Rahel Wasserfall, ed., *Women and Water: Menstruation in Jewish Life and Law* (that's really her name); and http://www.mayyimhayyim.org. There are three newish alternative *mikvot*, or mikvahs, in North America. There's the inclusive ImmerseNYC, a project of the Marlene Meyerson JCC Manhattan. Queer Mikveh (an alternate spelling) Project is based in the Bay Area and during the pandemic has conducted rituals over Zoom. In Toronto there's MKV, a mikvah for queer and trans people (http://radiodress.ca).

SOUTH FLORIDA, BEFORE

Names have been changed.

CREAM PUFFS

Chuck was a big eater, but not fat.

LATE NIGHT

I wrote the essay some time ago. It is a snapshot of my life and national sleep deprivation in the 1990s. For updates on our chronic short sleeping, see Jane Brody, "The Health Toll of Poor Sleep," *New York Times*, December 12, 2021 (online version has good links to the number of short sleepers and the dangers of same); and Olga Khazan, "The Uneven Health Toll of Sleep Deprivation," *Atlantic*, August 2017 (explores racial disparities in sleep deprivation effects). Now there's an annoying study that finds that going to sleep at 10 or 11 p.m. is best for heart health, especially women's: Shahram Nikbakhtian, Angus B. Reed, Bernard Dillon Obika, Davide Morelli, Adam C. Cunningham, Mert Aral, and David Plans, "Accelerometer-Derived Sleep Onset Timing and Cardiovascular Disease Incidence: A UK Biobank Cohort Study," *European Heart Journal—Digital Health* 2 (December 2021): 658–66. See also Lisa L. Lewis's new book *The Sleep-Deprived Teen: Why Our Teenagers Are So Tired, and How Parents and Schools Can Help Them Thrive*.

WE HAD PARIS

Azzedine's last name has been changed.

LUCK: IN THE VALLEY

The Joan Silber quotation is from *The Art of Time in Fiction: As Long As It Takes*.

IN WROCŁAW, FORMERLY BRESLAU

On Frida Kahlo and Jewishness, see Julia Weiner, "Was Frida Kahlo Jewish?" *Jewish Chronicle*, June 7, 2018.

FLOOD, MEYERLAND

Emancipation Park has many associations. Here are some relevant excerpts from a piece I wrote in *Newcity Chicago*:

"Emancipation Park was the site of Black Lives Matter Houston protests May 29 and 30, 2020, over the death of the Third Ward's most famous and tragic son [George Floyd]."

"Emancipation Park used to be on Dowling Street, named for Confederate war hero Dick Dowling. The street name was changed to Emancipation Avenue on Juneteenth 2017 as part of the dedication of a new recreation building in the park designed by Perkins + Will."

"In late June 1917 'colored' army troops came to Houston to guard the construction of a training camp. Racial tensions were high that summer in the United States—in early July there was a gruesome and brutal riot against African Americans in East St. Louis, Illinois. The Third Battalion of the 24th Infantry had never before been posted in Jim Crow territory. In Houston the men experienced police brutality, as well as the antagonism of racist streetcar conductors and construction workers. The soldiers especially objected to being called 'n******.' On August 23, 1917 the soldiers were due to have a watermelon party in Emancipation Park. Instead, reacting to a police assault on a corporal that day, more than one hundred soldiers rioted. Fifteen whites were killed, including four policemen, and four black soldiers died. (Numbers vary by source.) Nineteen soldiers were hanged and sixty-three were imprisoned in Leavenworth Penitentiary."

"Because Houston leaders remembered the 1917 riot, they were especially motivated to bring integration to Houston in a peaceful way."

"You could consider the Houston mutiny and riot to be part of a long stream of African-American rebellion."

Our part of Meyerland was made up of what David Biespiel calls in his memoir *A Place of Exodus: Home, Memory, and Texas* "plaid streets"— Loch Lomond, where he grew up; Braesheather, where I did. Other

Scottish-sounding street names are South Braeswood, Braesmont,
Dumfries, Rutherglenn, Glenmeadow. We were near the Brays Bayou,
named after a surveyor, not the hills of Scotland, though sometimes the
bayou is spelled "Braes."

A TRAVELER'S LEXICON

Unexpected pleasure no. 4: Cynthia remembers the details differently.

RESOURCES

Here are organizations that advocate and educate on the subjects of these essays. There are many other wonderful groups; this is just my list. I will update the list on http://slwisenberg.com.

MENSTRUAL EQUITY

First, a word about "menstrual equity" from Women's Voices for the Earth (https://www.womensvoices.org): the term refers "to the affordability, accessibility and safety of menstrual products." WVE's site is bilingual.

Period: The Menstrual Movement (http://period.org) is a youth-led organization that provides education, menstrual supplies to those in need, and advocacy for abolishing the "tampon tax" on menstrual products.

Period Equity (https://www.periodequity.org) litigates against the tampon tax; website lists states that do and don't impose taxes on menstrual products.

ASTHMA

Allergy and Asthma Network (https://allergyasthmanetwork.org) fights health disparities and provides information for people with allergies and asthma; website is bilingual.

American Lung Association (https://www.lung.org) has long been fighting against air pollution and tobacco use and providing information on lung disease. I donated my old car and got a tax deduction.

Asthma and Allergy Foundation of America (http://www.aafa.org) works on policy to help people with asthma and allergies.

Environmental Law and Policy Center (https://elpc.org) works to protect the air and water of the Midwest through litigation and advocacy.

Moms Clean Air Force (http://momscleanairforce.org) works against air pollution and for environmental justice.

BREAST CANCER

Breast Cancer Action (http://bcaction.org) is a feminist group that fights health disparities and pushes for regulation of cancer-causing toxins; it's also a leader in calling out "pinkwashing" by corporations and other groups that symbolically fight breast cancer while marketing or promoting carcinogenic products. BCA encourages people to Think Before You Pink—to critically examine pro-pink public relations campaigns. See also Gayle Sulik, *Pink Ribbon Blues: How Breast Cancer Culture Undermines Women's Health*; and Samantha King, *Pink Ribbons, Inc.: Breast Cancer and the Politics of Philanthropy*. And while you're at it, you might read or listen to my book, *The Adventures of Cancer Bitch*.

JUNIPER
JUNIPER PRIZE FOR CREATIVE NONFICTION

This volume is the third recipient
of the Juniper Prize for Creative Nonfiction,
established in 2018 by the
University of Massachusetts Press
in collaboration with the
UMass Amherst MFA Program
for Poets and Writers, to be
presented annually for an outstanding
work of creative nonfiction. Like its sister
awards, the Juniper Prize for Poetry
(established in 1976) and the Juniper Prize for
Fiction (established in 2004), the prize is named
in honor of Robert Francis (1901–1987),
who lived for many years at
Fort Juniper, Amherst, Massachusetts.